Felbrigg: the Story of a House

By the same author

THOMAS GRAY

HORACE WALPOLE

THE EARLY LIFE AND DIARIES OF WILLIAM WINDHAM

*

NORFOLK ASSEMBLY

COUNTRY NEIGHBOURHOOD

A NORFOLK GALLERY

NORFOLK PORTRAITS

THE WEST AND SOUTH FRONTS

FELBRIGG

The Story of a House

R. W. KETTON-CREMER

Published in collaboration with
The National Trust by
The Boydell Press · Ipswich

First published 1962
Reissued 1976 by The Boydell Press Ltd.,
P.O. Box 24 Ipswich IP1 1JJ

ISBN 0 85115 071 3

Printed and bound in Great Britain by Redwood Burn Limited
Trowbridge and Esher

TO THE MEMORY OF

MY FATHER, MY MOTHER

AND

MY BROTHER

CONTENTS

ILLUSTRATIONS

All the paintings, except that of William Windham III, were photographed by the Courtauld Institute of Art.

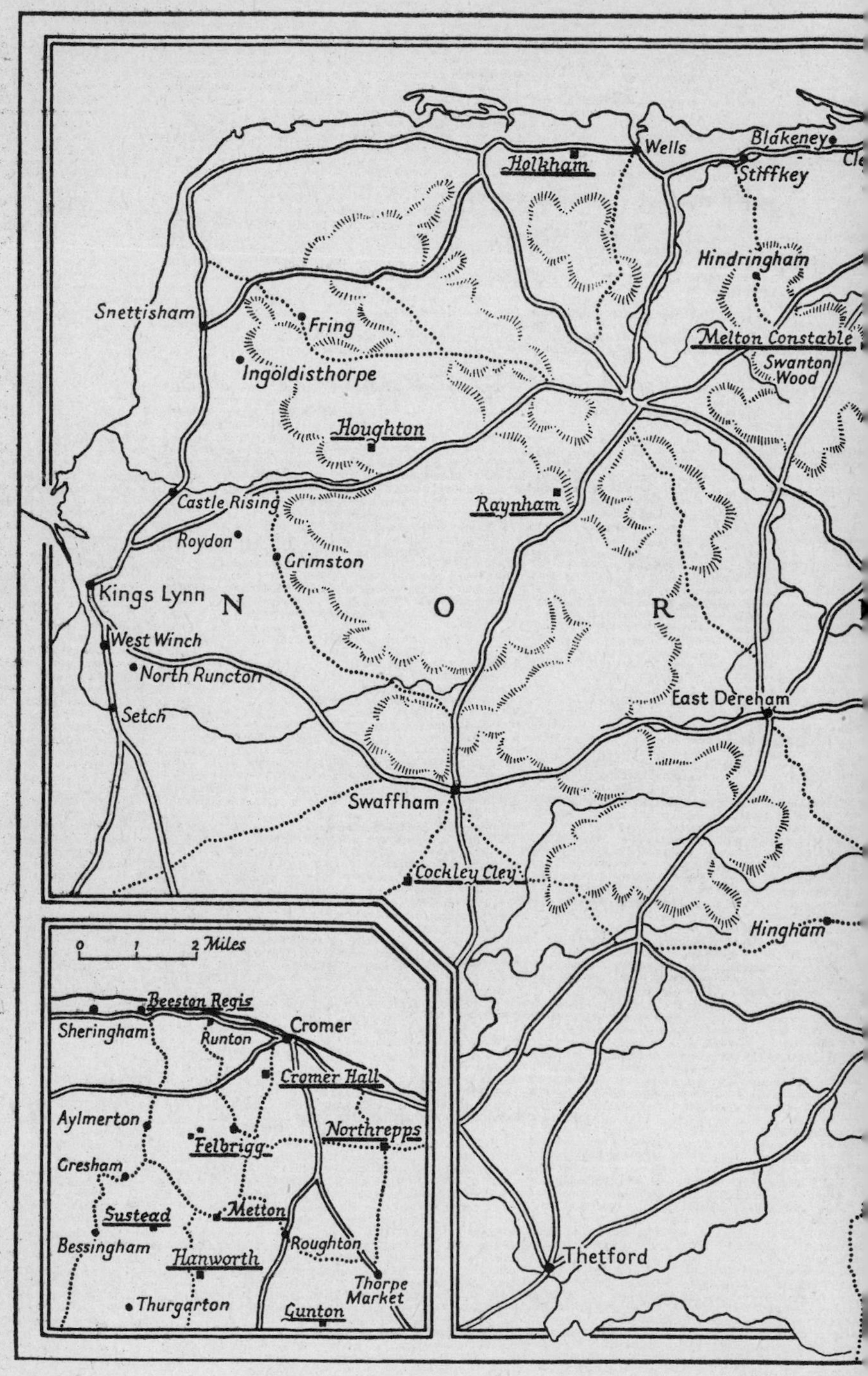

Wells
Blakeney
Holkham
Stiffkey
Hindringham
Snettisham
Fring
Melton Constable
Swanton Wood
Ingoldisthorpe
Houghton
Raynham
Castle Rising
Roydon
Grimston
Kings Lynn
N
O
R
West Winch
North Runcton
Setch
East Dereham
Swaffham
Cockley Cley
Hingham
0 1 2 Miles
Beeston Regis
Sheringham
Runton
Cromer
Cromer Hall
Aylmerton
Felbrigg
Northrepps
Gresham
Sustead
Metton
Bessingham
Roughton
Hanworth
Thorpe Market
Thurgarton
Gunton
Thetford

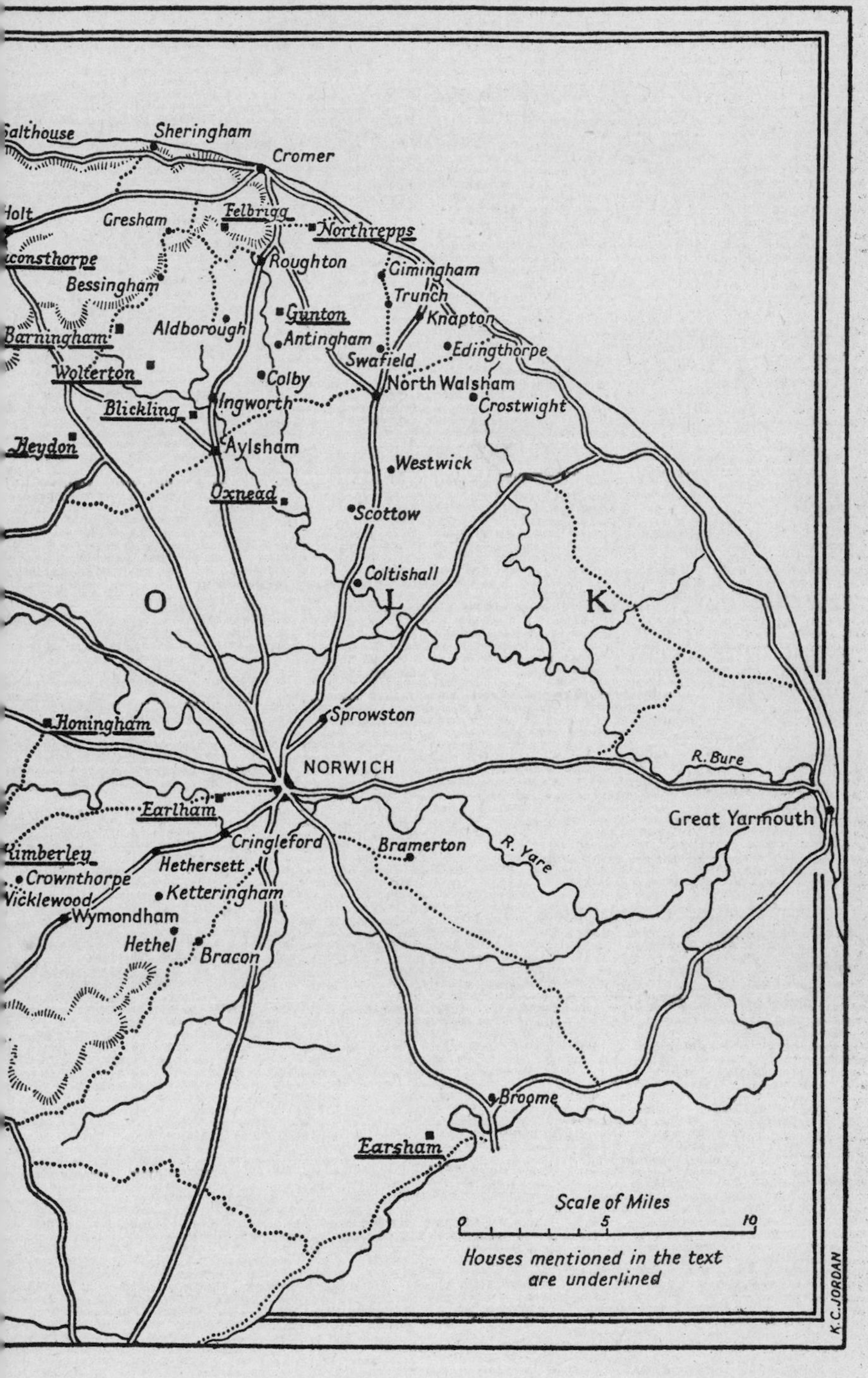
Salthouse
Sheringham
Cromer
Holt
Gresham
Felbrigg
Northrepps
Baconsthorpe
Roughton
Gimingham
Bessingham
Trunch
Gunton
Knapton
Barningham
Aldborough
Antingham
Edingthorpe
Swafield
Wolterton
Colby
North Walsham
Ingworth
Crostwight
Blickling
Heydon
Aylsham
Westwick
Oxnead
Scottow
Coltishall
O
L
K
Sprowston
Honingham
NORWICH
R. Bure
Earlham
Great Yarmouth
Kimberley
Cringleford
Bramerton
Hethersett
R. Yare
Crownthorpe
Ketteringham
Wicklewood
Wymondham
Hethel
Bracon
Broome
Earsham
Scale of Miles
0
5
10
Houses mentioned in the text
are underlined
K.C. JORDAN

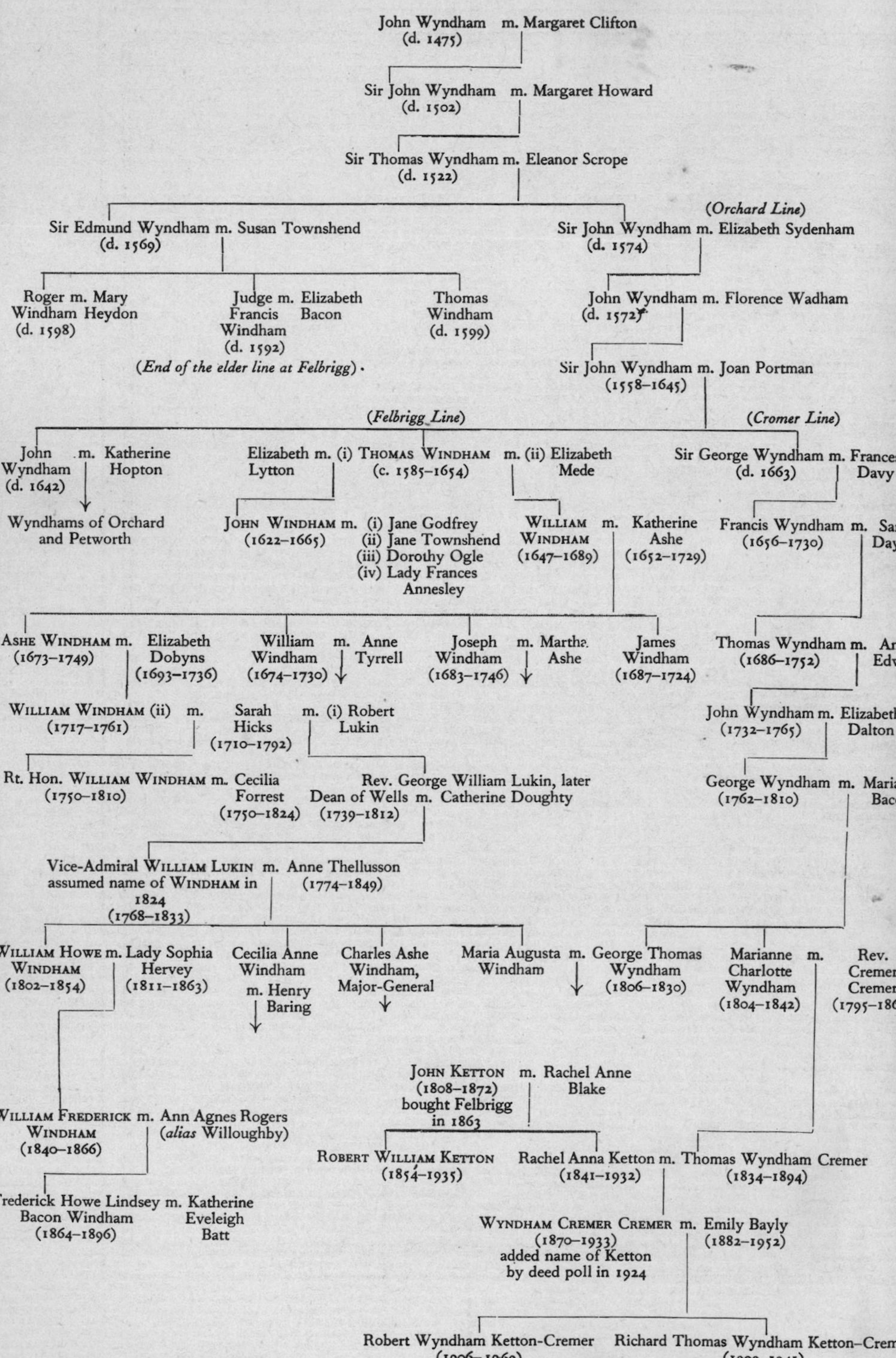

John Wyndham m. Margaret Clifton
(d. 1475)
Sir John Wyndham m. Margaret Howard
(d. 1502)
Sir Thomas Wyndham m. Eleanor Scrope
(d. 1522)
Sir Edmund Wyndham m. Susan Townshend
(d. 1569)
(Orchard Line)
Sir John Wyndham m. Elizabeth Sydenham
(d. 1574)
Roger Windham m. Mary Heydon
(d. 1598)
Judge Francis Windham m. Elizabeth Bacon
(d. 1592)
Thomas Windham
(d. 1599)
(End of the elder line at Felbrigg)
John Wyndham m. Florence Wadham
(d. 1572)
Sir John Wyndham m. Joan Portman
(1558–1645)
(Felbrigg Line)
(Cromer Line)
John Wyndham m. Katherine Hopton
(d. 1642)
Wyndhams of Orchard and Petworth
Elizabeth Lytton m. (i) Thomas Windham m. (ii) Elizabeth Mede
(c. 1585–1654)
Sir George Wyndham m. Frances Davy
(d. 1663)
John Windham m. (i) Jane Godfrey (ii) Jane Townshend (iii) Dorothy Ogle (iv) Lady Frances Annesley
(1622–1665)
William Windham m. Katherine Ashe
(1647–1689) (1652–1729)
Francis Wyndham m. Sar Day
(1656–1730)
Ashe Windham m. Elizabeth Dobyns
(1673–1749) (1693–1736)
William Windham m. Anne Tyrrell
(1674–1730)
Joseph Windham m. Martha Ashe
(1683–1746)
James Windham
(1687–1724)
Thomas Wyndham m. An Edw
(1686–1752)
William Windham (ii) m. Sarah Hicks m. (i) Robert Lukin
(1717–1761) (1710–1792)
John Wyndham m. Elizabeth Dalton
(1732–1765)
Rt. Hon. William Windham m. Cecilia Forrest
(1750–1810) (1750–1824)
Rev. George William Lukin, later Dean of Wells m. Catherine Doughty
(1739–1812)
George Wyndham m. Maria Baco
(1762–1810)
Vice-Admiral William Lukin assumed name of Windham in 1824 m. Anne Thellusson
(1768–1833) (1774–1849)
William Howe Windham m. Lady Sophia Hervey
(1802–1854) (1811–1863)
Cecilia Anne Windham m. Henry Baring
Charles Ashe Windham, Major-General
Maria Augusta Windham m. George Thomas Wyndham
(1806–1830)
Marianne Charlotte Wyndham m. Rev. Cremer Cremer
(1804–1842) (1795–186
John Ketton m. Rachel Anne Blake
(1808–1872)
bought Felbrigg in 1863
William Frederick Windham m. Ann Agnes Rogers (alias Willoughby)
(1840–1866)
Robert William Ketton
(1854–1935)
Rachel Anna Ketton m. Thomas Wyndham Cremer
(1841–1932) (1834–1894)
Frederick Howe Lindsey Bacon Windham m. Katherine Eveleigh Batt
(1864–1896)
Wyndham Cremer Cremer m. Emily Bayly
(1870–1933) (1882–1952)
added name of Ketton by deed poll in 1924
Robert Wyndham Ketton-Cremer
(1906–1969)
Richard Thomas Wyndham Ketton-Crem
(1909–1941)

Chapter One

PRELUDE

I

THE spring is always cold and late on the Norfolk coast. For weeks at a time the wind blows in from the sea, a chill drying wind, northerly or easterly. The trees—horse chestnut, sycamore, beech, oak, sweet chestnut, ash—come slowly into leaf under a reluctant sun. It is long before the blades of corn even begin to hide the tilth from view.

At Felbrigg the characteristic sound of spring is the crying of the lapwings, the restless plovers. To and fro they fly over the pasture and the young corn, wheeling and tumbling in the air, calling all the day long. There is no rookery as there used to be at Beeston, the home of my childhood; and every year I miss that familiar April sound. Jackdaws chatter as they make their nests in the hollow beeches. Cock pheasants, spectacular in their mating plumage, crow and drum their wings. In the trees near the church a pair of kestrels is sure to breed, and occasionally I hear their shrill mewing note. Late in April the cuckoos come. But the dominant note, always and inescapably, is the crying of the plovers.

There will be days, and sometimes even whole weeks, when the weathercock swings round to the south—days of continuous sunshine and bird-song, of leaves almost visibly unfolding, of the wild cherry blossom radiant along the rides and verges of the woods. Such days may come early, and touch the delicate flowers of peach and apricot along the garden walls. They may come late, and enrich the mounded pink and white of the apple-trees. But it will not be long before the wind goes back again to north or east, and the fog creeps in from the sea, and the blossom and the young foliage are lashed with rain.

Always, during April and May, my thoughts particularly return to my father, my mother and my brother. The spring months cover my mother's birthday and my own; my father's death at Felbrigg; my brother's death in the tragic confusion of the German assault on Crete. My parents lie in the churchyard at Felbrigg. My brother's grave in Crete will be for ever unmarked and unknown. Their memory is with me as I begin this book; and with their names it will close.

II

Felbrigg Church lies remote in the park, far from any house, with fields and pastures all around. Most of it, including the nave and the fine square tower—Norfolk flintwork at its best—was rebuilt by Sir Simon Felbrigg early in the fifteenth century. Within are the superb brasses of the Felbriggs, a long series of Windham monuments, square box pews, hatchments, Victorian tablets, an abundance of light. A ring of oaks and beeches surrounds the walled enclosure of the churchyard, with its grey headstones and a single weeping ash.

In medieval times much of the village must have clustered round the church. War-time ploughing brought to the surface all sorts of relics —bricks, tiles, mortared flints, fragments of kitchenware, the necks of those brown glazed jugs with the bearded "bellarmine" head. I do not know what brought about the change. Some epidemic may have compelled the removal of the houses to another site—at least one severe visitation is recorded in the Elizabethan parish register. More probably it was due to the eighteenth-century passion for unbroken stretches of parkland. Whatever the cause, the village is now grouped round the little green, half a mile away across the fields. Only two houses are even within sight of the church—the home farm and the Hall.

The church, in its latest and present form, was already two hundred years old when the Hall was built. There had been an earlier hall on the same site, where the Felbriggs had lived and then the first generations of Windhams. Nothing remains of it except some medieval arches and doorways in the cellars. And the people who inhabited it are shadowy figures, dimly perceptible through some wills and legal documents, a few letters, a few inscriptions, nothing more. It is with the building of the existing house that the story of Felbrigg begins to assume actuality and life.

III

This book, then, is the history of an English house, from the early seventeenth century until the present time. Like all such houses, it has known vicissitudes; prosperity and neglect, happiness and grief, good times and bad. But through all these changes, and despite the ownership in succession of four different families—the Windhams, the Lukins, the Kettons and my own—its fabric has undergone little alteration, and its contents have remained surprisingly intact. And from almost every generation of the four families a substantial body of papers—letters, diaries, inventories, accounts—has fortunately survived.

Owing to circumstances which will appear in due course, I scarcely knew Felbrigg until I was eighteen years old. Beeston, a couple of miles away, sheltering from the sea-winds behind its little grove of trees, was my childhood home—the home of my ancestors, in a sense that Felbrigg can never be. I loved every acre of its modest woods and fields, as I love them still. Felbrigg, with my father's eccentric uncle living a hermit's life in his two small rooms, was a place of mystery. But from the day when we moved there, in the spring of 1924, it has remained my home. I have sought to gather every detail of the lives of those who have lived there before me, the men and women whose story is recorded in this book. I have tried to hold the house and estate together during my own span of life. And I hope that in the course of time my ashes will lie in the churchyard among the plover-haunted fields.

Chapter Two

THE EARLIER CENTURIES

The early history of Felbrigg—the Felbrigg family—Sir Simon Felbrigg—acquisition of Felbrigg by John Wyndham—early history of the Wyndham family—the Elizabethan Windhams—the elder line comes to an end with Thomas Windham's death in 1599

I

THE parish of Felbrigg lies close to the northern coast of Norfolk, a mile or two inland from the sea. It forms a part of the wide belt of comparatively high ground, broken and hilly, an area of woods and heaths and rather light farmland, which stretches across the north of the county. The origin of its name is unknown. It is supposed to be derived from the ancient Scandinavian *fiǫl-bryggia*, a plank bridge. But even a plank bridge presupposes a river, or at least a stream; and since there is no watercourse of any kind in the whole parish, apart from a couple of tiny rivulets cut for drainage during the eighteenth century, the conjecture is somewhat doubtful.

At the time of the Norman Conquest the village was held by two freemen of Gyrth, Earl of East Anglia. He was a brother of King Harold, and fell at his side in the last desperate stand of the English at Hastings. When Domesday Book was compiled, Felbrigg had become part of the lands granted to Roger Bigod, a powerful Norman whose son was the first of the formidable line of Bigods, Earls of Norfolk. For more than two centuries the Bigods bore great sway in eastern England, and held their place among the leading barons of the kingdom. At Felbrigg they appear to have enfeoffed a family, possibly of their own kindred, who assumed the name of the place. In due course the heiress of these Felbriggs married a younger Bigod son, and their descendants continued to live in the manor house and were known indifferently as Felbrigg or as Bigod.

All this is confusing, and partly conjectural; but the mists suddenly clear in the fourteenth century, with the earliest of the brasses in Felbrigg Church. It lies in the chancel, just beneath the sedilia, and consists of four figures side by side, their hands clasped in prayer, with an inscription in Norman French at their feet. The first is Simon de Felbrigg, who died in 1351, an elderly man in the unpretentious dress of a civilian landholder. Next is his wife Alice de Thorpe, in correspondingly modest attire. Then comes their son, "Monsieur Roger de Felbrigg," a soldier in complete armour, his feet resting on a lion. This Roger fought in France and elsewhere beyond the seas, and died about 1380, whether in war or in peace we do not know, in distant Prussia—"*et là est son corps enterré.*" The last figure is his wife, a daughter of Robert Lord Scales, wearing a most elaborate *nebulée* head-dress, in striking contrast to the sober hood of the elder lady.

In their son, Sir Simon Felbrigg, the family reached its climax and, so far as their native parish was concerned, its close. As a young man he was high in favour with King Richard II and his first Queen, Anne of Bohemia, and married the Queen's cousin and maid of honour, Margaret, daughter of Przimislaus Duke of Teschen. Towards the close of the reign he was appointed King Richard's standard-bearer, and was chosen a Knight of the Garter. After the King's deposition and death he seems to have been little employed for several years; but he was able to retain the pensions granted to him by his late master, and returned in due course to royal favour and military activity.

Early in the fifteenth century he largely rebuilt Felbrigg Church. The buttresses of the nave, and the spandrels of the western door into his fine new tower, bear his coat of arms, *or a lion rampant gules*, and also the fetterlock, which was used as a badge by the House of York and its supporters. In 1416 Lady Felbrigg died, and Sir Simon placed in the church a brass of exceptional magnificence to her memory and to his own. Their figures, almost life-size, stand beneath a double canopy of splendid workmanship. He is in full armour, with the insignia of the Garter, and bears the standard of his dead sovereign—the cross and five martlets of Edward the Confessor, impaling the arms of England and France. She is a figure of great elegance, with her head-dress and veil, close-fitting kirtle and long flowing mantle, and the lapdog at her feet with its collar of bells. Above them are the arms of King Richard and Anne of Bohemia; their own arms, his rampant lion and her imperial eagle; and again the fetterlock badge. Between them, on a finial of the canopy, is King Richard's own badge, the white hart which he bore in honour of his mother the Maid of Kent—the lovely emblem which figures, together with the cross and the five martlets, in the Wilton Diptych, the greatest work of art that survives from his reign. The entire composition vividly brings to mind the refinement of Richard's art-loving, pleasure-loving, cosmopolitan court, in the carefree days before his follies had gained the upper hand and his adversaries closed in upon him.

But Sir Simon was not to lie at his wife's side beneath their sumptuous brass; and the space left in the inscription for the date of his death has remained for ever blank. He married a second wife, Catherine, daughter of Anketill Mallory of Winwick in Northamptonshire, and widow of Ralph Grene of Drayton in the same county. They became prominent benefactors of the Dominican Priory in Norwich; and when they died, Sir Simon in 1442 and his second lady in 1461, they were buried in the choir of its great church. At the dissolution of the monasteries the church was not destroyed, but was acquired by the city of Norwich, and under the name of St Andrew's Hall has been used for civic and secular purposes of all kinds ever since. If, as seems likely, a memorial was erected to Sir Simon and Lady Felbrigg in the choir—rechristened Blackfriars Hall, and used for many years as a church for the Dutch congregation in Norwich—no trace of it now remains.

By his first wife Sir Simon had two daughters, his only children. Anne became a nun at Bruisyard in Suffolk. The needlework cover of a psalter embroidered by her is now in the British Museum. Her sister, Alana, married Sir William Tyndall of Hockwold. In the reign of Henry VII her grandson, by virtue of his descent from Margaret of Teschen, was invited to prosecute his claim to the much-disputed throne of Bohemia. He was prudent enough to refuse.

Sir Simon in his will directed his trustees to sell Felbrigg and others of his properties after his wife's death. One of these trustees, Lord Scales, contrived to get the reversion of the properties into his own hands, and then sold the reversion to a certain John Wyndham. This transaction took place towards the end of 1450. About the same time Wyndham leased the manor-house at Felbrigg from Sir Simon's widow, and established himself there as her tenant.

II

As the reign of King Henry VI advanced upon its lamentable course, the county of Norfolk fell ever deeper into disorder. Powerful noblemen, such as the Duke of Norfolk and Lord Moleyns, conducted themselves as though they were above the law—as indeed, in the circumstances, they were. On a somewhat lower level, though occasionally coming into contact with them, a number of thrusting and ambitious figures ceaselessly manoeuvred for power and riches. Paston, Heydon, Wyndham—in two or three generations their families would be among the foremost in Norfolk. At this stage they were already beginning to fill the void left by the disappearance or decay of several of the older knightly stocks, the Erpinghams, the Felbriggs, the Fastolfs.

John Wyndham presumably derived his name from the town of Wymondham, some ten miles south-west of Norwich. The earlier stages of the family tree, which provided him with a lineage stretching back to "Ailwardus de Wymondham, an eminent Saxon," are now regarded as fanciful; and he is not in fact known to have possessed any land before 1436. In that year he bought the manors of Crownthorpe and Wicklewood, in the Wymondham neighbourhood; and shortly afterwards he made a propitious marriage with Margery, daughter of Sir Robert Clifton and widow of Sir Edward Hastings. The next stage in his upward career was less creditable, though perhaps even more profitable than the acquisition of manors and good family connections. He became associated with the nefarious practices of Norfolk's two leading trouble-makers, Sir Thomas Tuddenham and the lawyer John Heydon of Baconsthorpe. In the words of the historian of his family:

> Together the three succeeded in establishing a kind of legal racket, resembling in its working those recently brought to such perfection in the New World. Their chief weapon was the illegal practice of "maintenance," that is to say supporting litigants in whom they had no personal interest in order to damage others whom they desired to embarrass. Their secondary armament was to corrupt and overawe jurors and judges, threatening them with reprisals and attending court sittings with armed escorts of sometimes as many as four hundred men.[1]

Like so many personages of fifteenth-century Norfolk, John Wyndham is principally known to us through the medium of the *Paston Letters*; and it is perhaps unfortunate for his reputation that he was usually on the worst of terms with the Pastons. John Paston was pursuing much the same career of personal aggrandisement himself, and their interests conflicted more than once. They or their dependants indulged in several brawls in the streets of Norwich, during one of which Wyndham characterised Paston's mother and wife, who had hurried out of church on hearing the commotion, as "strong whores." But when every allowance is made for Paston prejudice, it still seems clear that Wyndham was an exceptionally turbulent and unpopular

[1] H. A. Wyndham, *The Wyndhams of Norfolk and Somerset*, p. 4.

figure. His coming to Felbrigg was by no means welcome to the commoners of the parish; and when he first appeared there as the tenant of Sir Simon's widow they seem to have made some sort of hostile demonstration against him.

The manor-house of the Felbriggs presumably stood upon the site of the present Hall, whose cellars contain masonry and brickwork which are thought to date at least from the fifteenth century. John Wyndham continued to occupy it, except when his various enterprises called him elsewhere, until the death of Lady Felbrigg, which occurred in 1461. The reversion then passed to him, and he became the absolute owner of the property. His title to it, however, did not go undisputed. Another branch of the Felbrigg family considered themselves to have a claim on the estate, and had never been reconciled to the transaction whereby Lord Scales acquired the reversion from his fellow-trustees and sold it to Wyndham. In 1461 the head of this branch, Sir John Felbrigg, suddenly appeared at Felbrigg with a band of supporters, at a time when Wyndham was away from home. Wyndham's second wife, Elizabeth Lady Heveningham, whom he had married a few years before despite the most strenuous opposition from her son, was in the house, and locked herself into her chamber in order to keep possession. Felbrigg promptly broke into the room, dragged her forth by the hair, and turned her out of the house. He then established himself at Felbrigg, and defied all Wyndham's efforts to eject him.

This was not an unprecedented occurrence in fifteenth-century Norfolk. A few years before, exactly the same thing had happened to Margaret Paston at the neighbouring manor of Gresham. Lord Moleyns and a large force had descended upon the little castle and, in the words of John Paston's subsequent petition, "mined down the wall of the chamber wherein the wife of your said beseecher was, and bare her out at the gates." The Pastons eventually re-established themselves at Gresham, and the Wyndhams at Felbrigg. Sir John Felbrigg continued in possession for several months, while Wyndham was reported by one of the Pastons as saying that "he will go get him a master, and methought by him he would be in the King's service, and he saith that he will have Felbrigg again ere Michaelmas, or there shall be five hundred heads broke therefor." Finally the King ordered the Sheriff of Norfolk to reinstate Wyndham, and a compromise was arranged, whereby Felbrigg renounced his claims, and made over all his interests in the property, in return for a payment of two hundred marks.

This settlement was final, and Wyndham continued in unchallenged possession of Felbrigg for the rest of his life. He died in 1475, and was buried in the church of the Austin Friars at Norwich.

III

This book is the story not of a family but of a house, and a house no part of which was built until the seventeenth century. I propose therefore to pass briefly over the intervening generations. The next hundred years saw a great consolidation and increase of the Wyndham fortunes, and the establishment of a flourishing offshoot of the family far away in Somerset. But the individuals seem even more remote from us than the Felbriggs, whose brasses bring them so vividly to mind: more remote than the first John Wyndham himself, as he is revealed in the letters of the unfriendly Pastons.

John Wyndham was succeeded by his son of the same name. This younger John married Margaret, a daughter of Sir John Howard, who was created Duke of Norfolk at the accession of Richard III in 1483. Although he received much advancement through the influence of the Howards, he did not share in their temporary eclipse after King Richard's death at the Battle of Bosworth, in which his father-in-law was killed.

Jockey of Norfolk, be not too bold,
For Dickon thy master is bought and sold—

the famous rhyme was used by Shakespeare. But John Wyndham came to no harm, and two years later was knighted by Henry VII for his good service at the Battle of Stoke. After the death of his Howard wife he made a second marriage with Eleanor, the widow of a Yorkshire knight, Sir Richard Scrope; and about the same time his eldest son Thomas married her daughter Eleanor Scrope. This double marriage brought the Wyndhams into close connection with Edmund de la Pole, Earl of Suffolk, who was also married to a lady of the Scrope family. Suffolk, as a possible claimant to the throne, was regarded with deep distrust by the King. When he fled abroad in 1501 and took refuge with Henry's adversary the Emperor Maximilian, a number of his friends and supporters were arrested. Among them was Sir John Wyndham, who was convicted of high treason and beheaded on Tower Hill on 6 May 1502. His companion at his trial and on the scaffold was Sir James Tyrrell, who is generally supposed to have confessed before his death to the murder of the two young princes in the Tower.

His widow retired to the nunnery of Carrow on the outskirts of Norwich, with her daughter Frances Wyndham, and three of her daughters by Sir Richard Scrope. One of these girls, Jane Scrope, owned a pet sparrow which fell a victim to the nunnery cat; and their friend John Skelton, from his parsonage at Diss, sought to console her with his delectable poem *The Book of Philip Sparrow*, which begins as a dirge for the vanished bird and closes with a shower of commendations of Jane herself:

She is the violet,
The daisy delectable,
The columbine commendable,
The gillyflower amiable:
For this most goodly flower,
This blossom of fresh colour,
So Jupiter me succour,
She flourisheth new and new
In beauty and virtue.

Sir John Wyndham's heir, Thomas, was able to win back all that his father had lost. Largely assisted by the influence of his Howard cousins, two of whom in succession were Lords High Admiral, he embarked on a most rewarding naval career. He saw service against the French in 1512 and 1513, was knighted, became Treasurer of the Fleet and presently an Admiral and one of King Henry VIII's Council. More important still, his father's attainder was reversed, and he was secured in the possession of all the estates of his family. Latterly he lived in considerable magnificence, so much so that when he died in 1522 his executors were unable to pay in full the legacies contained in his long and elaborate will. One of these provided for the repair of the Lady Chapel in Norwich Cathedral, in which he and his two wives were buried. The repairs were insufficient, and in Queen Elizabeth's reign the Chapel was demolished and his tomb removed into the Jesus Chapel, from which it has now disappeared.

Sir Thomas Wyndham left three sons and three daughters. The eldest son, Edmund, succeeded him at Felbrigg and in the favour of Henry VIII. At the dissolution of the monasteries he was able to obtain, on terms which were probably advantageous, a large share of the buildings and lands of the neighbouring priory of Beeston. He was knighted at the King's marriage with Jane Seymour, with whom he had a family connection through his step-mother, Sir Thomas's second wife Elizabeth Wentworth. But his career received an unfortunate check when he struck a Norfolk neighbour, Mr Clere, in the royal tennis-court. He was condemned to lose his right hand, the customary penalty for such an offence within the palace bounds, but was eventually pardoned. He was High Sheriff of Norfolk at the time of the rising headed by the Kett brothers, and made a vain attempt to disperse the rebels by the exercise of his authority in the King's name. When the revolt was finally put down by military force it fell to him to preside at the execution of the Ketts and their chief followers.

Sir Edmund's sister Margaret had married, during their father's lifetime, Sir Andrew Luttrell of Dunster Castle in Somerset. Her descendants still live in that romantic house on its precipitous hill; and her portrait still hangs there—a face full of individuality, faintly quizzical in expression. It was on a visit to Dunster that her second brother John Wyndham met Elizabeth Sydenham, the heiress of the neighbouring property of Orchard, just inland from the sea near the little town of Watchet. They were married in 1528, and Orchard Sydenham became Orchard Wyndham, as it remains to this day.

By his second wife, Elizabeth Wentworth, Sir Thomas had a son who bore his own name. He also became a naval commander, served with particular distinction in the Scottish wars, and was made a Vice-Admiral. But like other seamen of the age he was by nature a privateer, and was in frequent trouble with the authorities over the disposal of his prizes and their contents. In many of his enterprises, official and otherwise, he was associated with Sir John Luttrell, the son of his half-sister Margaret. These "two filibustering toughs," as Professor Ellis Waterhouse rightly calls them, were painted by Hans Eworth in 1550.[1] The pictures, with their emphasis on movement and action, were novelties in the portraiture of the age. Thomas Wyndham, "a bluff personage caught in a moment of repose from the battlefield," leans against a tree, burly and red-faced, with gun and helmet beside him. Sir John Luttrell, stripped naked to the waist, wades in a stormy sea, with a ship foundering in the background, and a profusion of allegorical figures, emblems and verses. The pair jointly planned a privateering expedition to Morocco in 1551, on the eve of which Luttrell died. Wyndham himself died two years later in the Bight of Benin, on an ill-organised venture in search of gold.

[1] Ellis Waterhouse, *Painting in Britain, 1530 to 1790*, pp. 15–16. The portrait of Wyndham is at Longford Castle, that of Luttrell at Dunster.

IV

Sir Edmund Wyndham died in 1569. He was the first of his line to be buried in Felbrigg Church. His predecessors lay in the religious houses of their choice; but now the Reformation had come, the monasteries and friaries had vanished, and rich men had no alternative but to be buried in their parish churches. His monument was on the north side of the church. A visitor towards the close of the century described it as "a faire toombe . . . not haveinge as yet anie mention of superscription, but spaces and scochons lefte to bee furnished: over the toombe his whole coat armoure with the achevemente, his sworde and pennon." It survived until the eighteenth century; then it disappeared, possibly when the church was fitted with the existing square box-pews.

By his wife Susan, daughter of Sir Roger Townshend, Sir Edmund had three sons, Roger, Francis, and Thomas. There were also two daughters, Amy, who married Henry Heveningham, and died young; and Jane, who married first John Pope and then Humphrey Coningsby, and was to outlive all her brothers. This generation of the family was, I think, the first consciously to adopt the spelling Windham, which thenceforward distinguished the line at Felbrigg from the branches elsewhere.

Roger Windham succeeded his father in 1569, and owned Felbrigg for thirty disastrous years. His predecessors had been forceful and ambitious men, peremptory, hasty-tempered, not overburdened with scruples—just the kind of people, in fact, who did establish new families during the Wars of the Roses and consolidate them under the Tudors. They were not always liked, but they were respected and obeyed. Roger, on the other hand, soon aroused the entire neighbourhood against him. He became a sort of local tyrant just at the time when law and order and fair dealing, under the wise government of Elizabeth and her ministers, were beginning to make substantial headway. He showed himself mean, grasping, vindictive, above all litigious to the point of mania. He persecuted clergymen about their tithes and small copyholders about their tenures. He went to law over every imaginable subject of dispute, from stranded wrecks to straying horses and broken fences. He sued his neighbours, his tenants, his tradesmen. When a nephew of his wife, Mary Heydon of Baconsthorpe, killed a deer in Felbrigg park he haled him into the Court of Star Chamber. In the course of sixteen years he brought actions against more than a hundred of his poorer neighbours, who in desperation appealed to the Privy Council and obtained some redress. Persistent litigation usually defeats its own ends. Roger Windham seldom met with much success at law, and suffered several humiliating reverses. His estate began to suffer too; and he was obliged to mortgage substantial portions of it to his cousin Sir John Wyndham of Orchard.

Roger's second brother, Francis, was a professional lawyer, and an extremely able one. He became Recorder of Norwich and for some years represented the city in Parliament. From 1579 until his death in 1592 he was a Justice of the Common Pleas. He married Elizabeth, a daughter of Sir Nicholas Bacon, the Lord Keeper, and step-sister of Francis Bacon. He had a house at Norwich in the parish of St Peter Mancroft, and his monument, with an effigy in his judge's robes, is still to be seen in that church.

Roger Windham had no children by Mary Heydon, and the Judge had also died childless. So the property was inherited, on Roger's death in January 1599, by the third brother Thomas, a bachelor. Nothing whatever is known about his earlier life; and before the close of that year he too was dead. But two documents, copies of which have survived, reveal that he was a man of ability and determination. He was confronted by a resentful tenantry, a neighbourhood full of confusion and strife, and an estate burdened with debt. He summoned a meeting of his tenants, and delivered a speech to the effect that he intended to return to the manorial customs of his father's time, and that no alterations made during Roger's reign were to be regarded as valid.

Since there is nothing [he began] that makes men thrive and prosper better either in their estates, or in their credits, than peace and unity: I make no doubt, but all who are wise, and have tasted the good effects and fruit thereof, will always practise and embrace it.

He assured them that he proposed to make no alteration in the customs or fines, although on sundry neighbouring manors the tenants had been dealt with in a very different way. He had much to say on the vexed question of rights of common. Here again

what ever was enjoyed, or taken by you, or your predecessors, in the times of Sir Edmund Wyndham, or other my ancestors that lived in the estimation of their country and love of their tenants, I will willingly afford and yield you. But for Mr Roger Windham's time, you may perceive by many acts of his, and conveyance of land, which he made, and have been overthrown, that permission and sufferance in his time will make no custom or precedent for any man to build or depend upon.

The other document shows that he next turned his attention to his brother's dealings with their cousin Sir John Wyndham. He took the line that although Roger had mortgaged a number of his Norfolk manors to Sir John, such a transaction was void, since he was himself the heir at law under his father's will and had never given his consent. Nevertheless he had no desire that his cousin "should be frustrate of such money as hath been by him disbursed for the saving of the inheritance of the said manors." He merely wished to safeguard his own interests, and those of any children born to him, "in case I shall like to marry, and to take wife." If he did not marry, he was content and indeed most willing that the reversion of his whole estate should pass to his cousin. He was already a bachelor well advanced in years, and Sir John probably had little anxiety about complying with the demands which he now made—that if he married and had a son, the estate should descend in his male line; that if he had daughters, adequate portions should be assured to them; that in any case the lands should be charged with the payment of Roger's debts; that allowance should be made to him for the necessary repairs to the houses and grounds occupied by his brother, "being at the time of his death in decay"; and that the interests of his sister Mrs Coningsby should be safeguarded if she survived him. All these conditions were embodied in a lengthy agreement, and it might appear that on some points Thomas was driving a very hard bargain; but the final clause suggests that both parties were well aware how things would eventually go.

Finally I do greatly desire that the said inheritance coming to my said cosin, the same might continually be inhabited, and the house of Felbrigg be dwelt upon, either by himself, or by some of his children of the name; so that the name might be continued with some countenance in this county, and in this lyneal succession, where the eldest house hath alwayes remained. Foreasmuch as otherwise if the lands should be alwayes in farm, and the rents continually be carryed out of the country, within a few years the name should there be utterly forgotten, hospitality abolished, and all come to ruine and desolation; which if I were assured should so come to pass, I would never agree that the right and title of the said inheritance should pass into that lyne and race of my said cosin.

Having done much, in the space of less than a year, to put the affairs of Felbrigg once again into order, Thomas Windham died on 20 December 1599. In 1608 his sister Jane Coningsby died also, without children by either of her husbands. The elder line at Felbrigg had come to an end; and the entire inheritance now passed to Sir John Wyndham of Orchard.

Chapter Three

THOMAS AND JOHN WINDHAM

Sir John Wyndham inherits Felbrigg in 1608, and presently settles his son Thomas Windham there—the building of the south front—the Civil War and the Commonwealth—Thomas Windham's death in 1654—the uneventful career of his eldest son John, and his death in 1665

I

DURING the reign of Queen Elizabeth, and throughout the long period of Roger Windham's malpractices at Felbrigg, the Wyndhams in Somerset prospered greatly. The marriage of John Wyndham and Elizabeth Sydenham had rooted the family at Orchard, where they remain to this day. The eldest son, another John, had married Florence Wadham, a sister of Nicholas Wadham who founded at Oxford the college which bears his name. One of their younger sons established yet another line at the neighbouring house of Kentsford. His descendants in the next century were to play a prominent, honourable, and sometimes tragic part in the Civil War.

A year after her marriage Florence Wyndham was taken ill, was thought to have died, and was buried in the family vault in St Decuman's Church at Watchet—that ancient church standing high above the waters, looking across to distant Wales. The same night a covetous sexton opened her coffin in order to remove her rings, and cut one of her fingers in the process. She had in fact fallen into some sort of cataleptic trance, and was now awakened by the pain and rose from her coffin. The sexton fled, leaving his lantern behind him; and with its aid she made her way home across the fields to her astounded family. Similar stories have come down from other centuries and other lands; but this tale of Florence Wyndham's resurrection has been so long a part of local tradition that one hesitates to dismiss it as legend. Soon afterwards she gave birth to her only child, a son named John, from whom every living member of the Wyndham family is descended, apart from a branch in the United States whose progenitor was Thomas, the tough and enterprising sailor.

Florence Wyndham's husband died young, and she was left to bring up her son, a boy of twelve, the third John in succession. In due course he married Joan, the daughter of Sir Henry Portman of Orchard Portman, and had by her nine sons and six daughters. He was knighted in due course, and lived to the age of eighty-six, passing the whole of that long span in looking after his property and the affairs of his own neighbourhood. He was a man of great wealth, since a substantial Wadham inheritance came to him from his mother in addition to his paternal estates. It was to him that Roger Windham mortgaged his lands in Norfolk; and it was to him that Thomas Windham expressed his hope, which proved to be virtually a dying injunction, that "the house of Felbrigg be dwelt upon, either by himself, or by some of his children of the name; that so the name might be continued with some countenance in this county, and in this lyneal succession, where the eldest house hath alwayes remained."

II

Whatever his cousin Thomas might hope, Sir John Wyndham had no thoughts of dwelling at Felbrigg himself. The Norfolk origins of his family can have meant little to him. Orchard Sydenham had now been Orchard Wyndham for three generations, and he had himself altered and enlarged it. Orchard lying sheltered in its rich valley, between the westernmost spur of the Quantocks and the eastern slopes of Exmoor, would always be his home, and there his eldest son would succeed him. But he decided that Thomas, his second surviving son, should eventually go to Felbrigg, and spell his name Windham, and if possible re-establish in Norfolk the "lyneal succession" which the other Thomas had desired.

Sir John did not succeed to Felbrigg immediately upon the death of Thomas, since the latter's sister Mrs Coningsby, now a widow of sixty, was still alive. In fact she was in residence at Felbrigg, where she may have come to cheer the solitude of her bachelor brother Thomas. She continued to live there after his death; and some account-books show that she maintained a considerable household. She had as companion a mysterious Jane Wyndham, who may perhaps have been a young cousin from Orchard. In the lists of articles of apparel bought by Mrs Coningsby, many items are marked as being purchased on behalf of Jane; and some of them suggest that in 1601, when the accounts begin, she was still a child. But children in that age were dressed with the same formality as their elders. Old Jane Coningsby and young Jane Wyndham alike wore the silk and taffeta and tiffany and riband and lace, the ruffs, masks, girdles and gloves of which the accounts are full. "Smith the taylor" must have had valued clients in both.

That is really all we know of the reign of Jane Coningsby at Felbrigg. She died in November 1608, at the age of sixty-seven; and with her death the entire Norfolk property passed to Sir John Wyndham absolutely. We hear no more of the younger Jane: she appears nowhere in the account-books of the new régime. But whoever she was, Sir John no doubt took good care of her, just as he took good care to commemorate Thomas Windham and Jane Coningsby in the church of their ancestors. He commissioned their effigies in brass, set in great slabs of Portland stone—Thomas in armour, Jane in hood and ruff and all the sober richness of Jacobean attire. Beneath the effigies were inscriptions to their "worthy memorie," and below the inscriptions were lines of verse. The brother's quatrain reads:

Livest thou Thomas? Yeas. Where? With God on highe.
Art thou not dead? Yeas. And here I lye.
I that with men on earth did live to die
Died for to live with Christ eternallie.

There are brasses of exactly similar style to Sir John's parents in St Decuman's Church, with verses of exactly the same degree of accomplishment. Did he write them all himself, one wonders? From the account-book of his steward in Norfolk it is possible to ascertain every stage of the progress of these slabs and their brasses from London, by ship to Yarmouth, by long-boat to Coltishall Bridge, in two carts to Felbrigg; and every payment, down to the one shilling and eight pence which two masons received for laying them down in the church and paving the floor around them. Unfortunately there is no record of the cost of the monuments themselves or the name of their maker, which would have been the most interesting details of all.

It is from account-books that virtually all our information about the next twenty or thirty years is derived. Sir John had a most capable servant named John Blinman, to whom was largely entrusted the taking over of the Norfolk property. He is at first the dominant figure of the new series of account-books, constantly riding to and fro between Orchard, London, and Felbrigg. From Orchard to London he would spend three nights on the road, usually at Wincanton, Andover, and

Bagshot. Between London and Felbrigg he would spend another three nights, at Ware or Puckeridge, at Newmarket or Barton Mills, and at Norwich. His supper and breakfast would cost him between fourteen-pence and eighteenpence, and his horse's fodder and stabling rather more.

At Felbrigg he surveyed the property, and made inventories of the farm stock, the bullocks, horses and swine, the sheep on the foldcourse and the unsold wool, the wheat, mislen, oats, barley, vetches and hay, the pigeons in the dovehouse, the hives of bees in the garden. He drew up lists of the tenants and commoners, and received their rents and dues. He paid wages, tithes, money for the poor. He took over from William Doughty, who had been Mrs Coningsby's steward, the contents of the house, jewels and plate, apparel and bedding and linen.

In the summer of 1609 Sir John paid his first and possibly his only visit to his Norfolk properties. There were great preparations for his coming, with the purchase of much claret and muscadine and sack, and the slaughtering of many pigs and lambs and capons. The neighbours and tenants sent presents of all kinds, and they or their servants, according to circumstances, were duly remunerated by John Blinman. Mr Doughty's man was given sixpence for bringing two ducks and two artichokes, Mr Linsie's man a shilling for bringing a haunch of venison, the miller of Ingworth a shilling for his offering of eels.

Among much other business Sir John decided which of the contents of the house were to be sent to Orchard, and which were to remain at Felbrigg. Mrs Coningsby's gowns of satin and velvet, her scarf of cypress with silver fringe, her new French hood, her lawn apron and her silk stockings, went off to his own wife and daughters; but much else of her wardrobe was left, and some was given to Anne, Dorothy and Alice, her maids. Linen and bedding were divided between the two houses. There was little jewellery—Mrs Coningsby had probably disposed of it in her will—but what there was went to Orchard. The three coach-horses, and the coach with all its furniture, went to Orchard also; but the twelve other horses—Grey Watte, the great mare, the little bay mare, Blacke Rone, the sorrell colt, Gill, Bartram, and the rest —remained at Felbrigg.

The plate, in which people of the sixteenth and seventeenth centuries invested so much of their capital, was also divided. Several pieces—among them a basin and ewer parcel gilt, a standing cup and cover gilt, a great broad bowl, a standing cup engraven—were sent to Orchard;

but the greater proportion was left at Felbrigg, and was presently "sent to London to Mr Thomas." It is clear that already Sir John not only regarded his son Thomas as the eventual owner of Felbrigg, but had determined to provide for him out of the Felbrigg property. For some time to come the bulk of the Norfolk rents were remitted to Orchard; but as early as 1610, and in every year thereafter, substantial payments out of them went to Thomas.

There has been much confusion about the date of Thomas Windham's birth, since the inscription on his monument in Felbrigg Church credits him with at least thirteen more years than he actually attained. He was probably born about 1586, and was destined for the law, being entered at Lincoln's Inn and called to the Bar in 1610. As a young man he was inclined to display the hasty temper of his family, and on one occasion was fined twenty shillings by his Inn "for striking a labourer on the works of the house with his fist." He was a promising lawyer, and it was with some reluctance that he finally abandoned his career and went down to take possession of Felbrigg at his father's behest. But his severance from the Bar was a gradual process. Every year he went to Felbrigg for a few weeks, sometimes in connection with suits heard at Norwich or on other legal business. In 1613 there are entries in John Blinman's accounts for "diett at ffelbrigge ffor Mr Thomas, his man and his ffoote boy and myself." Their diet was arranged for the first week with Thomas Cutlacke, who was in charge of the house; but for the next two weeks additional provision was also made "by Mr Thomas his appointment"—beef, lamb, mutton, beer, geese, pigeons, capons, a roasting pig, and a woman to dress the meat. It is clear that ever since Mrs Coningsby's death Felbrigg had had no regular occupant, but had only been opened up when some member of the family had to go there on business. It had grown antiquated, comfortless, outworn, ripe for rebuilding in accordance with the standards of a new age.

It is uncertain when Thomas Windham actually went to live at Felbrigg, but it must have been fairly soon after 1615, since his own account-book begins in that year. Its entries relating to farming, building, and wages are bewilderingly interspersed with small personal expenses—a plover-net, physic for his hawks, a bottle of sack, a shillingsworth of crayfish, a penny almanac—and all are scribbled in his exasperatingly difficult hand. Nevertheless, a picture emerges from these confusing pages of a man increasingly absorbed in country life, in the bullocks on his pastures and the sheep on his foldcourse.

In December 1620 he married Elizabeth, daughter of Sir Rowland Lytton of Knebworth in Hertfordshire. A few pages of the notebook are in her large Italian hand, laborious but blessedly clear in comparison with her husband's. He was evidently away from home for a few weeks in 1621; and in his absence she received the money for bullocks and wool and tallow sold from the estate. She also recorded her own expenses—wages to Joan and Nell, a pair of shoes for the boy, a groat to Goody Goodrife's girl, nine shillings to Mr Matthews for paving the cellars, cobweb lawn and bone lace, muscadine and sugar-candy and cinnamon and saffron. Then, on 15 March 1622, she gave birth to a son John; and less than four months later, at the beginning of July, she died. Apart from these few entries in her husband's account-book, no trace of her has survived.

III

About the time when Thomas Windham took up his abode at Felbrigg, his father resolved that a new house should be built there. It has already been explained that nothing is known of the house occupied by the Felbriggs and the earlier Wyndhams. The medieval masonry and brickwork, still to be seen in the cellars which extend below and in front of the present house, have led to the assumption that it was built more or less on the site of its predecessor. I think there can be little doubt that this was so, and that the older house was levelled to the ground. No trace of medieval ground-plan or building-fabric survives.

Sir John Wyndham is recorded as having given "divers great sums of money" towards Thomas's expenses in Norfolk, and in particular towards the building of the new house. Father and son clearly regarded it as a joint enterprise: and the arms of both—Sir John impaling Joan Portman, Thomas impaling Elizabeth Lytton—are beautifully carved above the main doorway. But it is impossible to trace the progress of the building in Thomas Windham's account-book. There are payments, especially in 1621, to brickmakers and masons, smiths and joiners and sawyers, Matthews the bricklayer, Stanyon the plasterer, Linacre the glasier, Stockdale who made the staircase. But the total amounts do not remotely approach the cost of erecting so substantial a house. Either there was a separate book of building accounts which has now vanished or else the main expenses were discharged by Sir John himself. Nor do we learn anything of the interior arrangement of the house, which has been greatly altered since that day. There are one or two tantalising entries, as when two shillings were paid "to the hardstone men for the stone of the harth pase in the chapell chamber." Where was the chapel chamber, and what was its appearance? There are many such questions that must always remain unanswered. It seems that the finishing touches were not given until 1624, when a carver named Smith was paid for two lions four feet high, presumably those which still surmount the gables to east and west.

Although the interior of Thomas Windham's house was very considerably altered during the eighteenth century, the façade remains virtually unchanged. It followed a characteristic Jacobean design, repeated with variations throughout the land. The central feature is a square projecting porch, flanked by spacious mullioned bow-windows, all rising through two stories to terminate in a parapet which screened the long gallery. The parapet bears in pierced stone letters the inscription GLORIA DEO IN EXCELSIS, and is surmounted by heraldic beasts in stone, with the lion and unicorn in the centre. The side-gables are curved in a manner suggestive of Flemish influence, a form which was adopted also a few miles away at Blickling, a more grandiose but exactly contemporary house. The structure is mainly of brick with stone dressings, although a certain amount of flint was also used. So capricious was this alternation of brick and flint, and so casual the finish round the windows, that I believe the façade was always intended to be plastered, unusual though such a surface may have been in East Anglia. The plaster, whatever its age, is now deeply weathered and lichened; and where it has fallen away the rosy brick shows through, forming a singularly attractive texture.

The house was built facing almost due south, so that the sun might pour into the wide windows and into the little solar chamber above the main door. It was a narrow house in proportion to its height, only a single room in thickness for most of its extent,[1] although at the western end it seems to have had other rooms which vanished when the new wing was built at the end of the seventeenth century. The large south-west room was the Great Hall, with the usual arrangement of screens, hatches, and buttery within the main doorway. The gallery at the top of the house was long ago partitioned into small attic bedrooms; and no other room retains any trace of its Jacobean aspect.

In this house Thomas Windham lived for the next twenty years or so as a widower. His little son John was placed in the care of "Nurse

[1] During repairs in 1952 and 1958 the original north wall of the house, built of carefully selected flints, and now deeply embedded in later alterations, was revealed at two widely separate points.

THE SOUTH FRONT

THE RED BEDROOM

Cutlacke," to whom payments appear in the notebook. Later the boy was sent to the Grammar School at Norwich, and payments for him are made to Mr Lovering, the master there. Thomas Windham's loneliness was somewhat mitigated by the arrival in the neighbourhood of his younger brother George, who married Anne, the widow of his neighbour James Underwood. From her husband Mrs Underwood had inherited the principal estate in Cromer; and Sir George Wyndham —he was one of Charles I's gentleman pensioners, and was knighted at his Coronation—settled with her at Cromer Hall, a couple of miles away from Felbrigg.[1]

There is little to record of the history of Felbrigg during the sixteen-twenties and sixteen-thirties. Scarcely a letter of any kind has survived from those decades, and Thomas Windham's account-book records his farming operations and little more. Each year he or his bailiff would attend at St Faith's Fair and Hempton Fair, those great occasions of meeting for the entire countryside, to which a multitude of drovers from Scotland and the north of England would bring their thin and hardy beasts. Substantial purchases would be made of "Skotch bullockes," "northerne bullockes," "steeres Yorkshire." They would be brought home to graze and fatten on the good pastures at Felbrigg, Metton, Sustead, Gresham, Beckham, or farther afield; and in due course the majority would be sold to local butchers on terms of agreement carefully recorded in the book. There are fewer details about the sheep: I think again that after the early sixteen-twenties these accounts must have been kept separately, and are now lost. But in 1621 there were more than nine hundred sheep on the Felbrigg foldcourse; and there is an interesting list of the wool delivered to a great number of local women for purposes of spinning—"Goody Maries, a stone"; "Goodie Doutie, halfe a stone"; "Widdow Waker, halfe a stone"; "ould Goody Cutlacke, seventeen pounds"; and so on throughout the whole neighbourhood.

IV

In the meantime the storm-clouds of the Civil War were gathering fast. In Norfolk the dominant feeling was strongly Puritan. The Laudian reforms, while acceptable enough to a considerable proportion

[1] Sir George Wyndham had no children by Mrs Underwood, but established the line of the Wyndhams of Cromer through his second wife Frances Davy, a connection of the Underwoods. It is from this marriage that I am descended, and bear my second name of Wyndham.

of the clergy, were highly unwelcome to the laity as a whole. They were, moreover, enforced with exceptional rigour during three critical years by an able and energetic Bishop of Norwich, Matthew Wren. The imposition of Ship Money was deeply resented even in a maritime county; and there were other causes of disaffection. It is significant of the general state of feeling that of the twelve Members returned to the Long Parliament in 1640 by the county and its five boroughs—Norwich, Great Yarmouth, King's Lynn, Thetford, and Castle Rising—only two adhered to the King when the great cleavage came two years later.

Thomas Windham was wholly in agreement with this Puritan and Parliamentarian majority in Norfolk. He was a man of moderate views, both in religion and in politics. But he could not accept the rites and ceremonies enjoined by Bishop Wren, the reverence paid to the altar, the bowing and "dopping-worship," the dangerous suggestions of Popery—or, for that matter, the Bishop's masterful interference with the rights of private patrons. And as a lawyer, bred in the high-mettled school of Edward Coke, he watched with misgiving the encroachments of the monarchy upon the liberties of Englishmen. Among his neighbours and friends were Cokes, Hobarts, Gawdys, the representatives of the great lawyers of an earlier generation, all strong in support of the Parliament. So were most of the leading gentlemen of the county—Sir Thomas Wodehouse of Kimberley, Sir John Holland of Quidenham, Sir Isaac and Sir Edward Astley of Melton Constable, Sir John Palgrave of North Barningham, Edward Walpole of Houghton, and the two Knights of the Shire in the Long Parliament, Sir Edmund Mundeford of Feltwell and Sir John Potts of Mannington. The Royalist elements were few and scattered—Sir William Paston of Oxnead, the L'Estranges of Hunstanton, the de Greys of Merton, the Heydons (fallen now on evil days, with their great house at Baconsthorpe already in decay), Catholic families such as the Bedingfelds of Oxburgh and the Cobbes of Sandringham. There was nothing that they could effectively do against their united and overbearing neighbours.

It is likely that the Parliamentarian sympathies of Thomas Windham were intensified by his experiences as High Sheriff of Norfolk in 1639–40, when it was his duty to collect Ship Money from a resentful and obstinate county. He did his best, on the one hand prodding the constables of the various hundreds, who were charged with the actual work of collection, and on the other hand explaining to higher authority that the people were recalcitrant and the times were bad, with a "general damp of industry and commerce with a despicable ebb and depression of the price of commodities." But he must have much disliked being reprimanded by the Privy Council for his inefficiency in this business of Ship Money, a measure which he tried hard to enforce but of which he entirely disapproved.

So when the war broke out in 1642, it is not surprising to find the name of Thomas Windham on virtually all the Committees by means of which the supporters of Parliament were organised and its cause so successfully advanced. He served on the committee for sequestering the estates of delinquents, on a whole succession of committees for levying money and raising troops, and on the very important Committee for the Eastern Association. This last was formed in August 1643 to co-ordinate the strategy and resources of the six eastern counties—Norfolk, Suffolk, Essex, Hertfordshire, Cambridgeshire, and the Isle of Ely—which had joined together in a sort of federation at an early stage of the war. The Eastern Association provided a unified area of territory, and a reserve of manpower and provisions, which proved to be of incalculable benefit to the Parliamentarian cause. Some members of its Committee were always in session at Cambridge; but they were a large body, and there is no means of knowing whether Thomas Windham often made one of them.

At the outset of the war, before any real organisation had been set up, meetings had been hastily convened by the Deputy Lieutenants at which contributions were invited from sympathisers with the Parliament. In the minutes of one of these meetings a note occurs in Thomas Windham's hand—"I doe hereby undertake to deposite for the publique service and good viii score ounces of plate: and to be ready to furnishe for defence of this county within ytselfe two horses furnished and two foote." His son John, now a young man of twenty, fresh from his studies at Cambridge and Lincoln's Inn, volunteered for service under Lord Grey of Werke, who had been appointed Major-General of the forces raised within the Eastern Association. He became a captain of horse; and in 1643 there are a few references to him, mainly in connection with the pay of his troop, in the accounts of John Cory, the treasurer of the Norfolk committee of the Association. Lord Grey was replaced during the summer of 1643 by a more vigorous and efficient commander, the Earl of Manchester, under whom John Windham presumably continued to serve. But absolutely nothing is known of his fortunes during the remainder of the war.

The sympathies of the Wyndhams down in Somerset were deeply divided, as was the case in so many families all over the kingdom. Thomas's father Sir John Wyndham, now over eighty years old, supported the Parliament. So did his Portman and Luttrell relations. On the other hand, his Wyndham cousins at nearby Kentsford and Trent were passionate Royalists. Sir Edmund Wyndham of Kentsford became Governor of Bridgwater, and held the town and its surrounding countryside for the King until he was obliged to surrender to Fairfax in 1645. Three of his younger brothers fell fighting in the King's armies. Sir Francis Wyndham of Trent seized Dunster Castle from its owner, his kinsman Thomas Luttrell, and from its almost impregnable security dominated western Somerset for years. On one occasion he swooped on defenceless Orchard, and plundered old Sir John to the tune of four thousand pounds. He held Dunster until the very end of the war, when it was one of the last Royalist strongholds to surrender, and then only after a siege of a hundred and sixty days.

Thomas's younger brother and neighbour at Cromer, Sir George Wyndham, as a Gentleman Pensioner of the King should have endeavoured to serve his master in the day of adversity. It has been stated that he was declared a delinquent; but there seems to be no evidence that his estates were at any time under sequestration. After the Restoration he claimed to have lived during the war on his estate at Cromer, "doing his utmost for the royal advantage." In fact there was little that he could possibly have done in that solidly Parliamentarian countryside. His name does not occur on the earlier Committees; but early in 1645 he suddenly appears as a member of the Committee then appointed under the ordinance "for raising and maintaining of Forces for the defence of the Kingdome, under the Command of Sir Thomas Fairfax." It may be that, as the war advanced, he yielded to the force of circumstances and the persuasions of his elder brother, and made his peace with the side whose success was almost assured.

To moderate supporters of the Parliament such as Thomas Windham, the progress of the war brought many anxious hours and some unpleasant surprises. His property lay deep in the unravaged territory of the Eastern Association. In fact, except for the three weeks' siege of King's Lynn in the summer of 1643, there was not so much as a skirmish on Norfolk soil. But the cost, even to a prosperous landowner, was formidable—a heavy and increasing burden of taxation, special assessments at times of particular crisis, the requisition of horses, the general dislocation of affairs. Furthermore there was the tendency, inevitable in all revolutions, for things to get out of hand, the pace to become too hot, the enthusiasts and the extremists to assume control.

These anxieties are illustrated in one of Thomas Windham's few surviving letters, written in December 1643 to Sir John Potts of Mannington, a Knight of the Shire for Norfolk. It seems that Windham was reported to have undervalued his estate for the purposes of the levy imposed, earlier in the year, for maintaining the Army and prosecuting the war; and that Potts had vindicated him. After all, old Sir John Wyndham still lived on at Orchard: he did not die until two years later: and it is apparent, from his son's letter, that he still retained interests in the Norfolk lands.

Honored Sir I thanke you for those kinde ffavors which I lately receaved from you in way of Justice, to rescue me from the Iniurie of that monster Reporte which in this wicked Age often takes the upper hand of Truth. Our joynt affections, leaning on the same pillar of Constancy to Religion and the Common Wealth, I doubt not shall alwayes preserve our Neighborhood unto the mutuall Comfort of our famelies. My personall Estate I have given up at 2000£ which is one more than I knowe that I am worthe (my Estate in Lands to the Uttermost) during my ffather's Lieff. The oppression practised by Jubs and his Associatts is very odious, their fury in Churches detestable. Mr Cooke and Mr Sutterton are in the morning for Cambridge to represent those greavances which nothing but our owne firme Union (who have served the State in times of most danger) can withstand. In this as I shall continue ever to serve my Cuntry soe God willing entierly remayne

Your Servant to be disposed
Tho: Windham.

ffelbrig 10 December 1643.

The reference to the misdoings of "Jubs and his Associatts," and their detestable fury in churches, is significant. There was at this time a Captain John Jubbes in Sir Miles Hobart's regiment of militia, who may in due course have blossomed into the Lieutenant-Colonel John Jubbes who proposed, at the critical Army Council of 1 November 1647, that the Parliament should be purged of its unreliable members, and that a Parliament so purged would be the more likely "to declare the King guilty of all the bloodshed, vast expense of treasure, and ruin that hath been occasioned by all the wars both of England and Ireland." But whoever he may have been, he and his associates represented the extremist element, whom Windham and his friends were already viewing with some alarm.

In the previous August an ordinance had been issued by Parliament directing that all crucifixes, crosses, images of the persons of the Trinity, images of saints, and superstitious inscriptions were to be ruthlessly destroyed. In this same month of December the Earl of Manchester issued warrants empowering William Dowsing and others to carry out a methodical scheme of destruction of such objects throughout the territory of the Eastern Association. Windham would not have been out of sympathy with the ordinance, or with Manchester's instructions to Dowsing. But random desecration and iconoclasm by people like Jubbes was more than he could endure. Early in the following year he was active, together with Sir John Potts and Sir John Hobart, in enforcing the ordinance for the taking of the Covenant, with its emphasis upon the utter extirpation of Popery, prelacy, and superstition. Nevertheless he took care that the "superstitious inscriptions" in Felbrigg Church came to no harm. The brasses of the Felbrigg family remained unmutilated, despite their Popish prayers for the souls of the dead.

The Rector of Felbrigg, the Rev. James Taylor, held the same views as Windham, and continued undisturbed in his benefice throughout the war and the Commonwealth years. Few of his clerical neighbours, however, were prepared to take the Covenant. There was indeed a particularly strong and compact group of loyal clergy in this area of Norfolk, where the squires were so predominantly Puritan. They included the incumbents of several livings of which Windham was the patron—Richard Talbot of Metton, Thomas Blofeld of Aylmerton, John Farmerie of Runton and Beeston Regis, and the spirited Richard Plummer of Sustead and Alby, who described the prevailing party as "Parliament Rogues, Roundheads, Rebells to the King, and Traytors," and flatly refused to pay the Parliamentarian assessments, asking "What, shall I pay Money to maintaine Rebellion?" All these were ruthlessly ejected, together with their brethren of Thorpe Market and Westwick, Roughton and Hanworth, Aldborough and Colby, Gimingham and Trunch, Knapton, Swafield, Scottow, Bessingham, and Edingthorpe. Few of them lived to return to their old parishes at the Restoration.

At last the war dragged to its close, in an atmosphere of perplexity and discontent. In the victorious party the cleavage between the moderates and the extremists, the Presbyterians and the Independents, grew ever wider. It is in this context that another letter from Thomas Windham must be read. It was addressed on the third of May 1647 to "my much honored ffriend John Hobart Esquire at his house in Norwich."

Honored Sir:

Seeinge that I have now by the earnest desier of the cuntry and my ffriendes condiscended to resigne my disabilities, to be disposed of by their well-wishes at the next Election for the County, I could not but deeme my selfe unworthie to appeir ther yf (with the first) I should not submitt my purpose to your frendly approbacion, and to such effects of your noble Curtesie as in your Judgment shall best agree with the Cuntrie's satisfaction and may give just occasion for me to be esteemed (as in truth, I am) and shall alwaie remayne

Your affectionat servant
Tho: Windham.

John Hobart was a cousin of Sir John Hobart of Blickling, and a staunch Parliamentarian and Presbyterian. Sir John had become one of the Knights of the Shire two years before, on the death of Sir Edmund Mundeford; and he himself died a few months after the date of this letter. Presumably his illness had already caused some influential persons in Norfolk to approach Windham as a possible successor. In the event the choice fell not upon Windham but upon his friend and neighbour Sir John Palgrave of North Barningham, who was returned to Parliament on 1 November. Clearly Windham had no strong wish to enter public life; and he would have been quite content to resign his claims to Palgrave, who was in all respects a man of his own way of thinking. But only a year later, in December 1648, Pride's Purge quietly but firmly removed all such temperate and responsible figures from the conduct of the nation's affairs. Sir John Potts, Sir John Palgrave, Sir John Holland, Sir Thomas Wodehouse, Framlingham Gawdy, John Spelman—such men had been the mainstay of the Parliamentarian cause in Norfolk; and from Parliament they were now cast out. Only the Rump, the extremists and fanatics and doctrinaires, remained, on the sufferance of a military dictatorship. Within the next few weeks they had judged and executed their King.

V

In 1644 or thereabouts Thomas Windham, having been for twenty years a widower, married a young wife, Elizabeth, daughter of Sir John Mede of Lofts in Essex. In 1645 his son John married Jane, daughter of Richard Godfrey of Hindringham in Norfolk, a girl of seventeen. He emerged unscathed from whatever part he may have played in the later stages of the war, and brought his wife home to live at Felbrigg with his father and his youthful step-mother. There was a difference of only four years between the ages of the two brides.

The eldest son of Thomas and Elizabeth Windham was born in 1645, and was named Thomas. He was followed by William, George (who died in infancy), Elizabeth, Joan and John. The younger couple, John and Jane Windham, were less fortunate. Their only son John was born in 1648 and lived for three months. He lies buried in Felbrigg Church under a single stone with his little uncle George—*infantuli duo*—who was born and died in the same year. Next year a daughter Ann was born to them, and she also died. They had no other children; and Jane herself died on the last day of 1652, after seven years of marriage. She is buried in the chancel beside her children, under a ledger-stone on which her husband caused to be inscribed an affectionate epitaph and a brief Latin *epicedium*.

Apart from the births of his second family of children, we know nothing of the last years of Thomas Windham's life. No more letters have survived, and there is no account-book to tell us of his later farming operations or his private expenses. In his last illness he was attended by Dr Thomas Browne of Norwich, already famous as the author of *Religio Medici* and the *Vulgar Errors*. He died on 1 March 1654, a few months after the birth of his youngest son John, and was buried in Felbrigg Church. Elaborate memorials were not in fashion during the Commonwealth; and it was not until many years afterwards that the remarkable monument on the north wall of the chancel, of which more will be said in the next chapter, was erected to his memory.

VI

From the very day of Thomas Windham's death and for four years thereafter an account-book, meticulously kept by two successive stewards, provides details of the receipts and expenses of his son and successor John. It is fortunate that it should be so, for apart from this book the records of John Windham are very few indeed. Not a single letter to or from him has survived, and there are scarcely any contemporary references to the twelve years during which he was the owner of Felbrigg. He married three times after the death of Jane Godfrey, but had no more children, and we know virtually nothing about any of his wives. No monument in the church commemorates him. A few signatures on documents are the sole personal relics of this rather mysterious man.

Yet the account-book shows that his life at Felbrigg during the sixteen-fifties was full and active, and followed the accustomed pattern. The transition from father to son produced no innovations of any kind. The bell was tolled "for my old Master." There were payments for making his grave, and later for his gravestone. Doctor Browne received thirty shillings for his fees. And then the life of the house and the estate went steadily forward—rents were collected, barns were built, the buttery boy had his new clothes; crayfish and crabs were bought, and oranges and sugar candy, fowling-pieces, powder and shot, hoods and bells for the hawks, and tobacco-pipes and tinder-boxes, and beagles and spaniels and a pet monkey.

John Windham's second wife was Jane Townshend, one of the sisters of Sir Horatio Townshend of Raynham. He will appear again in a later chapter; and it is sufficient to say at this point that he was a young man of considerable ability, and already of much influence in local affairs. He had been too young to take any part in the Civil War; and although privately he favoured a restoration of the monarchy, he was prudent enough not to announce his convictions at this time. The date of John Windham's marriage to Jane Townshend is unknown; but I am inclined to place it in the summer of 1654, when the account-book suggests a great deal of hospitality at Felbrigg. Towards the end of July provisions pour into the house—pigs, turkeys, chickens, duck-lings, lobsters, crabs, whitings; people are pa͡id for bringing trout, codlings, capons, partridges, peas; Sir Horatio Townshend sends a salmon, and his man receives half a crown. I think these preparations may well have been made for the homecoming of John Windham's second bride. If so, the marriage was sadly brief: she died less than two years later, and was buried in Felbrigg Church on 24 May 1656.

A little more may be gleaned about John Windham's life from the account-book, but nothing about his personality. He was evidently fond of hunting and hawking; he consumed a good deal of tobacco; he liked to visit his neighbours—the Pastons at Oxnead, the Hobarts at Blickling, the Townshends at Raynham—but seldom went farther afield. At various places on the estate he must have done a good deal of building; large purchases of brick and tile are frequently mentioned, and he bought many cartloads of stone and other material from the mansion of the Heydons at Baconsthorpe, then in process of demolition. He had inherited much wealth from his father, including substantial capital sums out on loan to his neighbours, upon which the interest was regularly paid: Clement Paston had borrowed £4000,

Sir Horatio Townshend £2500, Sir John Hobart £2000, Sir William Paston £1000, and so forth. His health may not have been good: Doctor Browne was summoned to Felbrigg on at least one occasion, and other doctors are also mentioned.

Then the book comes to an end at the close of 1656, and we are deprived even of these few lights on John Windham. At the beginning of 1660 he signed, as did most of his neighbours, the address to General Monck urging the recall of those Members of the Long Parliament who had been excluded in Pride's Purge in 1648—the essential prelude to the Restoration. He acted as a commissioner for the earlier subsidies raised on behalf of Charles II, and in various other matters of local business. At some unknown date he married a third wife, Dorothy, a daughter of Sir Thomas Ogle of Bardwell in Suffolk. She died in July 1664, and shortly afterwards he was married yet again, to Lady Frances Annesley, a daughter of Arthur, first Earl of Anglesey. The period between the death of his third wife, his marriage to the fourth, and his own death was exactly fifteen months. He died on 30 September 1665, and was buried in Felbrigg Church beside his three wives and his two small children. His eldest half-brother Thomas had died of smallpox in his fourteenth year; and William, the next brother, a young man of eighteen, was now the heir. With him began a new and eventful chapter in the story of Felbrigg.

Chapter Four

WILLIAM WINDHAM I

The Windham family situation in 1665—Elizabeth Windham marries Lord Maidstone—William Windham comes of age in 1668—his able management of the property—his marriage to Katherine Ashe—the building of the west wing—estate management and planting—Norfolk politics and the 1679 election—completion of the west wing—William Windham's death in 1689

I

A GENERAL family reorganisation followed immediately upon John Windham's death. Lady Frances, his widow, soon departed from the scene. In addition to a lavish settlement, she received all her husband's personal estate, including most of the furniture and household goods at Felbrigg. Before long she took a second husband, a young man named John Thompson, the son of Maurice Thompson, a well-known supporter of the Cromwellian régime. John Thompson himself became a prominent Whig politician, and was eventually created Lord Haversham in the reign of William III. He and Lady Frances had a family of one son and six daughters.

Thomas Windham's widow, the mother of the new owner of Felbrigg, had also remarried. She had fixed her affections upon a man twelve years younger than herself, Richard Chamberlaine, "descended of the Honourable Ancestors of that Name, Borne at Astley-Castle in Warwickshire, Heyre to a Fayer patrimony and proportion of the Gifts of Body, Mind and Fortune."[1] By him she had four daughters, three of whom survived. She now moved to Felbrigg with her husband and her two families—William, Elizabeth, Joan, and John Windham: Mary, Martha, and Katherine Chamberlaine.

This assemblage of young people was soon provided with some excitement by the eldest sister Elizabeth. In 1666 there was a serious outbreak of the plague at Cambridge; and young Lord Maidstone, the

[1] The quotation is from the inscription which she placed upon his tombstone in Felbrigg Church.

heir of the Earl of Winchilsea, at that time a fellow-commoner of St John's College, was brought by his tutor to the rural seclusion of Felbrigg until the epidemic had died down. The tutor, the Rev. John Talbot, was a nephew of Mrs Chamberlaine—his mother was her sister, Jane Mede—and he and his pupil boarded at the parsonage, which then stood close to the Hall. Lord Maidstone was only fourteen at the time; but he was thrown much into the company of Elizabeth Windham, whose age was sixteen, both at Felbrigg and later at her uncle Thomas Mede's house in London. Early in 1667 they were married.

Lord Winchilsea was at this time Ambassador at Constantinople, a post which he had been obliged to accept owing to his losses of fortune in the Civil War. Apparently the boy kept the marriage a secret until he went out to visit his father in the spring. It is not surprising that the Ambassador was enraged to learn that his heir had wedded a girl whose portion under her father's will was a mere £1500, instead of waiting for his parents to choose some suitable heiress. Furious letters were despatched to everyone of influence from the King downwards, asserting that the marriage was "the foulest piece of fraud and abuse that hath been acted in this latter age in the world." The girl's mother and the Medes had entrapped the boy into a match "no ways agreeable to his fortune or quality"; and anyhow it had never been consummated.

My son sweareth about two or three in the afternoon that he was then made drunk by their putting wine in his beer, and that as soon as the gentlewoman's mother went out of the chamber he took his clothes and ran out of the room, and that since he never was in bed with her, and that neither at that time when he was abed with her, or since, did he enjoy her, nor doth he know whether she be man or woman.[1]

Whatever he may have told his indignant father on this occasion, Maidstone remained faithful to Elizabeth. He soon returned to England and to his bride. But there was little enough for the young couple to live upon, and their straitened means were not the least among the problems which confronted her brother in the years to come.

[1] The story in its main details was related in a Latin diary kept from 1671 to 1673 by Thomas Isham of Lamport, Northamptonshire. I have derived much supplementary information from an appendix to the forthcoming new edition of this diary by Sir Gyles Isham, to whom my thanks are due for permission to make use of it.

WILLIAM WINDHAM I

By Sir Peter Lely

KATHERINE WINDHAM, wife of William Windham I

By Sir Peter Lely

II

William Windham was born on 13 February 1647. His father had directed by will that his younger sons were to be bred "in a schollerlike way of education, so soone as they shall be fitt, at Eaton, Winchester, or Westminster." These instructions were disregarded; and William and his brothers were sent to a small but reputable grammar school at Elmdon in Essex, close to their mother's old home at Lofts. She and her second husband Richard Chamberlaine seem to have spent most of their own time at Lofts, though later they had a house in Norwich. At the age of fourteen William was admitted a fellow-commoner at Christ's College, Cambridge. He came of age in 1668, and embarked at once with vigour and competence upon the management of his own affairs.

It soon became his custom to set down in a large volume, bound in green vellum and containing nearly six hundred pages, his business transactions great and small. He lost no time in coming to a settlement with Lady Frances and her new husband, John Thompson, who released all their claims upon John Windham's real estate for the sum of £4500. Out of his brother's personal estate, which had passed to the widow absolutely, he bought a considerable portion of the household goods which remained at Felbrigg. He received only £10 for his father's books, "which were decreed to me, and carryed away" by some misunderstanding after his brother's death. Their loss must have irked him greatly, since he was himself a great reader and buyer of books. He employed an excellent binder for many of his volumes, and placed his fine armorial bookplate in all of them.

At the same time he borrowed £2000 from Mr Chamberlaine, "to pay debts contracted in my minoritye upon my account, as my Mother pretended," mortgaging to him the lands in Crownthorpe and Wicklewood. He had further to pay his mother an annuity of £150 out of the estate; and he was able to provide his sister Lady Maidstone with an allowance of £50 a year after the payment of her portion. His other sister Joan died of smallpox in Norwich towards the end of 1669.

These heavy calls on William Windham's resources were met by methodical estate management; and it was not long before he improved his position by a marriage which, besides being fortunate in every other respect, was also financially sound. His bride was Katherine, the eldest daughter of Sir Joseph Ashe, and he married her during the summer of 1669. Her father was a rich merchant, who lived at

Twickenham and was Member of Parliament for Downton in Wiltshire. His business connections were with the Low Countries and particularly with Antwerp. Margaret Duchess of Newcastle records in her memoir of her husband that at the Restoration, when the impoverished Duke had returned to England and she remained stranded at Antwerp "as a pawn for his debts," it was only from Sir Joseph Ashe that they were able to obtain a loan wherewith to discharge them. His wife's generous portion, and the benefit of her father's experience and advice, proved invaluable to Windham during the difficulties of these early years.

Katherine Ashe brought much happiness to Felbrigg. She was gay, generous, warm-hearted, a devoted wife, a loving but thoroughly sensible mother to a large family of children. The impression made by her numerous letters and notebooks and account-books, and by casual references to her in the letters of other people, is altogether very attractive. And so is her picture which Lely painted at the time of her marriage, showing her in brown dress and lilac bodice, with pearls twisted in her fair hair, plucking the blossoms from an orange-tree. William was painted at the same time; and they certainly made a handsome pair.[1] But Lely's portrayal of their youthful good looks was surpassed by his rendering of the worn, experienced, sensitive features of the old merchant, Sir Joseph Ashe.

In one of her notebooks Katherine Windham recorded the births of her children, and the names of their godparents. The eldest was a daughter, born a year after her marriage and given her own name. A son followed on 17 February 1673, and was named Ashe: "my Lord Townshend, my Father and my Aunt Austin christened him." Then came William, Thomas (who was born in a coach at Bishop's Stortford, a weakly child who lived little more than two years), Mary, a second Thomas, Joseph, Elizabeth, and James. There were also two Johns who died in infancy. It was no small achievement, in the seventeenth century, to rear eight children out of eleven to a healthy maturity.

Katherine Windham's little black notebook contains other matters besides this list of her children and their godparents. She put down all the money affairs of these years, her allowance from her husband, the interest on her own holdings in the East India Company, card-money, occasional wagers, her outlay on laces and ribbands and shoes and stockings and orange-water and an Indian gown. There are in-

[1] In 1709 she made over to her son Ashe Windham "my dear Husband's picture and mine by Sir P. Lilly," valuing the pair at £100.

ventories of her furniture and linen, china and plate. There are lists of her books also—much divinity, many manuals of piety, Jeremy Taylor, Calamy, Barrow, *The Whole Duty of Man*; several books on physic, gardening, and cookery; and a more frivolous section which included "Galantry Alamode," "Mercury Galant," "Garagantua," works by Calprenède, Scarron, Madame de Scudéry, together with a stout volume of plays by Dryden, Otway, Wycherley and other contemporary dramatists, which still remains in the library.

It was not long before Katherine's sister Mary Ashe also married into Norfolk. Sir Horatio Townshend was briefly mentioned in the previous chapter as the brother of the second of John Windham's four wives. When the Commonwealth era was drawing to its close he had been foremost in swaying the opinion of the county in favour of the restoration of the monarchy; and King Charles II rewarded him with a peerage and the Lord-Lieutenancy. In this office his policy was invariably one of moderation; but when political rivalries grew sharper in the early sixteen-seventies he found it increasingly difficult to steer a course between the Country Party, whose leader in the county was Sir John Hobart of Blickling, and the Court Party, who were being enthusiastically rallied to the King's support by Sir Robert Paston of Oxnead, lately created Viscount Yarmouth. Townshend's first wife, by whom he had no children, died in 1673; and shortly afterwards he married Mary Ashe. Next year she bore him the longed-for heir, a son to whom the King stood godfather and who was christened Charles, the future statesman and agriculturist.

The presence at Raynham, only twenty miles away, of "my dear sister Townshend" brought much happiness to Katherine Windham; and it was all the more welcome in view of the tiresomeness of her husband's own relations. There seemed no end to the disputes and lawsuits into which they dragged him. Trouble first arose with that rather shiftless young couple, his sister Elizabeth and her husband Lord Maidstone. In 1670 they came to live with Mr and Mrs Chamberlaine, her mother and stepfather, who had retired to a house in Norwich at the time of William's marriage; and their doings there were described to Windham, who was staying at the time at Sir Joseph Ashe's house at Twickenham, in a warning letter from his man of business Robert Pepper. They apparently concocted a scheme to put pressure on Windham, who had already behaved to them with considerable generosity, by claiming that he had promised to pay Maidstone five thousand pounds if he acknowledged Elizabeth as his wife. They were joined in this enterprise by two Norwich neighbours, Dr Edward Browne and his sister Anne, who in the previous year had become Mrs Fairfax, the children of Dr Thomas Browne. Mrs Fairfax further asserted that Windham had injured her reputation, in what way it is unprofitable to speculate. Nor is it profitable to wonder whether these proceedings came to the notice of her father, perhaps even then contemplating the writing of his *Christian Morals*; and if so what he thought of them.

Robert Pepper wrote, on 19 December 1670:

The Lord Maydston and his Train continue still here and lie at Rack and Manger with poor Mr Chamberlin, and how they can ever make him amends, I know not; he is at a vast expence and charge, and so like to continue for aught I can perceive. I have been but once there since my Lord came, but I doe sometimes meet Mr Chamberlin abroad and he tells me all the stories that pass amongst them; and one thing I must acquaint you, which is a designe and combination against you, and the business is this: There are some of your nearest Relations next your Mother, will swear that you did absolutely promise that in case my Lord Maydston would ever owne your Sister for his Wife you would give him 5000£. And besides those of your own Relations, I understand that young Dr Brown and Mrs Fairfax will swear the same, and upon their Testimony it is resolved to sue you upon an Action of Promise. This much I thought fitt to acquaint you that you may not be surprised by an unexpected Arrest when ever you are at London, for they will lay an action of 10000£ against you. I hear farther that Mrs Fairfax is openly your Enemy, and pretends you have mightily wrong'd her and injur'd her Reputation, and she will have satisfaction too. Pray God preserve you from all their Malice, for I am afraid you will meet with a great deal of trouble.

Nothing came of all this. Probably the Maidstones thought it wiser not to press their foolish claims; and the grievances of Mrs Fairfax seem likewise to have been disregarded. In any case Lord Maidstone's life had soon run its brief course. Less than two years later, in the spring of 1672, war was declared against the Dutch. With many other young men of quality he joined the fleet as a volunteer, and was killed fighting gallantly at the Battle of Solebay. On the day of his death his wife had a curious psychic experience, which she described to John Aubrey. "The Lady Viscountess Maidstone told me she saw (as it were) a Fly of Fire fly round about her in the dark, half an hour before her Lord died: He was killed at Sea; and the like before her Mother in Law (the Countess of Winchilsea) died (she was then with child)."

These last words must refer to the occasion of her husband's death, for in September of that year she gave birth to her son. Charles, afterwards the fourth Earl of Winchilsea.

William's relations with his mother were never very easy, although there were considerable periods when harmony prevailed between them. She stood godmother, together with Lady Ashe, to his firstborn child Katherine in 1670. And she co-operated with him over the erection of a memorial in Felbrigg Church to her first husband. They jointly undertook this duty, which his eldest son John Windham had neglected, soon after William came of age. A Norwich mason named Martin Morley was employed; and his receipt for the £45 which he received, signed and dated 16 October 1669, is still in existence. Although the inscription characterises it as *marmor modestum*, it is in fact a highly pretentious affair, a large mural monument with the usual Renaissance details interpreted in a somewhat clumsy provincial idiom. The epitaph went sadly astray, and provides a warning to those who assume that memorial inscriptions of this kind are invariably correct. Thomas Windham is said therein to have died in his eighty-first year, whereas he was only in his sixty-ninth. He may well have seemed *annorum ac opum satur* to his young wife; but even so, it is a little odd that her estimate of his age should have erred quite so far on the adverse side. It is evident that her affections were by now wholly centred on her second husband, Richard Chamberlaine; and when she buried him, under a simple ledger-stone which now lies at the foot of Thomas Windham's great monument, she did not leave readers of the inscription in any doubt as to her preference. She set up the stone, she recorded, "both as a monument of her true love and constant memory of him, and as a mark or signature of her unfeined purpose, in death as in life, to repose herself in the same bed with him."

Richard Chamberlaine seems to have been an amiable peace-loving character, somewhat overborne by a devoted but masterful wife twelve years older than himself. He liked his stepson William Windham, and wanted to be on good terms with him. The situation is made clear in a letter which he wrote to Windham on 29 May 1671, the only one of his letters that has survived.

Honor'd Sir

I had your extraordenary kind letter of the 16th instant, for which and all other your dayly renewed favours I return you my hearty thankes.

Sir I confess your Mother hath wheedled mee into the vanity besides the charge of a needless sumer howse, which (as you well Guess) is more for Quietness sake and peace at home than any Content I can promise myselfe therein, when done: It is but one of a greate many such like Inconveniences shee hath putt mee upon (as you I presume well know) to my grate detriment; but I must and will have all the care imaginable for the time to come; otherwise I must necessarily bee undone. What enjoyments then dear Sir have I had, or can expect in this world to make mee covett long Life? If anything, an invoialable leauge of Love and Friendshipp betweene us; which I shall alwaies cherish as very neare and deare unto mee: and as the Foundation of it hath beene upon sound grounds, so I doubt not but the building will bee good and Firme to our Lifes ends, there being not any person I have so grate an honour and respect for as your selfe; and if in any thing I may bee serviceable unto you, freely command mee; and I will endeavour my utmost most faithfully.

Sir I am sorry I can't send you no good newes of your Mother's calmness or better apprihension of thinges as they stand betweene you, although all points as well on the score of naturall love and affection as of Law and reason hath been to her discours'd and press'd by Dr Pepper, as indifferently related to both your Interests; but hitherto in vaine. I will assure you Sir the more I disswade her from her erroneous opinions and unkind expressions, the more shee offends therein. What shee designes or can promise her selfe of good I neither can see nor apprehend; But if there must bee an unnaturall suite betweene you (which I declare of all thinges I abhorre and detest) I will do all I can to wash my hands of it; desiring nothing but to save my owne state. Bee confident Sir I have and will do all I can to prevent all unkindnesses that shall or may happen betweene you, there being none alive that delights more in a fayre Correspondency amongst friends and relations than my selfe: especially where there is so neare an alliance as Husband and Wife, Mother and Sonne. What then can I say or do more, onely entreate you to believe mee, and satisfye your selfe that I will labour all I can for peace . . .

Peace, however, was not to be achieved. It would be tedious to describe in detail the lawsuits which impended. Briefly, Thomas Windham in his will had directed that if his wife, then with child, gave birth to a son, the boy's eventual portion was to be £4000, charged upon his manor of Worle in Somerset. After William came of age, there was much disagreement between him and his uncle Thomas Mede, one of the trustees, about the management of Worle during his minority. Mrs Chamberlaine supported her brother, and also swore that on his deathbed Thomas Windham had expressed his intent that the unborn son should have a further £1000 out of his personal estate.

As soon as this son, John, came of age in 1675, his mother and uncle encouraged him to sue his elder brother for the £1000. At the same time William sued his uncle Mede for substantial sums that had gone astray from the profits and interest of the manor of Worle. Another lawsuit was threatened between them over a house in Norwich which Mede had bought for William during his minority, but this appears to have been settled by arbitration.

William won his case against Mede, but was defeated by his younger brother. He recorded indignantly in his Green Book that "23rd November 1675 my Brother John Windham had a Decree in Chancerye against me for 1000£ . . . upon my Mother's single testimonye," and noted further that his mother's examination took place twenty-two years after the event. But John was not destined to enjoy his £5000, that portion so favourable for a younger son that Sir Joseph Ashe referred to him as "young Benjamin." He died in London a few months afterwards, on 2 June 1676, of the smallpox, as his brother Thomas and sister Joan had done. It is not surprising that William, when summoned to quarter sessions at Norwich when an epidemic was raging there in 1681, wrote to excuse himself from attendance because "I have been long a little indispos'd, which makes me something the more fearfull of the small pox, fatal to our familye."

He placed monuments in Felbrigg Church to the memories of Joan and John, graceful mural tablets, beautifully lettered and richly framed in flowers and scrolls. Otherwise nothing remains of Joan but a few bills relating to her illness and her funeral—fees to the doctor and the apothecary and the nurse, the parson and the clerk and the bell-ringer; gifts to the servants and the poor; payments for torches, gloves, a great scutcheon, and forty-two lesser scutcheons. And nothing remains of John but a single book which bears his signature, a folio volume of bound-up poems and plays—the poems and tragedies of Mrs Katherine Philips, the Matchless Orinda; the dramas of Roger Earl of Orrery, *Henry the Fifth* and *Mustapha*, *The Black Prince* and *Tryphon*; and that play of which Pepys so heartily approved, *The Adventures of Five Hours* by Sir Samuel Tuke.[1]

[1] I think the Mr John Windham, whom Roger North describes as "encouraging him with the present of a yacht," and possessing "a plentiful fortune," was incorrectly identified by North's editor Dr Augustus Jessopp with this John Windham (*Lives of the Norths*, 1890 ed., iii, p. 27). The whole passage suggests an older and wealthier man, perhaps one of the West Country Wyndhams.

As the dust of these various lawsuits subsided, William and his mother gradually became reconciled. Once more she signed herself "your most affectionate mother." In December 1676 she wrote: "God's blessings and mine be with you and yours. I am sorey you went away, we mite have bene mearrey to gether. Now tis hard to write, trewley my pen ffrese in my hand. I thanke you ffor your kind invitation." Her husband Richard Chamberlaine died in August 1675, in his fortieth year; and soon afterwards she appears to have retired with her Chamberlaine daughters to the village of Bramerton near Norwich. Thereafter we know no more of her, until a note in her son's Green Book records that on 29 July 1679 "my Mother died of a painfull Cancer in her breast, aged 55."

III

By the standards which had come to prevail in the later seventeenth century, Felbrigg was by no means a large or spacious house. William Windham had no desire to rival his neighbours at Blickling and Oxnead, Raynham and the newly erected Melton Constable; but he determined to enlarge his own house by the addition of another wing. Early in the sixteen-seventies he called into consultation William Samwell, an architect of some note in his day, now almost wholly forgotten.

William Samwell was one of those "gentlemen by birth who supplemented their inadequate private incomes by acting as architects and artistic advisers," in the days before the architectural profession had become fully established and organised. The group included such men as Hugh May, Captain William Winde, and Henry Bell of King's Lynn; while the more illustrious figures of Sir Roger Pratt and Sir Christopher Wren came from precisely the same background. William Samwell's grandfather was Sir William Samwell of Upton Hall in Northamptonshire, and James Harrington of *Oceana* was his first cousin. John Aubrey included among Harrington's *amici* "his uncle, Samuel, esq: his son, Mr Samuel, an excellent architect, that has built severall delicate howses (Sir Robert Henley's, Sir Thomas Grosvenor's in Cheshire)." Sir Robert Henley's house, The Grange in Hampshire, has been altered almost beyond recognition. Sir Thomas Grosvenor's, Eaton Hall in Cheshire, has twice been completely rebuilt, although Samwell's design for it may be seen in *Vitruvius Britannicus*. He was also the architect of a house occupied by the King on his visits to Newmarket, which was viewed with some disfavour by John Evelyn in 1670.

Passing through New-Market, we alighted, to see his *Majesties* house there now new building, the arches of the cellers beneath, are exceedingly well turned, by the *Architect Mr. Samuel*, the rest meane enough, and hardly capable for a hunting house: Many of the roomes above had the Chimnies plac'd in the angles and Corners, a Mode now introduc'd by his Majestie which I do at no hand approve of.

This house was destroyed by fire in 1683. In fact Samwell's wing at Felbrigg is the only indubitable example of his work that appears to have survived.

It is most fortunate that his signed and dated plans have been preserved. If they had perished, there would not be a scrap of evidence to connect the building with his name. Not a single letter from him or about him is to be found, and there is no word of him in any of the ledgers or account books. This is mainly due to the fact that he died not long after the plans were drawn, and so can have taken virtually no part in the actual building of the house. The first ground-plan was dated August 1674, and a revised version was produced in February 1675. He made his will in April 1676, and it was proved exactly two months later. The erection of the new wing of Felbrigg proceeded in the leisurely manner of that age, and was not completed until its architect had been dead for ten years.

At the time when this addition was planned, the entire house consisted of what is now the south front. Samwell's first ground-plan retained this front, but enlarged the house greatly by adding new fronts to the west, north, and east, with a large rectangular courtyard in the centre. All the domestic offices, which lay (as they do now) in a separate range of buildings to the east, were to be brought within this block. The scheme was far more ambitious than anything that William had envisaged; and he asked Samwell to confine himself to a single new front on the west, with some additional rooms added to the north of the existing front. The revised design, dated 26 February 1675, showed an L-shaped house of two fronts, as it remains today.

Samwell appears to have resented this drastic pruning of his scheme. In all centuries feelings between architects and their clients have often run high; but in this instance they were carried to excess, for above the date and his signature he wrote something which can only be read as "This ill fourmed Beare . . .," at which point the paper has been torn away. Above it Windham wrote "I perswaded Mr Samwell to draw this against his fancye, by reason I thought his first designe too bigg, and not convenient, which caus'd him to write . . ." and then a line pointing to the offensive words. Lower down on the plan he wrote, "I like this very well, altering the Closet and Staires. W.W."

The third drawing, the elevation of the west front, is not signed by Samwell; but the similarity of the numerals leaves no doubt, I think, that it is also from his hand. In some respects, such as the number of windows, it does not exactly agree with either ground-plan; but it represents the exterior aspect of the wing as it was finally agreed upon. The most notable difference is the presence in the drawing of a statue of Hercules, in a niche between the central windows of the first floor. It is uncertain whether this detail was in fact carried out; but a slight difference in the texture of the brickwork at that point suggests that the niche may once have existed, and was later filled in. The windows have mullions and transoms, which were in due course replaced by sashes. Stone pineapples are somewhat uncomfortably perched on the hips of the roof; there is now no trace of them and they may never have occupied that position. Apart from these divergences, and one or two minor details of brickwork, Windham adhered to the design of his dead architect most faithfully, as the building rose gradually and with long delays during the coming years.[1]

IV

From William Windham's ledger in its green vellum binding, and a few subsidiary notebooks, much can be learnt of the way in which he managed his estates in Norfolk, Suffolk, and Essex. The green book was intended to serve both as a current record and as a guide to his successor; and the pages of figures are often diversified with his comments and asides.

He was a shrewd and practical landlord, and supervised the drafting of his leases with much forethought and care. But his policy of allowances for repairs and improvements was sensible and often generous; and the ledger records many instances of his consideration towards tenants in difficulty or misfortune. Robert Keeble, "he being a very

[1] William Samwell was born in 1628. He married Anne, daughter of Sir Denner Strutt of Little Warley in Essex, and had two daughters. About 1660 he bought the manor of Watton in Norfolk. After his death in 1676 his widow married John Wodehouse, a younger son of Sir Philip Wodehouse of Kimberley. Mrs Windham (Katherine Ashe) kept in touch with them, and wrote in 1699 explaining how to distill a water from snails and earthworms, which might benefit Mrs Wodehouse's consumptive daughter "Mrs Samwell."

ancient man, and the times hard," has his rent abated by £8 a year. A remission of rent is made to Isaac Jeckes, "in respect the last Summer was soe very dry." The widow Copland receives an especially large allowance for ditching and repairs done by her late husband, "more out of Charity, than Reason." One has the impression of a man full of kindness and forbearance. Only on one occasion, when a prospective tenant was making unreasonable demands, is it recorded that "I parted with him in anger."

Many of his transactions are described in some detail, and he writes of his less satisfactory tenants with an agreeably sardonic humour. Thomas Gosse of Haveringland hired the warren at Felbrigg at £22 a year for five years. He was also to supply Windham with 300 conies a year, and leave 1300 breeding conies upon the premises at the end of his lease. But after some years "Gosse grew rich, married, and woud no longer endure the hardship of a Warrener's life." Richard Selfe rented a farm in Felbrigg, but "wanted Stock, was a lazy fellow, and an ill husband," and had to be got rid of. Samuel Smith hired some land in Metton, was always in arrears with his rent, and finally "wasted what he had, quarrelling with his neighbours, and ran away about Michaelmas," owing Windham a balance of £12. The Rev. James Taylor, who had been rector of the parish before Windham was born, was supposed to pay 30*s.* a year for three acres adjoining his glebe at Metton. But "Parson Taylor is an old humoursome man, and to this day I could never get him to account." Windham did not, however, worry much about this, as he owed the rector as much upon the contrary account for tithe and herbage.

Few landowners nowadays are confronted with problems about mills; but Windham had endless trouble over those on his property, and in particular Ingworth mill in Norfolk and Brunden mill in Essex. The mill at Ingworth was let at a rent of £30 a year, sixty eels and two pullets. The miller left without notice in 1686—"he carryed away his goods in the night"—and there was much difficulty in finding a successor. "Corne is so low, and Millers doe so scramble for grist by fetching and carrying (which was not formerly done) 'tis hard to get a Tennant." Brunden mill was a constant worry. After the death of one tenant Windham wrote, "By this Account one may see how little Mills are worth"; and eventually he arranged that the tenant of his large farm in the parish should take it over. "The Poverty and Knavery of Millers made me earnest to bring him to the aforesaid Agreement."

Most of the widespread farms and holdings, however, were let on satisfactory terms to competent tenants. Rents came in punctually, and the estate prospered under Windham's capable management. He was well served in his early years by Robert Pepper, and later by a certain John Salman, who became his right-hand man in all his affairs. The business of his manor-courts was ably conducted by the various stewards; and their produce, in cash and in kind, went to sustain the increasing family and the large household at Felbrigg. Yet Windham, thoroughly versed though he was in all country matters, was not himself an enthusiastic farmer. For example, at Michaelmas 1676 one of his farms at Crownthorpe was thrown upon his hands, and he was unable to find a tenant until the Michaelmas after. During that year he lost on the farm the sum of £81. 13*s.* 11*d.*, and noted in his ledger: "I did looke as carefully after this ffarme as I could well doe, and kept a strict Account of it, that my Son may see the inconveniency of having ffarmes come into his hands."

In 1678 he even relinquished control of his farm in the park at Felbrigg. "The great charge I finde a gentleman must be at in husbandrye, more than a yeoman," determined him to enter into an agreement with a farmer named John Masters of Bodham, "by which I shall have the conveniencye of a Dairie near me, and bee free from the trouble of plow-men; and I don't doubt but to make more of my land, than if I had kept it in my hands." The agreement was a very detailed one. Masters was to live in "the Dogg-house in Felbrigg Parke," and was to manage the dairy and farm for his own profit but along lines strictly laid down bŷ his landlord. There were clauses covering the buildings, the cows and horses, ploughing and muck-spreading, the corn, straw, chaff, and calder, the peas and vetches, the tithes and parish-rates. The arrangement appears to have worked well; but unfortunately two years later "Masters' Wife died, which made him not fitt for the imployment," whereupon Mrs Windham herself took charge of the dairy until a suitable successor could be found.

Windham retained, under his own shepherd, the sheepcourse on the heaths of Felbrigg and Aylmerton, over which in 1673 he was running seven hundred sheep. He also kept a considerable head of stock on his various grazing-grounds. But his disinclination for active farming remained, and gave him the more time to devote to his other country interests—his deer-park, his fish-ponds, his gardens, and especially his woods. All these, in the seventeenth century, were important features of the economy of a large estate. The household consumed quantities of venison, fresh-water fish, pigeons from the big dovehouse in the garden, vegetables and fruit and herbs. Home-grown timber was used not only for general estate purposes but for the entire constructional work on the new wing of the Hall.[1] He noted that in the winter of 1683 his herd of deer numbered 236—16 bucks, 24 soars, 28 sorrells, 26 pricketts, 10 havers, 90 does and teggs, 30 fawns, and 12 of a category which I am totally unable to decipher. On an average he would kill about seven brace of bucks and six brace of does each year. There was a group of ponds in the park, most of which his eighteenth-century successors were to merge into a single sheet of ornamental water. He stocked these, and other ponds on the estate, with quantities of carp, many score of which were given by his neighbours Sir Robert Kemp at Antingham and Mr Tennant at Roughton.

He was an assiduous planter of trees, a disciple of Evelyn and a reader of his *Sylva*. His favourite tree was undoubtedly the sweet chestnut, to which the Felbrigg soil is excellently suited, and where in effect it takes the place of oak. His plantations of this species, and their use by his successors for estate purposes of every kind, were commented upon by Nathaniel Kent a century later. Even today a few old trees survive which must date from his time. Most of these are gaunt and stag-headed giants in the mixed woodland known as the Deer Park; but the largest of all, in the small paddock to the east of the Hall, is still in splendid condition.

The Green Book contains a few records of his woodland operations —I only wish there were more. He first established a nursery of his own in 1676. In that year:

I paled the Nurserye, (which I hope will bee carefully preserved, soe long as it please God to continue it in the ffamilye) and did then sow there 6 Comb of Acorns: 1 Comb of Ashe-Keys: 1 Comb of Haws: 2 bushells of Holly Berryes: 1500 Chesnuts: 1 bushell of Maple and Sycamore Keys: and a very few Beech Mast. I did then plant 4000 Oakes, 800 Ashes, 600 Birches, 70 Beeches, and 50 Crabs, which were all Small. Sir H. Bedingfeld gave me the Oaks, Sir John Potts the Ashe and Birch. The Beech came from Edgefield.

Two years later "I planted the trees on the west side of the fflower Garden, which Mr Earle gave me out of Cawston Nurserye." In 1681 "I inclosed the Corner of the Park by Aylmerton Gate to make a Cops

[1] "Anno 1675: I felled all the Timber used about my new building at Felbrigg."

for my Deer, and planted it with trees out of my Nursery." In 1682 "I inclosed a piece of ground upon the Hill behinde the Deer-house, and planted it with trees out of the Nursery."

There are records also in another notebook of smaller planting operations. In July and August 1681 he removed sixty-six Scotch firs "into the old Strawberry Bed." In July 1682 he planted the Pond Walk with forty-six Scotch firs given to him by Sir John Hobart. All these trees died, not surprisingly if they had been brought over from Blickling to Felbrigg in the heat of July. Foresters in the seventeenth and eighteenth centuries would often plant and move trees at seasons of the year which their successors of the present day would regard as quite absurd. Windham noted after this mishap that the sixty-six trees moved into the strawberry bed in the summer of 1681 "thrive as much as those which were not stirr'd." Nevertheless he was more cautious in future, and his subsequent plantations were always established during the winter months. In November 1683 he set in the park what must have been a particularly attractive group of trees—walnuts, chestnuts, oaks, and limes, forty-nine in all, standing seven-square each way, like "the Quincunciall, Lozenge, or Net-work Plantations of the Ancients" so eloquently discussed in *The Garden of Cyrus* by Sir Thomas Browne.

Except for the great sweet chestnuts, which must date from his time, and two or three huge but fragmentary oaks which are yet older, nothing remains of the trees which William Windham knew. No estate maps or plans of his time have survived; and I do not even know the position of "the Wood," which seems to have been of considerable extent. In 1687 he "inlarged the Wood from the third Cross Walk to the Wall, and planted it with trees of my sowing and setting Anno 1676"—trees from the acorns and ash-keys which he had sown when he established his nursery ten years before. Of all his country pursuits his planting gave him the most constant satisfaction. When in due course he found himself embroiled in politics, and had been defeated in an election, he wrote of the far greater delight which he took in "my Nursery and Garden." I cannot help wondering whether, at this particular moment of stress, he was thinking of his well-filled nursery of children or of his more tranquil and more tractable nursery of young trees.

V

The middle years of Charles II's reign brought bitter dissension to his kingdom, and nowhere did political and religious controversy rage more hotly than in Norfolk. The old Puritan tradition found new strength and new sympathisers. The resentments and suspicions of forty years before were reawakened by the sight of a Papist successor to the throne. As was mentioned earlier in this chapter, a clash of personalities developed between Sir John Hobart of Blickling, who had married John Hampden's daughter and sat in Cromwell's House of Lords, and Sir Robert Paston of Oxnead, presently created Viscount and still later Earl of Yarmouth, whose Royalist father had suffered immense exactions and losses during the Civil War. Hobart, in activity and enthusiasm a sort of local Shaftesbury, led the Country Party. Paston rallied the supporters of the Court.

The "Cavalier Parliament," elected in the first flush of loyal enthusiasm after the Restoration, lasted for almost eighteen years; but its complexion altered considerably during that time. At a by-election in 1673 Sir John Hobart, despite his Cromwellian associations, was returned for the county of Norfolk. Two years later the other county seat became vacant, and was filled by a second adherent of the Country Party, Sir Robert Kemp. In 1676, however, the Court Party received fresh heart when Lord Townshend, who had sought to exercise a moderating influence throughout, was suddenly dismissed from the Lord Lieutenancy of the county, and their leader Lord Yarmouth was appointed in his place.

Like other leaders, Hobart was always on the watch for promising younger men; and it had long been his hope that William Windham, with his Parliamentarian background and his considerable local influence, would take an active part in politics. Whenever a borough seat in Norfolk fell vacant—once at Norwich, and on another occasion at King's Lynn—he urged him to become a candidate. The King's dismissal of Townshend, Windham's brother-in-law, filled him with fresh hopes that this promising young recruit would come down decisively on the side of the Opposition. To the same end he tried to enlist the support of Windham's father-in-law, cautious old Sir Joseph Ashe.

Quantities of letters from Hobart on this subject have survived at Felbrigg, often endorsed on the back with William's reluctant and evasive answers. Early in 1678 one of the Members for Norwich was thought to be dying, and the older man at once set his influence at work on his young friend's behalf. "If you shalbe earnestly and affectionately importun'd to this Service by considerable Citizens," he wrote, "I doe passionately desire you will accept of such an address."

William felt certain that he stood no chance, and told Hobart that he would "doe well to thinke of some body of a more generous and publick spirit" than himself. When Hobart rebuked his faint-heartedness, he said that he had "thought my selfe in honour oblig'd to lay the notion aside, because (knowing my owne nature) I did foresee, I could not bring my ffriends off with reputation, which upon my word, I value as much as my owne interest in the case."

The Cavalier Parliament was at last dissolved on 24 January 1679. Hobart had much to say about a project that Windham should stand, with Townshend's backing, for one of the seats at King's Lynn. He finally warned Windham, however, that a contest there would prove both difficult and expensive.

> That evill spirit [he wrote] is raysed agayne in that Towne both in the Candidates and Electors, soe that the last are like the daughters of the horseleach, and the former like prodigall nurses who are willing to quiet their craving children though with an expence of milke above their strength.

Moreover, Townshend's influence at Lynn was not so powerful as they had supposed. "I perceive your noble friend's interest in that Towne is not much stronger than his present constitution of body." At the same time Sir Joseph Ashe made a "fatherly offer" to surrender his seat at Downton to his son-in-law. But in the end Windham did not stand at this general election at all.

Hobart himself stood again for the county, and was opposed by two adherents of the Court Party, Sir Christopher Calthorpe and Sir Neville Catelyn. In their support Lord Yarmouth exerted himself to a far greater degree than a Lord Lieutenant, even in that less scrupulous age, was supposed to do. He even addressed the electors in a most magisterial letter, to the effect that "I find the Inclination of the County to be most for Sir Christopher Calthorpe and Sir Neville Catelyn, which agrees with my Judgment and shall have my Concurrence." At the election in February the two knights were returned, and Hobart found himself at the bottom of the poll. Nothing daunted, he immediately launched a petition against them, alleging all sorts of irregular practices, and making the greatest possible use of Yarmouth's ill-advised letter. The House, with its substantial anti-Court majority, allowed the petition, and writs were issued for a new election.

All three candidates stood again; and with much difficulty Hobart persuaded Windham to accept nomination as his colleague. "The battle must be fought over againe," he wrote: "you must prepare yourselfe to be a Principall at the encounter." "I thinke it reasonable to desire you not to ingage for me beyond retreat, lest I should not have courage to offer my service," Windham replied. "You are engag'd beyond an honourable retreat," rejoined his pitiless mentor, and quoted Lord Townshend and Sir Joseph Ashe to the same effect. "When it comes to the day of battle you can not, you must not refuse the combat in person." Finally Windham overcame his diffidence; the two pairs of candidates confronted one another, and a formidable contest loomed ahead. "There is like to bee very great endeavoring for the places," wrote Sir Thomas Browne to his son, "which will still keepe open divisions which were too wide before, and make it a countrey of Guelphs and Ghibellines."

In the hope of healing these divisions, old Sir John Holland of Quidenham made a last-minute intervention. In his younger days he had been an ardent Parliamentarian, and he was destined to be the last survivor of all the Members of the Long Parliament, dying in 1701 in his hundredth year. He now wrote pointing out that "unless some healing way be found out, our poore County will be soe mischievously devided, that not one or two Ages will be able to reconcile it againe," and suggesting that Catelyn and Windham might provide the solution by withdrawing from the contest. But his moderating counsels were of no effect: and a few days later Hobart and Windham issued a commendably brief address to the electors.

The House of Commons having declared, that Sir Christopher Calthorpe and Sir Neville Catelyn were not duly elected to serve as Knights of the Shire for our Countye, and a Writ being issued out for a new Election, Wee thinke it reasonable to acquaint you, wee are incouraged to offer our services to the Country, and that wee will personally appeare upon the day of Election, which is the 5th of May. Iff you thinke us worthy of that imployment, wee desire you'll please to appeare for us with your interests, and if wee have the honour to be chosen, Wee will endeavour to acquit our selves as become

Your faithfull Servants
Jo: Hobart
Wm. Windham.

The actual contest was short but strenuous. All the voting took place on the Castle Hill at Norwich; and the main anxiety and expense of the candidates, in this as in all elections for the Shire, was to assemble as many of their supporters as possible from the more distant areas of the wide county, and to provide for them and their horses during their sojourn in the city. Money therefore had to be spent lavishly on accommodation, on victuals, and above all on liquor—"letting loose the tap," in the words of Roger North. The innkeepers looked to reap a rich harvest, and were seldom disappointed. The day before the poll Hobart sent Windham a letter which vividly illustrates this aspect of seventeenth-century electioneering:

Blickling Sunday morning
six a clock [4 May 1679]

Sir

Last night at 11 a clock Brewster came from Norwich, with a good account of all our concerne only as to one pointe, and that a great one, that he, Alderman Paine and severall of our friends had been almost all over the Towne, and could not provide quarters for Dr Jessop's men and the Lynn men, from whome by a messenger yesterday in returne to our last I heard that they depended upon our taking up houses for them; and I dispatch'd by 2 a clock this morning an other servant to Alderman Paine to use his utmost endeavours and to take up houses for them upon the best termes he could. We are necessitated to this, for our competitors and their friends doe spare for noe cost. They have already taken up most of the Inns in Towne, made great provisions, agree where they are at a certainety for 3^s a man, and by giving more by 3^s a horse have taken away some of our men at Lynn, and by that means will keep some of them at home. As we shall want houses, so we shall want provisions for our men. I have order'd the beife I had provided for tomorrow morning to be sent this night to Chapleyfeild, soe likewise I shall what mutton, lamb and other provisions I can possibly gett ready against that time. I wish you would do the same, for all we can doe within this time will be too little. I wish you could provide Lobsters for the better company.

Some of our men came into Norwich last night, and many will doe soe this night. I thinke to dispatch Brewster this morning, and to gett presently together what waiters and other helpers are necessary at present.

This is a season for consultation as well as action. By reason of my dispatches I cannot well come to you, I wish your health and leasure would permit you to come to me, for we have a great deale to resolve on and doe in a little time, and our interest and reputations are deeply engaged.

On the back of the letter Windham has drafted his reply:

Though my teeth ake and my face is swell'd, if I thought I could improve our interest or reputation I woud waite upon you; but considering, if I was with you, I should yeild to your better Judgement in the management of this great Affair, I desire you'll please to give such directions for the entertainment of our ffriends at our charge as you thinke necessary or seasonable. In my opinion 'tis best to be att a certaintye. I'le meet you to morrow (God willing) at Aylsham by 5 a clock, and will provide 6 peeces of roast Beefe, 3 Sheep, 3 Lambs, and Lobsters and Crabs against to morrow night.

Early next morning they met at Aylsham, and rode together into Norwich at the head of a train of their supporters. Sir Thomas Browne watched the election, as he watched everything that took place in Norwich, and reported it all to his son in London.

Our election was the last Monday . . . I never observed so great a number of people who came to give there voyces, butt all was civilly caryed at the hill, and I do not heare of any rude or unhansome caryadge: the competitors having the weeke before sett downe rules and agreed upon articles for their regular and quiet proceeding. They came not downe from the hill untill eleven a clock at night. Sir John Hobart and Sir Neville Catelyn caryed it, and were caryed in chayres about the markett place after eleven a clock, with trumpets and torches, candles being lighted at windows, and the markett place full of people. . . . These were the number of the voyces,

Sir John Hobart	3417
Sir Neville Catelyn	3310
Sir Christopher Calthorpe	3174
Mr Windham	2898

I do not remember such a great poll. I could not butt observe the great number of horses which were in the towne, and conceave there might have been 5 or 6 thousand, which in time of need might serve for dragoone horses, beside a great number of coach horses and very good sadle horses of the better sort. Wine wee had none butt sack and Rhenish, except some made provision thereof before hand, butt there was a strange consumption of beere and bread and cakes, abundance of people slept in the markett place and laye like flocks of sheepe in and about the crosse.

The result of the election, which in less agitated times might have been regarded as a welcome compromise, pleased the enthusiasts of neither party. Calthorpe at once petitioned against Hobart's return, but his petition was dismissed with equal promptitude. Hobart then urged Windham to petition against the return of Catelyn. But Windham was not, and never had been, in the smallest degree eager for parliamentary honours. He had stood from a sense of duty, and at the urgent plea of his more experienced relations and friends. At heart he welcomed his rejection by the Norfolk electors with considerable relief.

He thought at first that he would have to go through with the petition. "Though I am uneasy to be out of the House," he told Hobart, "nor am for my own particular sorry I had not the major voices, yet upon a publick account, I am willing to proceed so far as you and our great ffriend advise." And again:

> I confess I take soe much delight in my Nursery and Garden that I don't envye the Knight the honour of being in the house, nor (to use your owne words) provide Ammunition, Guns and Carriages to assault him, yet upon a publick designe, I will proceed soe far as Sir Joseph Ashe and you and our great ffriend advise. . . . When there is an opportunitye for me to serve my King, Country, ffriend or my selfe, you shall finde I will rowse up, and be as active and unwearied in the service as any bodye can be.

But although "our great friend"—Lord Townshend—had written after the election a warm-hearted letter of apology for the ineffectiveness of his support, he did not appear at all enthusiastic over the petition. This gave Windham the opportunity he desired: and he wrote to Hobart on 20 May declining to carry the petition any further. "I am so well assured of his ffriendship, if he thought I should come off with reputation, he would advise it"; but since he seemed so lukewarm, it was better to withdraw. Nor did Hobart's remonstrances—"I expected to have heard not only that you were a man alive at Felbrigg, but that you intended to be soe at Westminster"—produce any change of mind.

In any event there would scarcely have been time to present a petition, since very shortly the King prorogued Parliament, and soon afterwards dissolved it. At the next election, which took place in August, Hobart found a less hesitant colleague than Windham in the person of Sir Peter Gleane. On this occasion both Whigs—as they may now perhaps be called—were returned to Westminster, and likewise in the third of these short-lived Parliaments, the Oxford Parliament of February 1681. Windham retired thankfully into the background, and to the indulgence of what Hobart had once described as his "ease at home, love of privacy and good husbandry." He supported Hobart unfailingly at election times, and continued to receive voluminous letters about all his hopes and projects. But his heart had never been in politics, and he grew increasingly anxious to see an end to the party strife which was bedevilling the peace and good neighbourhood of Norfolk. At the end of 1681 he wrote to Hobart:

Here is a general discourse of uniting both interests at our next Election, which in my opinion would bee very happy for this poor devided County. And considering how our interest declynes, I feare wee shall never have a better, nor soe good an opportunitye. Yet if it can't be with your consent, I will be as earnest for you as ever I was, being truly your very affectionate servant.

The words are very characteristic of William Windham—the love of peace, the loyalty to his friend.

The Whig interest was indeed declining, in Norfolk as elsewhere, at the close of 1681; and soon the Tory reaction was in full flood. Despite his withdrawal from active politics, Windham received his share of misrepresentation from a party which was determined to press its advantage to the full. A letter remains among his papers, dated August 1682, in which he addressed to an unknown friend a good-tempered refutation of one particular slander.[1] The Tories had spread a report in Norwich that he had refused to drink the King's health on some convivial occasion. The truth was that when the cup came to him

I bid the footman not fill it full, but he did not minde me, soe I tooke it and dranke about halfe . . . and gave it away without the least notice then taken of it by any body; for if there had, I would readily have dranke it, and am contented the Bell-man should in the Market tomorrow cry Oyes, Oyes, Oyes, if any man or woman believe Mr Windham will not pledge the Kinge they may goe to ffelbrigg and be convinced of the contrary, or if that be too great a journey let them repaire to the next generall meeting at the White Horse, and they shall there see the King's health goe round as heartily and with as much ceremony as at the King's Head, though belike it may be drank oftener and in bigger glasses there. I don't care how such a silly story is improved, for 'tis noe crime with sober men to wave drinking brimmers, and I desire no credit with other. I thank you for your ffriendly intimation to be watchfull of my words and actions, which have long been enviously, maliciously, and treacherously observed by some, and at last they can find nothing to charge me with but this silly story.

There was not to be another election in Charles II's reign; and before the reign closed, Sir John Hobart's fiery spirit was at rest. He

[1] It is not in his own hand, but in the hand of a clerk whom he occasionally employed to transcribe documents. It was, I think, probably addressed to his prudent old adviser Sir John Holland.

died in the autumn of 1683, a few months before his adversary and neighbour Lord Yarmouth. Almost to the end Windham continued to receive his budgets of political intelligence and speculation; and in his brief replies to express, with no effect whatever on his voluble old friend, his own predilection for "quiet, which I think the chief ingredient of a happy life."

VI

Throughout these years the family of William and Katherine Windham was steadily increasing. James, the youngest of their children, was not born until early in 1688. His eldest brothers, Ashe and William, were sent to Eton about 1685. I do not know where Joseph, Thomas, and James were educated. All the boys, until they went to school, were taught by a French tutor, who also instructed the girls in his own language and probably in other subjects as well. He was an important figure in the household for many years, and perhaps deserves a few lines to himself.

His original name was Guillaume Martinant de Nevar, but in England he always called himself William Nevar. He was not a Huguenot by birth: in his own words, "God Almighty was pleas'd to call me from the darkness of the Roman Superstition to the light of the true Religion." I do not know how he came to be established, when quite a young man, as tutor to the children at Felbrigg. During his residence there he composed and wrote out, with an elaborate heraldic frontispiece and many exquisite flourishes of his pen, a treatise on the text: "Let us therefore follow after the things that make for peace." The little volume was dedicated to "the good and vertuous Lady, Mrs Katherine Windham," and was completely in line with the views of her husband and his Whig associates, tender towards the "modest dissenters," rigid in its aversion from the Church of Rome.

I profess myself [he wrote] a member of the Church of England, and I thank God for so great a blessing, but I hope thus much I may say without being suspected to be either a Papist, or a Phanatick, that rather than divisions and quarrels should in so strange a manner rend the Church of God, and so furiously rage amongst us, it were much better for the happiness of this Nation, for our own peace and quiet, and for the credit of the Protestant Religion in the world, that such opinions as are not material should be conniv'd at, than that Peace and Charity which I take to be the fundamentals of Religion should be broken, and lost, and I don't question but any Sober and Peaceable Christian will be of my opinion, and judge as I do.

By now the rector of the parish, that "old humoursome man" the Rev. James Taylor, had grown very feeble in body, and needed a curate to perform his duties. He had always been difficult and cantankerous: far back in the time before the Civil War the churchwardens' accounts show him refusing to pay his poor-rate, year after year.[1] Windham was anxious that Nevar should be appointed to the curacy; but squire and parson had seldom been on friendly terms, and Taylor advanced the claims of a friend of his own, Mr Nobbs. Both parties therefore appealed early in 1686 to the Bishop of Norwich, Dr William Lloyd.

Windham was able to enlist the services of his former man of business, Dr Robert Pepper, who was now the Bishop's Chancellor. Pepper felt confident that he could manage the business, and referred to Mr Nobbs contemptuously as "a small Levite." Taylor's son, however, had an interview with the Bishop in company with Nobbs, at which they asserted that Nevar "was not well understood when he pray'd and preach'd, having not the English tongue perfectly." They also made the most of Windham's differences with the rector on the subject of tithe. The Bishop wrote to Windham on 8 March that he was satisfied the parishioners wished to have Nevar as their curate, and that he would endorse his appointment, on condition that he undertook the curacy of Metton as well. As for the tithe dispute, he had told the younger Taylor, "I was confident you would referr the whole Controversie to an amicable determination rather than wage Law with your minister."

Windham replied that, despite the extravagance of Taylor's claims, he would readily refer the matter to arbitration rather than go to law with him, "which is so contrary to my temper, that tho' he have had two Sutes with the Parishes, where my interest was at Stake, I was not in the least concerned in either." Two arbitrators were appointed—Sir Roger Potts of Mannington on Windham's behalf, and Dr Hildeyard, the capable and officious Rector of Cawston, on Taylor's; and in

[1] For example, in 1640 the churchwardens of Felbrigg complained to the justices to whom they submitted their accounts: "Wee doe affirme to your Worships that Mr Taylor, Clarke, the minister of our Towne do refuse to paye to this Rate upon our accompt, and he refuseth likewise to paye to the Rate of our laste yeare's accompt."

due course they settled the dispute. But Taylor did not relinquish his friend Nobbs, and accept Nevar as his curate, without a further struggle. He told the Bishop that:

> he thought it was a great hardship putt upon him that he might not have the liberty to name his owne Curate, and by which means the greatest Comfort of his life was taken away: for he did intend that Mr Nobbs should live in his house with him on purpose to read and pray by him, which he has great need of one for, at this time of day: and therefore he did hope his Lordship would have some regard for the good of his Soule, which might be in great danger to miscarry if he had not the help and assistance of a Spirituall Guide in this extremity of Old Age.

These aspirations were duly reported to Windham by Dr Pepper, with cynical comments on "this Cant of the old Gentleman," and forebodings that trouble would continue "so long as this vexatious man continues thus perverse and obstinate, which I fear nothing but death will ever amend in him."

The draft of Windham's reply is in the elegant hand of Mr Nevar, and one or two turns of phrase suggest that he may have had a share in its composition. After instructions to Pepper about the arbitration proceedings, it concluded:

> If Mr Taylor had lived as becomes a Clergyman, his Soul would not have been at this age in great danger; tho in his letter to the Bishop he seem now desirous to provide for it, his Practice is far from it. When his Lordship have been a little more acquainted with his dissembling canting way of writing, he will only open his Letters when he is at . . . Leisure.

Mr Taylor died in 1688, after an incumbency of fifty-five years. It might have been expected that Nevar would succeed to his livings, but it was not so. They may already have been promised long ago to the clerics who now took possession of them, Benjamin Beck at Felbrigg and John Oliver at Metton. Towards the end of the same year, however, Windham presented Nevar to the living of Crownthorpe; and a few weeks later he was appointed to Swafield, a living in the gift of the Duchy of Lancaster. The two parishes are many miles apart, and he probably continued to live at Felbrigg and served them by deputy. But he soon resigned them, Crownthorpe in 1689 and Swafield in 1692; and he appears next, and for the last time, in a letter addressed from Eastwell, the home of the young Earl of Winchilsea, the son of William Windham's sister Elizabeth Lady Maidstone.

Unfortunately the letter is undated; nor do we know in what capacity he was installed at Eastwell. He may have become the vicar of the parish. He may have been tutor to Lord Winchilsea's only son, a child who did not live long and predeceased his father. Anyhow, at Eastwell he was, writing to his former pupils in Norfolk on his wedding day. In September in some unspecified year he addressed this letter to Ashe Windham, with a postscript to his brother William.

Sir

I date this Letter from the happiest day of my life, a Levitical Conjurer transformed me this morning from an Insipid, Unrelishing Batchelour into a Loving Passionate Husband, but in the midst of all the raptures of approaching Joys, some of my thoughts must fly to Felbrigg, and tho I am calld away 17 times in a minute to new exquisite dainties, yet I cannot resist the inticing temptation of conversing with you, and acquainting you, with tears in my Eyes, that I am going to lose my Maidenhead, but you'll think perhaps of the old Saying, that some for Joy do cry, and some for Sorrow sing. Colonel Finch, who honours us with his merry company, tells me of dismall dangers I am to run before the next Sun shines upon me, but the Spouse of my bosom being of a meek, forgiving temper, I hope she will be mercifull, and not suffer a young beginner to dye in the Experiment. I commend myself to your best prayers in this dreadfull Juncture, and wishing you speedily such a happy night, as I have now in prospect

I remain
Your most humble and
most obedient Servant
W. Nevar

Dear Billy I am yours without reserve, and so says my Bride too.

VII

The west wing, for which William Samwell had drawn out his plans in 1675, was not completed until more than a decade later. The rainwater-heads are dated 1686, the ceiling of the drawing-room is dated 1687. But although the progress of the work was slow, it was carried out, from cellar to roof, with great exactitude and skill. The warm red bricks, probably baked on the estate, have remained extraordinarily sound—far more so than those with which the stables were built 130 years later. After the passage of almost three centuries the edges of the cut bricks which form the quoins and string-course, and frame some of the windows, are still sharp and firm. A few of the richly carved wooden modillions of the great overhanging cornice have had to be renewed. As has already been mentioned, the mullion-and-transom windows of Samwell's drawing were presently replaced by sash-windows, whose thick heavy glazing-bars in some instances gave way late in the eighteenth century to lighter work; and if the suggested statue of Hercules ever formed the central feature of the façade, it soon vanished without trace. Otherwise the external aspect of his west front has undergone no change.

Since Samwell died in 1676, it is not likely that any part of the interior decoration can be ascribed to him, or anything beyond the admirable proportions of the rooms. Indeed comparatively little seventeenth-century decoration survives at all. The wainscoting of two bedrooms, and the plasterwork cornice of one, are original. The chimney-piece of the Drawing Room, in grey marble with a deep bolection moulding, was later removed to the Library. Nothing else within the house remains as William Windham left it, except for the ceilings of the Drawing Room and the Cabinet.

These ceilings display the plaster-work of the late seventeenth century at its best, richly moulded and deeply undercut. That in the Cabinet was altered somewhat when a north bow-window was added to the room in the seventeen-fifties. The wreaths of fruit and flowers, the panels with their branches of vine and almond were retained; but some lighter and airier designs of eighteenth-century rococo were mingled with them. The Drawing Room ceiling remains absolutely untouched. Here the central panel is enclosed in a great rectangular border of roses and orange-flowers, pears, grapes, quinces, apricots, lemons, almonds, bursting gourds and pea-pods and pomegranates, ears of wheat, oak-sprays with their acorns, pine-cones and sea-shells. The same motifs, and more besides, figure in two wide oval wreaths, and in some smaller wreaths and subsidiary panels. The four corner panels are filled with luxuriant foliage, surrounding beautifully moulded figures of birds—pheasants, partridges, mallard, woodcock, plover. There are also William Windham's initials and the date 1687; and next to the initials a little figure of a pelican in her piety. I do not think there can have been any significance in the rather unexpected intrusion of this medieval emblem, in which the pelican wounds her own breast and nourishes her young with the blood. But in fact Windham was destined to live in his fine new rooms, and beneath his sumptuous ceilings, for barely two years. He had been building not for himself but for his posterity.

Both externally and internally the new wing was in uncompromising contrast to the existing Jacobean building. The roof-lines and the window-heights approximately correspond in the two fronts: otherwise they are poles apart in architectural style, and it is hard to realise that little more than sixty years separated them in time. The point was not lost on critically minded neighbours. Roger North, when discussing in his essay *Of Building* the alteration of old houses and the fashion of making imposing additions out of scale with existing work, remarked:

> This mistake I have not seen so conspicuous as in Mr Windham's hous at Fellbrigg, where is added to an old hous, a stately Appartment, raised as high in the first floor as the ceiling of the old hall, which hath made an ostentacious staircase: but the flights are so long, and the ascent so high, and the whole so different from the rest of the house, that I am not, though the generality are, pleased with it.

Later in the same treatise he maintained that the upper floor of a house, with its great rooms, should not involve too great an ascent—

> because it takes mightily off from the beauty, to endure a fatigue in the access. Mr Windham's hous at Fellbrigg in Norfolk hath this fault; for a new apartment is layd to the old so as the upper floor might range with that over the hall, which is 16 or 18 foot. And the staircase however pompous and costly in the frame and finishing, doth not stupifie the sense, so as to make the paines of mounting three or four stretching flights insensible.

This staircase is indicated clearly enough in Samwell's drawings, filling the area now occupied by the Dining Room and the bedrooms above it. But we can no longer judge of its merits or defects. It was swept away entirely during the eighteenth-century alterations described in a later chapter. Only a fragment of its ceiling survives, still in position in a curious little loft above one of the bedrooms—plasterwork of the same quality as the ceilings in the ground-floor rooms, and presumably by the same hand.

VIII

Despite their preoccupations at Felbrigg, William and Katherine Windham used to spend a certain amount of the year at the house of the Ashe family at Twickenham—a fine house close to the river, which became well known in the eighteenth century as the residence of that amiable gossip and man of letters, Richard Owen Cambridge. Katherine's sister Lady Townshend had died in 1685; and the death of Lord Townshend two years later left their three sons orphans. The eldest boy, Charles, was now at Eton, as were his cousins Ashe and William Windham, and the house at Twickenham became a convenient place for holiday visits. Sir Joseph Ashe died in 1686, "leaving a fair estate to a very feeble son, as well in land as the East India Company." The son, now Sir James Ashe, presently disobliged his mother by "his perversenesse to mee, and crossnesse in not marrying where I desired"; and she took infinite pains to ensure that no part of her own fortune should ever come into his hands. She continued in possession of the house at Twickenham, living there with her unmarried daughter Martha, who was blind, but nevertheless as forceful a character as her mother.

Windham's absences were sometimes the subject of comment in Norfolk. His half-sister Martha Chamberlaine, writing to thank him for the loan of £70 and to describe the gaieties of the Summer Assizes of 1688, wrote:

> All the nuse I heard upon the walke was a place you have got of Lady Ash of a thousand a year, and severall reasons were given why you doe not return yett to ffelbrige: the first your fear of being made parlement man, the next your desire to se how things will goe in these times, the third your hopes of the place, and to doe Lady Ashe some service, to whom you have sworn to live and dye with, the fourth and last to shake off Lady Maidstone from living with you. These I thought so much nuse I could not omitt it.

Much of this was sisterly chaff. Lady Ashe was certainly in no position to dispose of places of a thousand a year. Perhaps Windham's main reason for spending so much time at Twickenham was connected with the young Townshends. A certain amount of coolness, political and personal, had arisen between him and his late brother-in-law. After Lord Townshend's death it was found that he had appointed as the guardians of his sons not Windham, as might at one time have been expected, nor indeed any of his Whig friends, but a couple of Tory gentlemen of Norfolk, James Calthorpe and William Thursby. The future of the young Lord, soon to be the dispenser of so much influence and wealth, was a matter of high importance to his relations; and the Windhams and Ashes made it their business to win for themselves the boy's affection and confidence.

The story emerges from some agitated letters between the guardians. On 31 May 1688 Thursby told Calthorpe that the young Lord, now aged fourteen, and his brother Roger had been at Twickenham a week without leave from either guardian. They would be better at school. A week later they were still away from school, and Thursby had written to Lady Ashe to hasten their return there. He had also had a brush with Windham over an appointment to one of the Townshend livings. "Wee must all arme against Mr Windham's designs."

In a later but undated letter Thursby again lamented to Calthorpe his "peck of troubles and discontent" about the Townshend children. Windham had taken them away from Eton a fortnight before the holidays began; and now he had brought them up "in this sickly time" from Twickenham to London. What could Thursby do? He had reprimanded Charles's tutor, "who ought not to suffer them to be carryed up and downe nor from school without his guardians or one of their leaves"; but the tutor replied that he could not prevent the boy's own uncle from removing him. He then went to see his charge, and found him in bed with Ashe Windham. He said that he had come up to see his aunt and go to a play, and refused to leave London. An altercation then developed between Thursby and Windham, during which "my Lord lay in bed and said nothing." In fact the Twickenham party had "got a great step into the government of the young man." And there the letters end. For all these wranglings between his relations and his guardians, the young man came to no harm. His career as a politician and an agricultural improver is a matter of history. He remained on terms of close friendship with his Windham cousins to the end of his days.

At this time William Windham was full of vigour and the enjoyment of life, happy in his wife and children, his house, his estate, his garden and woods. The political events at the close of 1688, the Glorious Revolution and all that it implied, must have brought him heartfelt satisfaction. He might have reasonably looked forward to many years of contentment and peace in the home which he loved. But it was not to be so. Nothing is known of the circumstances of his death a year later, on 9 June 1689, at the age of forty-two—nothing beyond the mournful entry in Katherine Windham's little book, that on that date "my Dear Dear Husband left me, Having made me hapy 20 years."

Chapter Five

ASHE WINDHAM

Ashe Windham's education and early years at Felbrigg—careers of his brothers—his love for Hester Buckworth and his marriage to Elizabeth Dobyns—his years in Parliament—birth of his son William in 1717—his marriage collapses—the South Sea Bubble —William's upbringing and his tutor Benjamin Stillingfleet—they set out on the Grand Tour

I

AT the time of his father's death Ashe Windham was sixteen and a half years of age, and still at Eton. He and his brother William and their cousins Charles and Roger Townshend, formed a small family group there. Among the Norfolk boys of their acquaintance was a colleger named Robert Walpole, a neighbour of the Townshends at Raynham. His family was neither rich nor influential; and he was then a younger son, with his own way to make in the world. He was destined to be the virtual ruler of England for more than twenty years; and his career was to be linked with Townshend's, for the greater part of its length in staunch and intimate alliance, and at the end in bitter enmity.

Another friend of Ashe Windham's was Charles Goodall, a youthful prodigy who published a volume of poems at the age of eighteen, just after he had left Eton.[1] The poems were odes, pastorals, and translations, strongly influenced by Cowley and to a lesser degree by Dryden. Three of them were inscribed "to his dear Brother Mr Ash Wyndham," who figured there as Corydon to the author's Thyrsis. One was a pastoral exercise or "Propitiatory Sacrifice" addressed to the shade of John Milton. Another was a Cowleyesque ode on Solitude, and the pleasures that the two friends might enjoy in some remote Arcady, wandering beneath its trees and carving in their bark the names of Thyrsis and Corydon.

[1] *Poems and Translations written upon several Occasions, and to several Persons*, by a late Scholar of Eaton, 1689.

Each Dryad *that is* worthy *of the* Wound,
Each Tree *that's* worthy *of the* Mark,
Our mutual Friendship *know,*
Under our Auspice *grow,*
Thyrsis *and* Corydon *on the* Bark,
Thyrsis *and* Corydon *the* Woods *resound.*

But above all, the Ash *aspiring shoots,*
Thy Badge *of* Honour *proud to wear;*
The Ash, *a* Tree *for* Jove,
The Ash, *itself a* Grove,
Proud thy Name in hers *to bear,*
She nods her trembling Head, *and strouts her swelling Roots.*

The third lamented a temporary parting between the friends:

Oh! I could almost wish that Fate *would try*
How unconcerned for thee I durst to die;
How at the fatal Altar *I could smile,*
Griev'd only at thy absence for awhile.

Poor Thyrsis! it was as though Fate took him at his word. He went up to Oxford in 1689, the year of the publication of his book, and died shortly afterwards. He was buried in the chapel of Merton College.

Early in 1691 Ashe Windham left Eton for King's College, Cambridge, where he became a fellow-commoner. He remained there until the summer of 1693, and then embarked upon a prolonged Grand Tour. The exact course of his travels is uncertain, and so is their duration; but he saw something of France and Italy, Switzerland and Germany, travelling in comfort on an allowance fixed at the substantial figure of £600 a year.

He was accompanied on his Grand Tour by a tutor or *cicerone* named Patrick St Clair, who was to figure prominently on the Felbrigg scene for more than half a century. It is curious that William Nevar, a French Catholic who became a clergyman of the Church of England, should soon have been succeeded in the Windham circle by a Scottish Presbyterian who likewise obtained admission into Anglican orders. Patrick St Clair was a son of the Rev. John Sinclair, a Presbyterian divine of some distinction who had found himself unable to comply with the Test Act, and had therefore withdrawn to Holland. His son Patrick, a graduate of the University of Edinburgh, had gone into exile with him, and probably continued his studies at one of the Dutch universities. He seems to have accompanied several young Englishmen on their travels, and to have acquired a wide knowledge of the European scene, before he was engaged as companion to Ashe Windham. His name first appears in the Felbrigg accounts during 1692, when Ashe was still at Cambridge, as receiving a yearly salary of £20. He had embarked upon an association which altered the whole course of his life.

Ashe Windham came of age in 1694, when he was still abroad. It was not until early in 1696 that he returned to England, and entered upon his inheritance at Felbrigg. His mother continued to live there, and so did his brothers and sisters until their careers or their marriages took them elsewhere. St Clair likewise was established at Felbrigg, and lived there as the friend and confidant of the family, and as tutor to the younger children, for many years to come. He took orders in the Church of England, and Ashe Windham presented him in 1696 to the adjacent living of Aylmerton. Five years later he received from the Bishop of Norwich the neighbouring benefice of Thurgarton. He was able to combine the oversight of these parishes with his duties at Felbrigg, where his grasp of business and his shrewd Scottish common sense soon made him indispensable. He helped Ashe Windham with the management of the estate, and could be depended upon to supervise everything when pleasure or politics took his young patron elsewhere. He put the whole series of manorial records into admirable order—"took great pains among the old writings at Felbrigg," wrote Thomas Tanner, who also found him "a well-wisher to English antiquities." At the same time he did not allow his Greek and Latin to rust, and eagerly read the latest works in divinity, philosophy, and history. Ashe Windham himself was, even more than his father, a reader and a buyer of new books; and during these years the size and scope of the Felbrigg library greatly increased.

In 1696 Sir Godfrey Kneller, a neighbour and friend of the Ashe family at Twickenham, painted his attractive if rather conventional portrait of Ashe Windham—a pleasant-looking, fresh-faced young man in a long flowing wig, a blue coat, and a brown cloak, with trees in the background. His mother paid Kneller the sum of £15 in August of that year, and later £1. 2*s*. 6*d*. was expended on a frame. There is no record in the accounts of the small oval portrait, signed with Kneller's initials, of her second son William, in the red coat of the soldier which he had now become. She had already commemorated her husband in the church of his forefathers. An entry under the year 1691 shows that

THE WEST FRONT

ASHE WINDHAM
By Sir Godfrey Kneller

£50 was paid to "Gibbons for a Monument," with a further note of £1. 19*s.* for "bringing home the Monument." It may be that this work, which was placed on the south wall of the chancel in Felbrigg Church, was not executed by Grinling Gibbons himself. To quote Mr Rupert Gunnis, "having once found fame, Gibbons proceeded to employ a number of skilled assistants, so that much of the work in wood, marble, stone, and brass for which he received the pay, and later the credit, was in fact carried out by others."[1] But the design and workmanship of the memorial are admirable. It is a beautifully proportioned monument of white and grey marble, its central tablet supported on a massive projecting base, surmounted by weeping *putti* and an urn, and flanked by swags of fruit and flowers for which Gibbons must surely have furnished the models. The memorial to William Windham's father-in-law Sir Joseph Ashe, now placed in the tower of Twickenham Church, is closely similar in design. Only three years separated the deaths of the two men; and their monuments unquestionably came from the same workshop, and may even have been commissioned at the same time.

Like his father before him, Ashe Windham was regarded by the Whig interest in Norfolk as an eligible candidate for Parliament. As in his father's time, also, the party warfare in the county continued to be aggravated by personal rivalries. The Lord Lieutenant, the Duke of Norfolk, seldom visited his house—known as the Duke's Palace—in Norwich, where he used to vex the sober elements in the city by arranging performances of stage-plays. When he did appear there, rumours sometimes arose of forthcoming alterations in the political representation of the county. He made such a visit in the winter of 1699, and the situation was then discussed by that irascible letter-writer Humphrey Prideaux, a leading Prebendary of Norwich Cathedral and soon to become its Dean:

The Duke of Norfolk hath been here; and some will have it that his only businesse was to fix Dogget and his players here, who have now their stage up at the Duke's Palace, and are helping all they can to undoe this place, which, on the decay of their weaveing trade, now sinks apace. But I suppose his Grace had some other designe in this journey than for the sake of those varletts. The only caballeing designe here is for a new election; for it is resolved to think of neither of the old ones any more, and I find they are at a losse whom to fix on for the new. Mr Windham I reckon will be one, who is a young gentleman of

[1] Rupert Gunnis, *Dictionary of English Sculptors*, 167.

a very considerable estate in this countrey, but, haveing had an Italian education, is all over Italiz'd, that is, an Italian as to religion, I mean a down right atheist; an Italian in politics, that is a Commonwealths man; and an Italian I doubt in his moralls, for he cannot be perswaded to marry. He is about 25 years old, of a tolerable good understandeing and an estate of 4000£ per annum. His mother and the Lord Townshend's mother were sisters, both beeing daughters of Sir Joseph Ashe, I reckon this was part of what was caballed on this journey.

Prideaux had harsh words for almost everyone, and his strictures on Ashe Windham need not be taken very seriously. In religious matters the young man may well have been attracted, as were many of his generation, towards the latitudinarian side of the argument. He was no more a "Commonwealth's man" than any other moderate Whig of Parliamentarian ancestry. And his reluctance to marry, although the subject of increasing and outspoken annoyance to his mother, was certainly not a symptom of Italian morals. In fact he seems early to have embarked on the *liaison* with an unknown lady which resulted in a daughter known as Mary Phillips, for whose welfare he made careful provision.

The two Knights of the Shire at this time were Sir William Cooke of Broome and Sir Jacob Astley of Melton Constable. At the next election, in January 1701, Astley retained his seat, and Cooke was replaced not by Ashe Windham but by his cousin Roger Townshend. Indeed Ashe's political ambitions were not very fervent. There was a possibility of his standing for the shire in the election of 1705, and he did some preliminary canvassing; but in the end it was arranged that another Whig, the younger Sir John Holland, should stand together with Roger Townshend, and both were duly elected. The Townshend influence, which the Windhams faithfully supported, was growing ever stronger. In 1701 Lord Townshend had succeeded the Duke of Norfolk as Lord Lieutenant, and had never ceased to consolidate his power in the county and in the boroughs of Norwich and Great Yarmouth. He was in firm alliance with Robert Walpole, who could now command King's Lynn and one of the seats for Castle Rising; and their joint influence was immense.

The Lord Townshend flourisheth much among us [wrote Prideaux in 1708], for the whole countey is absolutely at his beck, and he hath got such an ascendant here over everybody by his courteous carriage that he may doe anything among us what he will, and that not only in the countey, but alsoe in all the corporations, except at Thetford, where all is sould. The election there is among the magistracy, and fifty guineas for a vote is their price.

Ashe Windham divided his time between Felbrigg, where he and St Clair jointly managed the estate, and his London house, which was in Soho Square. He was perhaps a less enthusiastic countryman than his father, at all events in these earlier years; but he gave close attention to his property nevertheless, keeping careful accounts and making many improvements. In matters of family business, such as the affairs of his Chamberlaine relations and their rather feckless husbands, he showed much patience and consideration. Throughout his long ownership of Felbrigg he made no additions or alterations to the house; but he was responsible, with some assistance from his mother, for the Orangery, which stands a little way from the west wing and at right angles to it.

The drawings for the Orangery survive, unfortunately without the signature of the architect, who designed it in exact harmony with Samwell's work. From these drawings it was possible in 1958 to reconstruct the roof, which had fallen into great disrepair, and the cornice, which had entirely disappeared. It is a well-proportioned building of red brick, severely unadorned, seven bays wide, with tall sash-windows rising almost to the eaves. Its date is probably 1705, since on 24 February of that year Katherine Windham announced to Ashe the part she proposed to play in its building. She was sorry that his pockets were so low.

I design to find sashes, workmanship, shutters, doors, pavement for the orenge house, you to find bricke, lime, timber, tile and cariage, but all the mony must be deducted out of what you owe me, which is at least 350£, for I can't supply my children on your account and find mony for everything, wish I could and it would be at your service.

The needs of her other children were much on her mind; but despite their occasional disagreements, Ashe was always, I think, her favourite. She loved Felbrigg dearly, and spent much of her time there. A letter of 12 August 1707 describes a visit after a long absence:

Felbrigg lookt like the land of Goshen, so full of everything that was good, abundance of fruit, the peaches not good anywhere this year, but this weather will make them better. I eat some excelent green gages, they are admirable, an excelent nectrine that comes from the stone, excelent white figes, the orenge trees full of large fruit, the Gardner pulled off the blossoms, they bearing too much the year before, that there is few small ones, the vines in the paled yard thrive extreemly, and the trees without the court yard.

It was now almost twenty years since her husband had died; but until Ashe married, which he still showed little inclination to do, Felbrigg would remain her beloved home.

II

The rest of the family moved out into the world. William went into the Army, and was soon a lieutenant in a regiment of horse. Thomas was also in the Army; he became Standard Bearer of the Yeomen of the Guard, and later rose to be their Lieutenant. Joseph chose a life of commerce, and became a rich and successful linen-draper in Austin Friars. He was most useful in looking after the business affairs of the family, acting as a sort of London clearing-house for those who lived in the country or whose duties took them abroad, honouring their bills, arranging their remittances, making investments on their behalf. James, the youngest boy, went to sea at an early age. Of the sisters, Katherine died in 1701, in her thirty-first year; Elizabeth married a Norfolk gentleman of good estate, Thomas de Grey of Merton; and Mary remained unmarried.

William was on active service from the outbreak of the war with France, and was badly wounded at the Battle of Blenheim. His leg had to be amputated, an ordeal about which he wrote to his mother most cheerfully and reassuringly soon afterwards:

Nordlingen Augt 23^{d} O.S. [1704]

Madam

I was Loath to write very soon after my first account I gave you of my being shott in the Legge in the Late Engagement, because truly my Surgeons could not tell well what to think of the Matter, but upon my Arrivall to this Place (which is the Hospitall for all our Wounded) I have got all the help I can desire, and on Tuesday last was fortnight my Legg was Doom'd to be cutt off and accordingly it was that Day, since which time I thank God there has not happened the least ill accident that could be, but all goes on full as well as ever any thing did. My Greatest pains are all over and in 10 Days I hope to get out of Bed now and then, and in three weeks to be going towards Mayence in order for Holland by Water.

I Bless God that During this whole affair I have not had one uneasie Minute or thought for the Loss of my Legg. I have not the least apprehensions of being a poor Criple but that I shall be able to Walk, Ride and go on as well as my Collonel has done tho not so fortunately.

Our Major was Kill'd, that if they do me Justice I shall succeed, as I have some hopes of.

Surely a Greater Victory was never Gained. They were 11000 foot stronger and we were 5000 stronger in Horse. They were so strongly Encamp't that they Laughed to see us a Coming.

On 13 September he wrote again:

Madam

I received the favour of yours from Twittenham of August the 22nd ... I never faile writing once a weeke, this is wrote out of my Bed. I begin to Sett up morning and evening an hour or two. My Stump goes still on to admiration. The bone must Scale off at the end before it can be healed up, or else one week more would do the Business, which now may take three, but there is no Danger nor much trouble in that.

I am in hopes to be well enough in a week to remove towards Mayence, for if I stay much longer here the Bad Weather will come and I shall not be able to stir all winter; now when I am at Mayence there is all the conveniency in the World to get by water to Holland. Here are not now left about 15 or 20 officers of I believe 200 which were here of our small English Army. There has been 2000 in the Hospitall, there is admirable Surgeons and good care taken of everybody.

Pray will my Brother be in London to buy me some more Horses? I shall hardly cross the Sea this bout I believe. I have had a small feavour this last week which I hope is now gone, and the wind in my Stomach is not so bad as it has been, which has given me more trouble than my Stump.

I long to hear a full account how every thing does at Felbrigg. Pray do you spend the Winter there?

On 13 October he wrote from Nimeguen in the same good spirits, to his cousin Roger Townshend:

It was no small grief to me that I was not in a statu quo to give an account to you that you might hear of the fate of your old Friends as well as the Victory, but now all that is old, and so is the loss of my legge, but I can assure you I make no doubt of being in a condition to serve her Majesty and my most dear Benefactors at Rainham, as well as ever, but I pray God to send it more in my power. Coll. Palmes who was the day after the battle made a Brigadier gott himself and the Regiment the greatest Honour and Reputation that you can well think, and truly I believe hardly any one was more instrumental to the Success of that Day ... Your Expression of Concern for me totches me as sensibly as an Amputation, but I must desire that you will have no further Pity of thought of that matter, for I have not the least Notion but of being as easy and happy as ever.

In due course William returned to England, and in September 1705 he married Anne, the daughter of Sir Charles Tyrrell of Heron Manor in Essex. It was a happy and successful marriage, and the children of it will appear later in this narrative. The loss of his leg did not bring William's service in the Army to a close. He obtained the promotion to Major which he desired, took part in most of the great actions of the war,[1] and was still with his regiment in Flanders at least as late as 1708, although by that time his disability and the strain of campaigning were having their effect on his general health. He was in due course promoted to Colonel, and his final retirement did not take place until after the end of the war.

In the meantime Katherine Windham had continued her efforts to find a suitable wife for her eldest son. Early in 1705 his reluctance to marry seemed at last to be overcome. A draft letter to an unknown gentleman runs:

Sir

I have formerly acquainted you with the great desire I had to see my son married: and tho' I have proposed several great matches to him could never prevail with him to listen to any, till the Lady I mentioned to you; and upon sight I find he is so extreamly taken with her, that I most earnestly wish it could be brought about. Shall think it so great a happiness to see him so well settled to his own mind, that if you can assist him in it I shall not fail to gratify you for your trouble according to your own desire, and I dare ingage for him he will answer all you can say in making her happy. My son will be leaving the town if this don't prevent, so that I desire your answer as soon as possible. Do assure you your service in this will for ever oblige . . .

Nothing seems to have come of this affair; and it was not until three years later, at the beginning of 1708, that Ashe Windham fell suddenly and violently in love with a young girl named Hester Buckworth. She was the daughter of Sir John Buckworth, a London merchant who also had a property at Cockley Cley in the south-west of Norfolk. A group by Kneller, now in the possession of Sir Arthur Bryant, shows her

[1] His memorial inscription in Earsham Church states that "he distinguished Himself in many great Actions in the late Wars, and Lost a Limb in the Defence of his Country at the Memorable Battle of Blenheim."

with her family—a fair-haired girl in a yellow dress, little more than a child, standing on a terrace with her opulent father, her fashionable mother, and her two small brothers.

She was in no sense an heiress, and Katherine Windham thought that Ashe might have done a good deal better. His infatuation had put an end to all her schemes for "great matches," and she could not conceal her disappointment. She made herself very disagreeable in a number of letters about the intended settlements. "You act a most improper part with a small fortune to make an unreasonable joynture and too great presents . . . every body thinks you have undervalued your selfe." At her own marriage she had received far less in jointure, although her fortune had been a better one, she was of a better family, and had better expectations. He was also being absurdly lavish in his gifts of jewels—"your selfe is jewel enough," she protested with a mother's partiality. Nevertheless she would surrender her own Norfolk jointure on reasonable terms, to make things easier for the young couple, and would hand over the family jewels and some of her own.

Still grumbling, she journeyed to London to inspect the bride, on the way visiting Braxted Lodge in Essex, a house which she had hired for a term of years for her own residence. She had no intention of living with a daughter-in-law, although she appreciated Hester's suggestion that she might like to remain with them at Felbrigg—" 'tis a sign she means well." Indeed she was bound to admit that Hester "has every body's good word as to her selfe, and hope you will alwaise find it so." No, she would withdraw to Braxted, which could be a home for her other children, and for their children, whenever the need arose.

It is a large new built house, not above 30 year, yet rooms but 12 foot high and but one sash window, all things convenient about it, a parke of 300 acres, 200 deer that I may kill as I please, stockt with rabits, plenty of pheasants, woodcocks and game; good ponds full of carp, perch and tench at command in stews; royalty of a river within halfe a mile; no great best garden, but well planted with excelent fruit, and a well furnisht kitchen garden. This is all too great for me, but with a hay meadow not dear, and here will be devertion for my Children when they will spend any time with me.

On arrival in London she despatched on 5 May to her son at Felbrigg another letter of misgivings and complaints. He was giving way to his bride in everything.

You are as fearfull to displease as if you had a Catch, when every body thinks you very much lessen your selfe . . . You may make me very coy to your Mistress if you please. Have not sent [to Sir John Buckworth] yet, been in spleen and vaupers ever since I came, thought she was so modest, cared for no finery, but Beautys are seldome so.

Moreover she thought the girl was probably too young to live contentedly in the country. She soon overcame her spleen and vapours, however, and sent her footman with a message to Sir John, just at the time when he had sent his man to her. An interview was arranged, and it is evident from a scribbled postcript that Hester had on the whole made a satisfactory first impression on her exacting mother-in-law. "Was to see your Mistress just now, Sir John and my Lady came over, we talkt only of Elections, she is extreame pretty and looks good humourd, too much of a town air to like the country, talkt very well, and no fault if that don't prove one."

Elections were all the talk in May 1708. A general election was in progress, and the tide was running strongly in favour of the Whigs. Roger Townshend, who had been one of the Knights of the Shire for Norfolk in several Parliaments, had been offered a less exacting contest in the borough of Great Yarmouth; and Ashe Windham was invited to stand in his place, in company with the other sitting Whig Member, Sir John Holland. They had the full backing of the Townshend and Walpole influence, and defeated their Tory opponents by a handsome majority. The poll was declared on 26 May; but Ashe's day of triumph was darkened in a most cruel fashion by the news of Hester's death. She had been seized with a sudden and violent attack of smallpox, and had died on 21 May.

The news must have reached her lover at the height of the election campaign, a day or two before the poll. It was followed by a letter in which his mother expressed her "very great concern on your account for the losse of one in all probability likely to make you so hapy, had not this fatall desease so violently seased her." She added the comment, not an infrequent one in the centuries when smallpox was the particular menace of youth and beauty, that even if his bride had lived "her charmes must have be gon however"; and mentioned also that she had told the attorney not to forward the marriage settlements, and had given orders to stop the painting of the coach.

Hester's death was lamented at greater length, and with more conventional expressions of woe, in a poem entitled *Threnodia Virginea* published later in the year and dedicated to Ashe Windham. It was a pamphlet of sixteen pages, and the author signed himself C.G. He has been identified with Charles Gildon, a minor figure of the *Dunciad* in years to come, but the attribution is quite tentative. It is a very bad poem.

> *Clogg'd with a mournful Gloom, arose the Day,*
> *And the Sun mounting shed a sickly Ray,*
> *For Beauty's Self, alas! expiring lay.*
> Buckworth*! the Glory of the* British *Plains,*
> *The Pride of Nymphs, and Idol of the Swains;*
> *In her first charming Bloom, unripe for Death,*
> *To cruel* Febris *now resigns her Breath!*

In turn her parents and her lover bewail her loss, until finally the apparition of Hester, in "a sudden burst of Glory," consoles them with the promise of reunion in a state of eternal bliss.

A painting of Hester Buckworth remains at Felbrigg, a version of her portrait in the Kneller family group. It was presumably done after her death, and perhaps by Kneller himself. It shows the same beautiful fair-haired girl, but a little older and rather more pensive in expression.

Frustration and grief can have unexpected reactions. Within little more than a year of Hester's death, Ashe Windham had married. This time he had chosen an heiress and a fortune, but in every other respect the marriage was a disaster. His wife was Elizabeth, the only surviving child of William Dobyns of Lincoln's Inn, an extremely rich Chancery lawyer. Her father was dead, and she had been brought up by her mother, who alone seems to have had some control over her. Certainly her husband had none at any time. Even before their wedding, a note of foreboding had crept into Katherine Windham's letters about a daughter-in-law who on worldly grounds must have appeared more acceptable than poor Hester. It is clear that Elizabeth had already displayed the unaccountable perversity of temperament which led to disaster later on. But other brides, the older lady observed, had been "melancholy," and she had promised to overcome this condition—"you will see if she can keep her word to be chearfull . . . I am of your mind it will be difficult breaking, especially since you like." "Liking"—physical attraction—and Elizabeth's fortune combined to overcome the doubts which Ashe had evidently expressed to his mother; and the marriage took place in the summer of 1709.

A year later things were already going hopelessly wrong.

Dear Son [wrote Katherine Windham], you know when anything I can offer to serve my friends I am alwaise ready, especially with my pen, and having this opertunity must offer to your consideration some things in relation to your wife.

She then embarked upon a long and vehement letter. It is too incoherent, and too full of intimate medical advice, to be quoted in its entirety, but a few sentences will indicate its drift.

Though a great deal is humour, her habit of body is accessory, and a wrong education, and ill principles . . . certainly crossing her may make her ill, but what flesh and blood can live with her without it? . . . when she strives to please, you may better bear with her infirmitys, and since it is your fate must make your selfe easy . . . her behaviour is now known in all the neighbourhood, every body pitys you, but I hope she will redeem all when she comes next . . . she should read some fine books, the Government of the Passions, Thomas a Kempis, receive the Sacrament &c . . . she that everybody alowes has so good sense may desire to have a good name with it . . . the fresh air, horseback or a coach in the country are good; playes, ill howers and much company where the spirits are exhausted, very pernicious . . . the Bishop knew of that dispute about trouts and pitied you, as you have gain'd ground, hope you will go on and study to overcome all by degrees.

Another letter, also of 1710, speaks of hystericks and whimsies, and an invariable refusal to accept medical advice of any kind. It reinforces the impression of a discontented, hypochondriacal wife; a perplexed and disappointed husband; and a marriage rapidly coming to grief.

III

Ashe Windham sat in Parliament for rather more than two years. Throughout that time two problems were exercising the minds of all, the succession to the throne and the ending of the war with France. In a hopeful endeavour to solve the first of these, Ashe associated himself with a motion recommending Queen Anne, whose numerous children had all died young and who was now an ailing woman of forty-five, to marry again. The incident was described by Peter Wentworth, a Tory letter-writer:

The Address the House of Commons have prepared to present the Queen to desire her to think of a second marryage accations a world of discourse. The persons that move it help out the jest, Mr Watson who is commonly called the fillet of veal was the first, little Lord Lumley was the second, Ash Windham the third, a young spark not less comical than either of the other two—as I am told, for I don't know him by sight. The House came into it very unanimously, but I have heard gentlemen of both parties laugh at it. . . . Sometime ago the Queen in Council order'd the Prayers for her having children to be put out and used no more.

This address was moved in January 1710; and it was, so far as I know, the only occasion on which Ashe distinguished himself in any way in the House of Commons. All that year the Whigs steadily lost ground, and the Tory reaction, aided by such episodes as the prosecution of Sacheverell, gathered overwhelming strength. The Queen dissolved Parliament towards the end of September; and the Whigs, in Norfolk as elsewhere, faced almost certain defeat. Ashe Windham stood again for the county; and on this occasion his fellow-candidate was no less a personage than Robert Walpole, who had risen to be Secretary-at-War in the late Government. Walpole felt that his own candidature was the only chance of rallying the county to the Whig cause. He was wrong: the two Tory candidates won an easy victory, Ashe Windham came third, and Walpole himself was at the bottom of the poll.[1] It was a humiliating reverse, but it did not keep Walpole out of the House. He had been elected for both King's Lynn and Castle Rising, and chose to sit for the former. The Windhams, however, possessed no borough influence, and Ashe was not to return to Parliament again.

The triumph of the Tories was short-lived. Their period of ascendancy lasted for less than four uneasy years, and then the Hanoverian succession brought them half a century of eclipse. Their councils were distracted by the rivalry between their leaders, Harley and Bolingbroke, and by the Queen's uncertain tenure of life. The Whigs rallied their forces, and nowhere more hopefully than in Norfolk, where their unity was cemented in 1713 by the marriage of Townshend, lately become a widower, to Walpole's sister Dorothy. There are echoes of this event among the letters at Felbrigg. Katherine Windham, when staying with her daughter Mrs de Grey at Merton, wrote to Ashe that "Coll. Walpole and Mr Bacon went away yesterday after dinner. The first came to acquaint me from my Lord [Townshend] his design of marrying his Sister. I wisht them a great deal of

[1] The figures were: Sir John Wodehouse, 3217; Sir Jacob Astley, 3200; Ashe Windham, 2783; Robert Walpole, 2397.

hapinesse." Her letter was undated; but Walpole himself wrote to Ashe soon afterwards on the same subject.

London

Dear Sir April 21st 1713.

I am sorry it was my misfortune to misse of seeing you at Merton. I proposd great satisfaction from enjoying your company, and meeting you in better health, and wanted an opportunity to assure you, that among all the advantages I promise myself from the honour my Lord Townshend designs to doe my Sister, nothing gives me more pleasure than to think it may be a means of securing to my family your friendship, which I was allways most desirous of cultivating.

Our new project for a County Election I am afraid is quite at an end, that I think you and your Brother de Grey ought to be press'd into the service, but this I have never hinted to any body but your self. My service to Tom and Joe.

I am Dear Sir
Your most affectionate and ffaithfull servant
R. Walpole.

During all this time the marriage of Ashe and Elizabeth continued on its unsatisfactory course. There were periods of separation, when she would live with her mother in London while he remained in the country. "I am sure I doe not thinke her worth anybody's care," wrote old Mrs Windham to her son in 1714. "One wou'd thinke you might injoy your selfe and friends, and let her alone." Then there would be a reconciliation, and they would once again spend a few months together. For seven years, apparently, there was no sign of a child; but at length, in 1716, Elizabeth found herself pregnant. "I am indifferently well and live more regularly, and Baby I suppose grows, for I do," she wrote in an unwontedly cheerful letter on the first day of 1717. A son was born a few months later, and was named William.

Instead of bringing them together, as might reasonably have been hoped, the possession of a child precipitated their final quarrel. For perhaps a couple of years everything went well. When Elizabeth was visiting her mother in London early in 1719, Ashe's letters to her were happy and equable.

My Dear, I hope this will find you well got to Town: and I cannot congratulate you better than with the News of the Boy's being purely well: he says Mama is gone to see Gran-Mama. There came this day a Rarée Shew, which pleased him much, there was George of England, Lewis of France, and so many curious things that the Boy is full of 'em: he came for money for this Shew in the prittiest manner.

And again: "I have been out with the child this afternoon in the coach: Nurse Wheedler with us. He is intirely well: and looks extream pretty." He called Elizabeth "Dear Nymph," anxiously enquired whether she believed herself with child again, begged her to write more often. But when at length she came back to Felbrigg they had violent disputes about William's health and manner of upbringing. On one particular occasion something took place which Ashe regarded as an act of cruelty to their son, and for which he never ceased to reproach his wife. Presently Mrs Dobyns fell ill, and Elizabeth went to London to be with her. The kind and sensible old lady died, but for months her daughter would not return to Felbrigg. Letters of recrimination went to and fro between them.

My Dear [Ashe wrote finally on 19 August 1720], I might well say, You do not care one jot for my Son or Me; when all the Pain, all the Torment which I had the last time you was here, by your cruel usage of him, could not prevent your using him so but the night was filld with his horrid Shriek, terrible to every Ear, but his Mother's; and stabbing every Breast in the family, but your own . . . I cannot possibly account for such behaviour to him, unless it was out of pure hatred to me, even tho' you greatly indanger'd the very life of your only child, who to me is more valuable than the riches of the Universe. I do not say this to quarrell, but the thing is notorious, and I will not be run down in it. And tho' your Person is the most agreeable to me in the world, and your capacity excellent, yet unless you resolve to use me for the future with some Regard, and my Son with some Humanity: I will never, by the living God, make the Speech you expect I shoud do, before you will come down, even tho' you could bring the Mines of Peru along with you.

There were further attempts at reconciliation, further scenes and upbraidings, and then a separation which proved final. Elizabeth went to live in Hertfordshire, first at Aldenham and then at St Albans. Ashe remained at Felbrigg, watching over William's upbringing with devoted care. Letters continued to pass between them; but it is unnecessary to pursue this story of hopeless incompatibility. It is all summed up in a letter from Ashe, written some years later.

London Aug 16 1728

My Dear

Our Son is a Charming Youth, and I always own that the fine parts of his mind are owing to you: the care of him shall be the buissness of my Life; and, God willing, I will travel with him: if this has any merit in it, I shall be happy in obliging you: and you may depend upon it, that no Care, nor Expence shall be wanting in me, to make him worthy of that Esteem and Love of yours, which his unhappy Father could never be possesst of, tho always

With the utmost affection
Yours
A.W.

IV

The other marriages of this generation had proved happier. William, now retired from active service, and his wife Anne Tyrrell were living at Braxted with their four promising children, William, John, Charles and Anne. Braxted, it will be remembered, was the Essex village in which Katherine Windham had bought a house in anticipation of Ashe's marriage. It is not clear whether she had made this place over to William and his family, or whether they occupied another house in the same parish. He had subsided contentedly into the occupations and amusements of country life. The loss of his leg did not prevent him from hunting and shooting, but his greatest pleasure was in fishing, and especially the netting of his ponds, with their abundance of perch, tench and "most delicate large carp." At times he suffered severely from gout in his foot, and was frank enough about its cause. "This is the second time punch has brought it—I don't think I am in much danger of having it again that way." His letters to "the Squire," the name by which Ashe was known to all his brothers, are full of affection and the enjoyment of life.

Of all people in the Earth [he wrote in 1712], I believe I have the least notion of burying any body. I think Providence has so order'd it that the weak bury the strong almost as often as these do them: and so now a days do the old the young, which before the Flood seldom hapened. I say Dear Squire keep out of the cold and wet, and I won't be unmindfull of my constitution; and we may chance to outlive many a hale man.

Joseph, the linen-draper, had married his cousin Martha, the daughter and heiress of Sir James Ashe. The match met at first with opposition from Sir James, and for some while he refused to see his son-in-law. But matters were soon adjusted, and Joseph and his wife were accepted as the future occupants of the family home at Twickenham. They had two daughters, Mary and Katherine; their only son William died young. Her two younger daughters-in-law were a great comfort to Katherine Windham. Both were sensible and sweet-tempered women; and she appreciated their dutiful letters, sent money and gifts and loving messages to their children, and could not fail to contrast their demeanour with that of her dear son Ashe's wife.

The other brothers, Thomas and James, did not marry. Thomas was still in the Army. James was still at sea. He was an amiable and contented young man: "I live happy and easy" was the burden of all his earlier letters. But as the years went by, he began to grow a little restive at the slowness of his promotion. "Really I am ashamed to be a Lieutenant any longer," he wrote in 1714. Of the surviving sisters, Elizabeth and her husband Thomas de Grey were bringing up their large family at Merton, while Mary lived in contented spinsterhood with her mother.

The death of Queen Anne in 1714, and the succession of the Hanoverian line, heralded a favourable turn in the fortunes of the Windham family. Their cousin Lord Townshend and his brother-in-law Robert Walpole were prominent among the Whig leaders, in whose hands the real power now lay. It was not an opportunity that the younger Windhams could afford to let slip. "I am turn'd a Sollicitor," James wrote to his eldest brother: "there is seldom a day but I wait on my Lord and Mr Walpole." He hoped to be appointed Equerry to the Prince of Wales, a place worth £300 a year but attended by a "great deale of charge." He did not get this post, or another on which he subsequently set his heart. His equable temper was ruffled, and he became very angry with his powerful cousin.

I cannot but conclude [he wrote] that notwithstanding all his promises and protestations, he has not made any one effort, which he himself can possibly suppose to be of more consideration than pulling off his Hat to the Chimney piece; what makes this the more touching is, I lose this just as I lost the Equerryship, that is without having any chance; and when the thing is gone, my Lord enumerating the mighty steps he made in it, and how he exerted himself: so that you must suppose me bowing and cringing for what I have the utmost detestation of.

In due course, however, he was provided with a comfortable little post in the office of the Commissioners of the Duties upon Salt.

Thomas did not have so long to wait. Early in 1715 he was appointed Standard Bearer of the Yeomen of the Guard. In that capacity it was his duty to attend the King on many public occasions. In November 1715, for example, he wrote to his brother Ashe that:

on Monday wee performed our Cavalcade into the Citty; which was very fine; and the entertainment there very magnificent. Wee had great contests for 2 or 3 days between the Equerys and my Command; which the King, after a full hearing, gave at last in my favour, so that Lord Leicester rid on one side the Coach door, and I, on the other. Thus you see, wee dispute here upon Trifles, about rideing on the out side, while you comfortably enjoy yourself in the inside of one.... I forgot to tell you I was twelve hours on horseback on Monday, which I think qualifys me for a more military Employment; but keep this as a great Secret for fear the woemen shoud think me more vigorous than I am.

For a few years they all sailed onwards through calm and prosperous waters. Then in 1720, like countless other families throughout the kingdom, they found themselves involved in the catastrophe known as the South Sea Bubble. Dazzled by fantastic hopes, deluded by the prospect of unlimited gain, all sorts of people left their normal vocations and plunged into the wildest speculation. Of the Windhams both William and Joseph hastened to take a hand in the game; but James, whose chief at the Salt Office, Arthur Ingram, was one of the South Sea Directors, plunged in head over heels.

The South Sea Company had been empowered, by an Act of Parliament passed in April 1720, to take over the greater part of the loans which represented the National Debt. The Company successfully outbid the Bank of England for this fabulous concession, for which it paid more than seven million pounds. The scheme had not gone through without opposition in Parliament, and Walpole in particular had pressed the claims of the Bank; but even before the Act was finally passed, the price of the Company's stock was soaring. Katherine Windham had already joined her sons in active speculation.

South Sea is all the talke and fashion [she wrote to Ashe on 4 April]. The Ladys sell their Jewells to bye, and hapy are they that are in. The Collonel almost every day at London to take premiums, but the first dealers wear the greatest dealers and gainers. Jemy so pleased with his good fortune, his grave face is turn'd to a smiling, he can't looke on you without a Simper ... Mr Witworth gave me 200 Ginys for the refusall of South Sea at 500 in two months, for 1000 Stocke; I am afraid he will not take it, and I be a rich widow at last. Never was such a time to get mony as now.

Some calculations in a postscript show that she had lately bought on Ashe's behalf £1500 of stock at 350. At the beginning of the year the stock had stood at 130.

In May the Company made an offer to holders of government annuities to exchange into South Sea stock. The terms, in view of the ever-rising price of the stock, appeared most advantageous; an immediate and considerable capital gain was assured; and great numbers of annuitants made the exchange, to their subsequent bitter regret. The price of stock soon reached 500, and James wrote urging Ashe to subscribe immediately and largely at this price. "I grow rich so fast that I like Stock Jobbing of all things." His letters were almost incoherent with prosperity, excitement and success. The impoverished young naval officer of a few years back, ashamed to be any longer a Lieutenant, was now in a position to discuss the buying of an estate.

I have a mind to buy land, for I think land will rise in a little time, so he that buys speedily I take will have a pennyworth. I like to buy in Norfolk because land is cheap in comparison of nearer countys to Norfolk. I would not give much for a House because I don't reckon I shou'd ever live in it. But I want an Estate that will bring Rent, if it is in a pleasant Country so much the better . . . Tho I owe a great sum of money, I have a great deale of money at Command. I wou'd willingly buy a clever Estate in Land if it cost 10 or 15 or 20,000 pounds. You will say, where will you get the money? I can do such a thing to my likeing either with my selfe or with a partner. I mean if I can't do it myself I can get a partner—I don't mean a matrimony.

He had had some thoughts of buying the le Gros property at Crostwight, but was deterred on hearing that Robert Walpole contemplated buying it—which he eventually did. So he resumed: "You will see by this whole letter what a mind I have to purchase, so pray if you hear of any thing that is good, pray buy for me, for land will be dearer if Stocks rise, so whether I buy Land or Stocks 'tis the same thing." The plea was repeated in a postscript:

Dear Squire, the whole of my letter is, if you hear of a good estate near you, buy it for me, and don't stand about price. If we had bogled about your South Sea you would have lost £1000 by it. You are not to think I have got above 5 or 6000, but I have now a good deale of Interest and power of money, and so I woud buy an Estate.

And in yet another postscript he concluded this engaging but foolish letter: "As every Subscription has immediately been worth above the price subscribed, so woud I give £1000 more for that estate than he that buys it will pay for it."

It was true about the subscriptions—for a little while longer. There was a fresh issue of stock in June, four and a half millions of it at 1000. But this time even the most cautious members of the Windham family had succumbed to the general hysteria. They bought lavishly at this fantastic price: and even then, so great was the demand, they had to use their influence with Townshend and Walpole to obtain all they required. And still the boom went on. "Stocks are much on the rise," wrote James in July. "I fancy it will be 1200 soon; if that happens, [the new] Subscription will at least be at 1500."

With every £100 of their South Sea stock worth well over £1000 in the market, all the Windhams began to look about for suitable investments in land. Ashe and William both became interested in Honingham, a few miles west of Norwich: while James's ambitions soared still higher. He heard that Heydon, the Earles' fine property with its beautiful Elizabethan house, was likely to come into the market. "If that shou'd come to be sold, I verily think I shou'd bid like a South Sea merchant for it." If, on the other hand, his brothers should find the price of Honingham too high, he blandly suggested that he might buy it himself. "If they outbid you in Chancery, I think 'tis likely I may outbid them; for as I think you know the value and will not give much above that, I that have no Terra Firma may bid handsomely for it."

The rise of South Sea stock had been accompanied by a wave of speculation of every kind. People were prepared to invest in anything; and innumerable companies were floated, some with reasonable aims and reputable backing, others with objectives of the most lunatic nature—the importation of Spanish jackasses for the propagation of unusually large mules, the wheel to solve the problem of perpetual motion, the gun which fired square bullets against infidels and round bullets against Christians, and the undertaking whose purpose was only to be revealed after the first instalment on the shares had been paid up. The Windhams did not concern themselves with any of the lesser companies. Their personal connections with Directors and with leading politicians gave them a good place in the scramble for South Sea stock; and they referred to these rival enterprises, with lofty detachment, as "bubbles." But it was the bursting of these lesser bubbles that brought their own inflated stock crashing hopelessly to the ground. The South Sea Directors had in fact lost all control of the situation which they had themselves created. Nevertheless they continued to pose as models of financial orthodoxy. In August they persuaded the Government to take proceedings against a number of the "bubble" companies, on the ground that they had no chartered or other legal status. A widespread panic and loss of prices followed at once, and many of the lesser companies collapsed or vanished overnight. Even South Sea stock began to fall ominously.

The majority of its holders still saw little cause for alarm. Writing to Ashe on 23 August, Katherine Windham could refer to the casualties among the lesser companies with the detachment of one whose own investments were still impregnably secure. South Sea stock had fallen to 825; but there seemed no need to worry—its price had fluctuated considerably from time to time during the past months, but had always advanced to a higher level. If stocks fell, so would the price of land; and Jemmy would get his estate at a cheaper rate.

> The fall of stocks and bubles will make land doe so. The Bubles, instead of a milion, have by underhand wayes projected to increase their stocks to milions without end, and have forct the Government to goe about to supresse them; and if they canot doe it, the Parliament must, or milions must be undon; for how can Lutestring, Copper, Thames Water or Insurance imploy milions?

She then turned to the buying of estates by her sons.

> If Jemy does not purchase Heydon, he thinks he shall like Honingham. You comend the place, have you seen it? The Collonel sayes it stands in a botom, in wet weather horses go up to the bely in the court yard, the garden wet and full of springs.

A few more days put an end to Jemmy's hopes of purchasing any of these fine places, and to all his golden dreams. In a month's time his paper fortune had vanished beyond recall. South Sea stock fell catastrophically, day after day, with everyone rushing to sell and no one prepared to buy. On 20 September the price had fallen to 410; by the end of the month it was at 150.

> Dear Brother [wrote William to Ashe on the 27th of that month], I have not wrote to you a long Time. I have been out of order, and there has been no good news to send—and indeed I might stay a good while longer if I should stay until there was. There never was such distraction and such undoing in any country. You can't suppose the number of familys undone. One may almost say every body is ruin'd, who has traded beyond their Stock. Many a 100000 man not worth a groat; and it grieves me to think of some of them. I have no contracts against me, only they upon whom I have obligations are bad paymasters. If I get enough to pay for Earsham, it will be well.

On 25 November he wrote again.

> We are here in a most sad state between Hope and Despair.... Poor Jemmy's affairs are most irretrievable I doubt; and as to the Misery which I think will attend this Affair, we do not yet see a hundredth part. Allmost all one knows or sees are upon the very Brink of Destruction, and those who were reckon'd to have done well yesterday are found stark nought to day. Those Divells of Directors have ruin'd more men's fortunes in this world, than I hope old Belzebub will do souls for the next.

Almost all the Windham family had sustained considerable losses. Precise details are lacking, but Katherine Windham had certainly exchanged at least a substantial portion of her holdings of government annuities for South Sea stock. Her notebooks, at no time very lucid, contain pathetic little entries such as: "Michaelmas 1722. I lost so much by the South Sea, and my affairs wear so intangled, I could finish no account." Her daughter Mary had suffered in the same way. Joseph the merchant brother, the experienced man of business, undoubtedly lost a great deal of the money which his shop had brought him over the years. Ashe had lost money too, and no more was heard of his intention of buying Honingham or any other estate. William managed to collect a reasonable amount of the money that was owing to him, and was able to complete the purchase of Earsham. It was not a cheap acquisition. The previous owner, a proficient amateur architect named John Buxton, who had lately designed and built the fine red-brick house which went with the property, boasted to a friend many years later that he had disposed of it "in the South Sea float to one of the Felbrigg family of the Windhams, being paid as he told this relator for every nail in it."

In fact James was the only member of the family to whom the events of 1720 brought absolute disaster. He had hopelessly over-reached himself in his stock-jobbing operations, and had lost all his own money and a good deal entrusted to him by other people. To one of these, a Norfolk neighbour, after explaining that he must default to the tune of £20,000, he remarked that "the Directors have brought themselves into Bankruptcy by being cunning artfull Knaves, I am come into the same State for being a very silly Fool." On 3 January 1721 he wrote to Ashe: "Dear Brother, I am sorry you have been under so much concern for me. I write this to ease your mind as much as I can." He gave reassuring details about the Salt Office and a bond that was due to

Ashe, and continued: "I dare say I have not lost your good opinion, and you may depend on what I say. . . . I am extremely sensible how much I am obliged to you for what you have done for me, and shall ever be your most affectionate James Windham." In a postscript he mentioned that he might be able to obtain, through Robert Walpole's influence, the place at the Salt Office from which Arthur Ingram had been expelled. (All the South Sea Directors had now been removed from any place of trust.) But, he added, "the Sea is fittest for an undone man, and so I am for that. Really the only reluctance I have is that I shall lose the happyness of spending a great part of the rest of my life with you."

So back to sea he went. He resigned his place at the Salt Office, in which, thanks to the intervention of Robert Walpole, his brother Joseph was enabled to succeed him. In May 1721 he was given the command of the *Solebay*, a vessel of twenty guns. He cruised first towards Sweden, and then returned to Scotland. Joseph Windham wrote to Ashe on 26 August: "Brother James has not been seasick in going, and coming home he was in a great storm, and had not time to think of any such things. His being the cause of so much vexation and care to his relations is his only concern." Soon afterwards he distinguished himself by the capture of no fewer than twelve smuggling vessels, some of which he brought into Newcastle and others into Yarmouth. The usual altercation about prize-money followed, but he was able to obtain, once again with the aid of the invaluable Walpole influence, the useful sum of £1000. His good service on this and other occasions led also to the command of a larger ship, the *Diamond*, in which he sailed to the West Indies, and harried the pirates of the Caribbean instead of the smugglers of the North Sea. In one action he saved eight merchant ships from a pirate, and retook one ship of Bristol; but the pirate got into shallow water and could not be taken. Soon afterwards, on 3 January 1725, he died in the Bay of Honduras and was buried at sea. He had not quite completed his thirty-eighth year.

V

Despite various overtures towards a reconciliation, Ashe Windham and his wife did not live together again after their great quarrel in 1720. Their son William remained at Felbrigg, where he was brought up with all the indulgence due to the only child of a lonely and saddened father, and with all the disadvantages as well. The rest of the family offered good advice and expressed their misgivings freely. "This is the cheife age to correct Master," his grandmother wrote during the South Sea summer: "am very glad he is so good natured, but a sure sign he will be pationate. Does he learn his booke and Catichism?" His uncle Joseph wrote a little later: "The Esquire's child is as fine a child as ever I saw, but spoilt in the bringing of him up—perhaps it may be overcome, if not the consequence fatall to all that have anything to do with him."

In 1721 his father had an illness or possibly a nervous breakdown, and went to drink the waters at Bristol, a visit which he found it necessary to repeat several times. So old Mrs Windham, accompanied by her daughter Mary, came to look after the house at Felbrigg, and continued there to the end of her days. Far from "correcting Master," she proved the most indulgent grandmother imaginable. She would have preferred him, at the age of four, to study *Télémaque*; but when his attention began to wander, she had no hesitation in substituting *Robin Hood.*

Many letters bear witness to William's liveliness, charm, and extreme precocity. The latter quality is attested by a list, in his father's handwriting, of "Tunes that Billy knew before he was 2 years old—January 26 1719." The tunes numbered no fewer than sixty-four and covered a strikingly wide field, ranging from the overtures to *Pyrrhus* and *Hydaspes*, through *Greensleeves* and *Bonnie Dundee*, to such songs as *Bouncy Doxy* and *Who got the Maid with Child?* At an early date Nurse Wheedler gave place to a French valet called Monsieur Ruth, who looked after the boy for a number of years. Thomas Windham wrote from Felbrigg to Ashe at Bristol on 8 July 1722: "Dear Esquire, Master Billy takes a great Pleasure in learning French and he pronounces it very well. Mr Ruth is very carefull of him; and they are best pleas'd when they are together." Other instruction was given by Patrick St Clair, still living close by at Sustead with his wife and daughter, and in constant touch with all that went on at Felbrigg. But in 1723 a regular tutor arrived in the person of a young man named Benjamin Stillingfleet, lately a scholar of Trinity College, Cambridge, who had now come down after taking his degree.

Edward Stillingfleet, the famous Bishop of Worcester, had married Andrea Dobyns, a sister of the rich lawyer William Dobyns, Mrs Ashe Windham's father. The Bishop's elder son displeased his father by professing Jacobite sympathies and marrying a woman without a fortune; and in consequence he could obtain no better preferment than a small living in Norfolk. He died in 1708; but his widow and children were befriended by Ashe Windham and his wife, who took a particular interest in the son, her promising young cousin Benjamin. His engagement as tutor to little William was at first regarded as a temporary post, since he had reasonable hopes of obtaining a Fellowship at Trinity in a few years' time. But he had somehow antagonised the all-powerful Master of Trinity, Richard Bentley, who caused him to be rejected. "Mr Stillingfleet is too fine a gentleman to be buried in a College" was the Master's supposed explanation. But Benjamin Stillingfleet was not a fine gentleman at all. He was a gentle, modest, rather unworldly young man, not averse from social life, but by temperament a scholar and an amateur of letters. After his rebuff at Trinity he showed no further ambition, but was content to act as tutor and companion to his young kinsman for as long as his services were required.

He proved an admirable tutor in every way. He gave William as good a grounding in the classics and mathematics as he would have received at any school. But he was also a man endowed with a wide-ranging intellectual curiosity, which he imparted to his pupil. They studied science and natural philosophy, music, mechanics, perspective, several European languages and their literature. The boy also profited from his tutor's predilection for husbandry, botany and natural history. Their personal relationship was a completely happy one throughout the many years of their association.

Nevertheless William's mother, critically examining him during the occasional visits he paid her, found much cause for complaint. In 1729 she thought that his religious instruction was being neglected, and urged her husband to remedy the omission. "You know better than I do what are my Cosen Stillingfleet's principles, and Ruth knows as little of that as of any other matter. . . . I must lay this matter home to your thoughts and conscience; a contrary behaviour you can ill answer to God, your son or your self." She could not judge the boy's progress in Latin and Greek, but "he never as I heard on read other books except voyages or Bawdy plays." He stooped in his gait. His manners at table were far from perfect. And what were the plans for his future? "The World is indeed extreamly bad, and difficult I believe it is for a young Man to live in it with inocence."

Stillingfleet's religious principles appear to have been perfectly orthodox, and there can have been as little ground for her other criticisms. Ashe Windham wrote to defend the régime at Felbrigg:

> I am sensible my Son is far from being perfect, but I comfort my Self that there is not *One* to be found, of near his Age, who for universal knowledge, cleverness, and manly conversation, can match, or come up to him. He is constant at family-prayers, and at Church: on Sunday Evening, he reads either to me or Mr Stillingfleet one of Dr Tillotson's Sermons: after reading it he can give a just, and surprizing account of it.

And although William never went to school, or for that matter to either university, his education at home had no softening effect whatever on his physique or his character. He grew up tall and athletic, vigorous and self-reliant, a first-rate horseman, fencer, and boxer. As his grandmother had foreseen, in manhood he became what she described as "pationate"—headstrong, excitable, amorous. But these qualities were equally conspicuous in many of his friends and contemporaries who had been through a more conventional schooling at Eton or Westminster.

Katherine Windham died on the Christmas Eve of 1729 in her seventy-eighth year, the matriarch of her widely scattered family. At Felbrigg, except during the short period of her eldest son's married life, she had been the dominant personality for sixty years. After his wife's departure, and in view of his long absences at Bristol or Bath, Ashe had thankfully made over to her the control of his establishment. The last letter she ever wrote to him was about the prospects of fruit, the acquisition of a new cook, and the difficulty of finding a man to break his colts. At Felbrigg she remained till her death, a shrewd and active manager, writing her affectionate but downright letters to her other children, scolding them severely at times and sometimes provoking indignant replies—especially from Joseph, whose handling of her money affairs often dissatisfied her. Of all her grandchildren, it was in William that she took most pride; and when he was with his father at Bristol in 1728, the year before her death, she addressed to him one of the most charming of all her letters.

> My Dear Child
>
> It is pleasure to me to hear you are so well, and your papa. You are now able to partake all the divertions of persons of your age, and as you now keep better Company than old women and old maids, I hope you will indevour to be upright and strait as they are. Every letter is filled with your health, but none mention the cheif fault you have, and I love you so well I would have you all perfection.
>
> I have been very bisy in directing the new wood, we have planted 4200 Chestnuts, 300 Beeches, 300 Birches, sowed 3 bushels of Accorns

and some Hawes. They tell me it makes a preety figure, and I please my selfe in time to come as you ride by you will remember me, and live to reap some profit of it.

All the local news follows. His fox and pigeons are well. Mr St Clair has got the son of Lord Breadalbane's gardener living with him to learn husbandry. Mr Earle of Heydon had died, and had been buried under the communion table, "to be as far from his kindred as he can." There was a report that "a quarel for a souldier's wife put him in a pation and killed him." The fruit was not keeping. Venison and woodcocks had been sent, but they could not get a hare.

I forget you are now full of divertions. Tho I am so delighted with a paper conversation, you will be tired if I doe not finish with the sincerest affection of

Your Grandmama
K. Windham.

VI

From this time onwards, for the next twelve years or so, a steady light is thrown upon life at Felbrigg by the letters which Patrick St Clair wrote to Ashe Windham during his frequent absences from home. I have printed them, with a connecting narrative and a good deal of annotation, in my book *Country Neighbourhood*; and it is unnecessary to quote from them again. They form the chronicle of a quiet countryside in the reign of King George II, during the latter half of Sir Robert Walpole's long ministry. In their modest way they reflect and endorse Walpole's own ideals of prosperity, consolidation and peace.

About the time of Ashe Windham's marriage St Clair had likewise married, and had gone to live at the Old Hall in the nearby village of Sustead. He continued to take the closest interest in the fortunes of the Windham family, and an active part in the management of the Felbrigg estate. His wife died in 1727: she and two of her near relations had all been swept away "near the same time, in the year terrible for Fevers," as their family monument in Hingham Church bears witness. St Clair was left alone with his daughter Elizabeth, "my dear child who is belov'd and esteem'd by all that know her, the greatest comfort of my life." The tutor and his former pupil had met with the same fortune. Both had lost their wives; the hopes and interests of both were centred upon an only child. The long-established bond of sympathy between them was strengthened by circumstance.

Ashe Windham's illness, at the time of his final separation from his wife, was evidently long and serious. There are many references thereafter, especially in his mother's letters, to the state of his health and the weakness of his nerves. For a long time an annual visit to Bristol or Bath was a necessity. Gradually he recovered strength and spirits, and survived into a robust old age. Even so, he liked to diversify his country life with visits to London, where he lodged in Suffolk Street in the house of an obscure landscape-painter named Walter Grimbaldstone; or with his brother Joseph when he succeeded in his wife's right to the Ashe house at Twickenham; with his brother William at Earsham, or his sister Mrs de Grey at Merton. To each of these places St Clair's letters would follow him, with all the business of the estate and all the gossip of the neighbourhood.

Throughout the letters the personality of St Clair is naturally predominant: but Ashe Windham's pleasant easygoing character is reflected in them as well. The two men understood one another perfectly—except on one single occasion, when some trifling matter had brought an expression of annoyance from Windham, and St Clair retaliated with a justification that covered several pages. But this was soon put right, and the correspondence flowed on. Both were scholars as well as men of business: some lines of Horace, or an apt quotation from Petronius, would alternate with news of the declining fortunes of the Pastons at Barningham, or the progress of the stately house which Horatio Walpole was building at Wolterton. The quiet social life of a country district was depicted in all its detail—that little circle of friends and neighbours, restricted always by undependable roads and the resources of a modest stable. The doings of the Wyndham relations at Cromer Hall and the choleric but kindly Colonel Harbord at Gunton; echoes from the great houses farther afield, Blickling, Raynham, Houghton, the rising magnificence of Holkham; more intimate news from a score of parsonages and small manors close at hand; and always in the background the farming and grazing, the rent audits and the manor courts on which everything was based.

During the period covered by St Clair's letters there were several changes in the family circle of the Windhams. William, the Colonel, died in 1730. He had complained now and then of suffering from the stone as well as from the gout; but in general his letters remained until his death as cheerful and buoyant as when he lost his leg at Blenheim a quarter of a century before. For several years he had been one of the Members of Parliament for Aldeburgh, a little Suffolk borough where the influence of the Treasury was predominant. He was succeeded in its representation by his eldest son William, who was pursuing his fortunes at Court as Under-Governor to the King's second son, William Duke of Cumberland. This William married Mary Countess of Deloraine, a widow somewhat older than himself, who occupied at Court a position officially parallel with his own. She was Under-Governess to the young Princesses; but she was also a favoured mistress of the King, the only woman, according to Lord Hervey, "that ever played with him in his daughters' apartment." Sir Robert Walpole much distrusted her influence, and spoke of her as "a very dangerous one"; and Pope's line *Slander or poison dread from Delia's rage* was supposed to have been directed against her. None of these alarming characteristics are suggested by the few references to her in the letters at Felbrigg, which show her moving quite normally in her husband's family circle. Hervey was perhaps nearer the mark when he described her in 1737 as "one of the vainest as well as one of the simplest women that ever lived." She was, however, a famous beauty: he went on to say that "to this wretched head there was certainly joined one of the prettiest faces that ever was formed, which, though she was now five-and-thirty, had a bloom upon it, too, that not one woman in ten thousand has at fifteen."

The close of 1733 witnessed the death of Sir James Ashe, "whose Estate of 4000£ *per annum*, and a great Sum of Money, falls to his Son-in-law *Joseph Windham* Esq., a Wholesale Linnen-Draper in *Austin-Fryars*." Joseph, it will be remembered, had married his cousin Martha, Sir James's daughter; and although the baronet had become reconciled to the match after a time, he had proved a difficult and cantankerous father-in-law to the end of his days. Little aid seems ever to have been forthcoming from his coffers towards the repair of Joseph's fortunes after the South Sea Bubble, until this great accession of wealth completely restored them. Joseph added the name of Ashe to his own, and as Joseph Windham Ashe soon became one of the Members of Parliament for Downton, the Wiltshire borough where his wife's family had held influence for so long. Shortly afterwards his daughter Mary, the only survivor of his three children, married her cousin John, the second son of Colonel William Windham of Earsham.

Thomas Windham died in 1736, still holding the rank of Lieutenant of the Yeomen of the Guard. He had never married, and apart from half a dozen short letters, few vestiges of him have survived. But he had been a pleasant member of the family circle and was remembered with affection, not least by St Clair, who observed during his solitary dispute with Ashe Windham that "your brother Thomy us'd to say you were generous to a fault to some people, but poor St Clair you grudg'd to pay him his due."

Ashe Windham's wife died in the same year. Throughout their long period of separation they had continued to exchange occasional letters; and as late as 1730, during one of his illnesses, she had written to ask if she might return to him. She had heard that he was alone, with only servants to look after him, and offered her affectionate care and attendance. In earlier days, she admitted, "youth and folly had made me behave with less submission than I ought." But now that she was older and wiser, "if any thing on my part can be to your happyness or advantage to the utmost of my power, I will not be wanting in any part of my duty." Even so, she was not able to resist one or two bitter allusions to the unhappy past; and it is clear, from the rough notes for his reply which her husband jotted down on the back of the letter, that his mind was absolutely set against her return.

> Not say any thing of my Sufferings nor by way of Retaliation. Whatever opinion she has good of me by starts, and occasionally, she will find me full of Imperfections: and as so many years older, so much more disagreeable to her. Sister would have come but I discouraged it.[1] A man so sick is the most offensive animal that lives.

So Elizabeth Windham remained in London, or at her country retreat in Hertfordshire, to the end of her days. She died at her house in Southampton Street on 5 March 1736, at the age of forty-three, and was buried at St Albans. Her son, now a young man of eighteen, had been with her for several weeks. He kept his father informed about her declining health; but he had more to say about the astronomical lectures of Desaguliers which he was attending, and the fine Paris edition in which he was reading Polybius with Stillingfleet. After her death it fell to him to examine her possessions, and to make an inventory of the bonds and deeds in her walnut chest of drawers, the jewels in her crimson velvet casket, the trinkets in her japanned cabinet. Among the relics of her past life this unloved woman had preserved a miniature of her mother-in-law, Katherine Windham, the woman whom everyone had loved so well.

[1] This was presumably his sister Mary, who after her mother's death in the previous year had gone to live, like so many East Anglian widows and spinsters, in the sociable town of Bury St Edmunds.

VII

It appears from St Clair's letters that two rival beauties shared the admiration of the Felbrigg neighbourhood during the seventeen-thirties. One of them was his own daughter Betty, about whose suitors a good deal is heard—for example, the "handsome, ingenious and sober clergyman," with the excellent living and satisfactory temporal estate, who heard of her perfections from afar, and came to stay with their neighbour Mr Cremer "with no other design but to see her." But Betty's health was delicate, and her attachment to her widowed father extreme. It was not until after his death, many years later, that she married the Rector of Stiffkey, the Rev. Theophilus Lowe, who makes a fleeting appearance in the pages of Boswell as a schoolfellow of Samuel Johnson. In those far-off days at Lichfield, according to the great man, "they never thought to raise me by comparing me to any one; they never said, Johnson is as good a scholar as such a one; but such a one is as good a scholar as Johnson; and this was said but of one, but of Lowe; and I do not think he was as good a scholar."

The other local beauty was Miss Anne Barnes. Her brother was the Rector of Felbrigg, but she lived at Northrepps with her father, a retired Norwich lawyer. She had many admirers, some of them men of wealth and standing, others of humbler degree. Among the latter was Benjamin Stillingfleet, who fell passionately in love with her. He would walk at night to Northrepps for a glimpse of the light of her bedroom candle. His ardent letters, signed Damon and addressed to Celia, reached her almost every day. He wrote some lines to her with a diamond upon a window-pane of the china-closet at Felbrigg.[1] Gradually, and against her better judgement, she gave way to his importunity, and "promisd him that if he ever was in a way that could maintain me in the manner I had been usd to, and he shoud like to live in, I would marry him." Unfortunately he never showed any resolve to improve his fortunes, and it seemed highly improbable that he would

[1] The pane has survived the intervening centuries, and the lines shall be quoted for that reason rather than for their intrinsic merit:

Could Lammy look within my breast
She'd find her image there exprest
In characters as deep as here
The letters of her name appear
And like them ever will remain
Till time shall break my heart in twain.

ever be able to maintain a wife at all. He refused to take orders in the Church, or seek some other form of preferment, or do anything but drift along at Felbrigg as tutor to Billy Windham. At the same time he was intensely jealous, watching her every action with a vigilant and critical eye. Anne confided her difficulties and misgivings to Ashe Windham in a number of letters.

> If he can't conceal his unhappy temper from me, now he has no authority over me, what am I to expect from him when he has, but the greatest unhappyness? for I am too sensible, that no behaviour on my side can ever cure him of his unjust suspicions, or make him easy with me, unless I was to retire from all the World, and live with him in the Desarts of Arabia, which I am not yet romantic enough to do.

It was an impossible situation, and everyone else at Felbrigg was relieved when the affair was brought to an end in 1735. But Stillingfleet was deeply wounded, composed a *Philippic against Woman* in blank verse, and persisted in regarding himself as a much injured man. Fortunately the course of Billy Windham's education took them increasingly to London; and in due course Ashe Windham decided that his son should not be sent to either university, but should embark instead on an unusually protracted Grand Tour. It was arranged that Stillingfleet should travel with him; and Windham also recognised the tutor's past services, and created for him some measure of independence, by settling upon him an annuity of a hundred pounds for life.

Certain people, conspicuously unpractical in the management of their own affairs, are perfectly competent to advise and even to admonish others. Stillingfleet was one of these, and he now addressed to Windham two works containing the final precepts which he desired his pupil to bear in mind on his entrance into the great world. The first was a long didactic poem, *An Essay on Conversation*, which he published in 1737, and allowed to be reprinted later in the first volume of Dodsley's *Collection of Poems*.

> *The Art of Converse, how to sooth the Soul*
> *Of haughty Man, his Passions to controul,*
> *His Pride at once to humble and to please,*
> *And joyn the Dignity of Life with Ease,*
> *Be now my Theme. O Thou, whom Nature's Hand*
> *Fram'd for this best, this delicate Command,*
> *And taught, when lisping without Reason's Aid,*
> *At the same Time to speak and to persuade,*

WINDHAM, with Diligence awhile attend,
Nor scorn the Instructions of an older Friend;
Who, when the World's great Commerce shall have joyn'd
The deep Reflection, and the Strength of Mind,
To the bright Talents of thy youthful State,
In turn shall on thy better Lessons wait!

After this invocation Stillingfleet went on to deal with all the aspects of Conversation, in its wider meaning of the social intercourse of civilised human beings. He was by no means untalented as a poet, and in fluent and graceful couplets he explained how a man of good sense and sound morality should conduct himself as he moves through the varied scenes of life.

Stillingfleet's other production was a prose letter addressed to Windham on his coming of age. It extends to ninety-four pages, and still reposes, handsomely bound, in the library at Felbrigg. "You are now compleatly become a member of society," Stillingfleet told his pupil, "capable of answering all its purposes, and invested with all the power which it grants on account of age, and accordingly as you make use of that power you will deserve the name of a pernicious, an useless, or a good one." He began by describing the primary importance of religion in life, and the grounds for belief in the Christian revelation. He then turned from man's duty towards God to his duties as a social being—the distribution of charity both in money and other forms of beneficence, and the conduct of relationships in household and neighbourhood. There was some very frank speaking on certain questions of sexual morality, and on the importance of framing and adhering to a fixed plan of life. Frequent residence in the country was advocated, as most suitable for a man of large estate, and some study of farming—"the want of which tast . . . has fill'd this nation with gamesters, dancing masters, fiddlers, French taylors and Italian singers, the disgrace and ruin of common sense and vertue." The pursuit of learning, and especially of philosophy and history, would no doubt remain in the forefront of Windham's interests; and might he long continue to benefit from the advice and example of his "prudent and kind parent."

Some of his tutor's precepts Windham took to heart; others he notably failed to observe during the years to come. But Stillingfleet's discourse shows how intimate was the confidence and friendship between the two men who had already passed so much of their lives together, and who now set out on their travels to foreign lands.

Chapter Six

WILLIAM WINDHAM II

William Windham on the Grand Tour—his collection of paintings—the Common Room at Geneva—marriage contract with Elisabeth de Chapeaurouge—mountaineering—return to England—friendship with Garrick—liaison with Mrs Lukin—disagreements between William Windham and his father—death of Ashe Windham in 1749

I

As the eighteenth century progressed, the Grand Tour came increasingly into favour as the final stage of a rich young man's education. In Ashe Windham's youth it had still been quite exceptional. Half a century later his son's generation flocked abroad almost as a matter of course.

Their travels were mainly in France and Italy,

To where the Seine, obsequious as she runs,
Pours at great Bourbon's feet her silken sons;
Or Tyber, now no longer Roman, rolls,
Vain of Italian Arts, Italian Souls.

They would divert themselves for a few weeks or months in Paris, discovering new standards of elegance, luxury, and enjoyment. Then they journeyed southward across the Alps, in quest of the antiquities of Rome, the galleries of Florence, the dissipations of Venice. A few went farther afield, to Vienna or to some of the German Courts. Some would voyage down the Rhine, and visit the Low Countries before returning home. And a considerable number, more perhaps than is generally realised, made a prolonged stay in Switzerland, usually at Geneva. Many parents, especially those of the Whig persuasion, wished their sons to study the institutions of this Protestant republic, to attend the lectures of the eminent scholars who gave lustre to its Academy, and to acquire the French tongue in an atmosphere uncontaminated by Popery. There was much to be said for the visiting of classical sites, the purchase of pictures and statuary, the study of *virtù*;

WILLIAM WINDHAM II
By Barthélémy du Pan

THE CABINET

but many of these young men were not being educated as collectors or *dilettanti* at all. They were the future legislators of Great Britain.

So William Windham and Benjamin Stillingfleet, after a brief stay in Paris, established themselves at Geneva in the spring of 1738. They seem to have lodged, for a time at least, in the house of one of the Syndics, Monsieur Gallattin. A small number of letters survive from William to his "Dear Papa," mainly about the method of government in the republic. The question of remittances occasionally arises. In April he wrote: "This place is not near so cheap as I imagined before I came here, and the strangers especially the Germans have a vile custom of dressing vastly fine; but the English do not do it near so much, and always affect to dress the plainer the finer the Germans go."

He soon made a most congenial friend in another young Englishman, Robert Price of Foxley in Herefordshire. They were of the same age, and their interests, both intellectual and athletic, were closely similar. Price was a quiet youth, while Windham was restless and exuberant. He lacked Windham's passionate love of reading, but was a good musician and could draw and paint with skill. Both were outstanding horsemen, boxers, and tennis-players. Stillingfleet was equally pleased with Price, and here again a lifelong friendship was formed. In October the three men set out for Italy together.

They spent almost a year in Italy, but virtually every record of their movements has vanished. The earliest stages of their journey are mentioned in St Clair's letters. "It is dismal passing the Alps, when they are covered with snow," he wrote, recalling his own travels with Ashe Windham all those years ago. He hoped William would stay at least a fortnight at Turin, since the King of Sardinia's court was now the politest in Europe.

> You will not refuse your son the £500 he desires above his allowance, for no doubt he desires to lay it out in books, and pictures, and perhaps medals, in short to please himself; and it were great pity, that a Gentleman of his present fortunes should not have it in his power to do acts of Generosity, or to satisfy his curiosity, when he has a mind.

It seems unlikely, in view of William's lavish purchases of pictures and books in Italy, that the extra £500 was withheld.

By February the travellers had moved on to Florence. St Clair was anxious that William, when he went to Siena, should enquire whether his old friend Signor Gabrieli was still alive.

If he is, your son will be delighted to see his Air pumps, which perhaps are as fine as any in Europe; he made such a Meridian line in the church of Siena as is in the church of Bologna; and there is at Siena likewise one Signor Gigli who is worth his acquaintance; and at Rome desire him to enquire after Monsieur Bianchini, your acquaintance, and the best Astronomer in Italy, and likewise for Monsignor Fontanini, now a Bishop, with whose conversation your son will be extreamly pleas'd, and likewise Signor Campani from whom you bought your microscopes; he is worth your son's acquaintance.

At this point, unfortunately, there is a gap of many months in the sequence of St Clair's letters, and it is impossible to reconstruct Windham's movements from any other source. We only know that he spent several months in Rome, bought many pictures there, and made some new friends.

Both he and Price were much impressed by the work of Giovanni Battista Busiri, sometimes known by the nickname of Titarella, an artist now little remembered, but then held in some esteem. Busiri, who was born in 1698 and died in 1757, was one of the many eighteenth-century followers of Gaspar Poussin. He specialised in paintings, gouaches, and pen-drawings of landscapes and classical ruins in Rome and the Campagna, those scenes which English travellers had come so far to view, and wished to recall in the years to come. Price took lessons in drawing from Busiri, and he and Windham were generous purchasers of his work. Windham bought six large landscapes in oil —views of Frascati, Civita Castellana, the cascades at Tivoli, the falls at Terni—and twenty-six smaller paintings in gouache. These little pictures, still gay and fresh in colour, are enchanting representations of eighteenth-century Italy—fountains and wayside shrines, ancient tombs and temples, waterfalls and bridges, peasant girls and fishermen and goatherds. To the end of Windham's life they would serve to recall for him the contours of the Alban hills, the cypresses and umbrella-pines against the Roman sky.

Other paintings, still at Felbrigg, were acquired in Rome at this time—two landscapes with classical figures by Jan Glauber, another follower of Gaspar Poussin who worked in Italy; two flower-pieces by Karel van Vogelaer, known to his Roman patrons as Carlo dei Fiori; a *Christ in the Garden*, ascribed without much justification to Carlo Maratti; two gouaches by Pietro Bianchi; and a beautiful Joseph Vernet, cool and grey in tone, of a Mediterranean harbour on a hazy morning. Windham also made a large collection of engravings, and bought numerous works on architecture and classical antiquities.

The further course of Windham's travels in Italy is uncertain, and so is their duration. He and Price are known to have gone to Naples; and few young Englishmen failed to devote some weeks of their Grand Tour to the splendours and delights of Venice. They may indeed have journeyed to Vienna, seen something of the Austrian Court, and perhaps even spent a few weeks with the Imperial Army. Certainly Windham, at some time during his years abroad, acquired a very handsome and exotic uniform, Hungarian or Croatian in aspect, in which he was later painted by John Shackleton. This may be the origin of the story, for which I can find no other evidence, that he served for a considerable time as an officer in Maria Theresa's Hussars. We only know that towards the end of 1739, or during the early months of 1740, he and Price and Stillingfleet returned to Geneva.

During their months in Rome they had made the acquaintance of certain young men and their tutors, who now joined forces with them at Geneva. These were Thomas, seventh Earl of Haddington, and his brother George Hamilton, who had taken the name of Baillie from his mother's family; their tutor the Rev. John Williamson, an amiable and slightly eccentric character who had much in common with Stillingfleet; Benjamin Tate of Mitcham in Surrey, like Price an enthusiastic amateur musician; and his tutor Thomas Dampier, a youngish scholar who had not yet taken orders. Another agreeable Englishman had lately come out to Geneva, Richard Aldworth of Billingbear in Berkshire. He was an exact contemporary of Windham and Price, a stout young man with a round cheerful face and an inexhaustible store of good nature. This group of congenial spirits soon established a sort of club, known as the Common Room. Other English visitors were welcomed to the club, and acceptable foreigners were sometimes introduced. Its activities greatly enlivened the sober atmosphere of Geneva, and the high spirits of the young English became almost proverbial. But to its founders—Windham, Price, Haddington, Baillie, Aldworth, Tate, and the three tutors—the Common Room meant more. They constituted a more intimate circle, known to one another as "the Bloods"; and they remained a close-knit and united sodality to the end of their lives.

One of the chief activities of the Common Room was the production of plays. They acted *Macbeth* and *The Siege of Damascus*, and pantomimes and harlequinades of their own composing, to delighted if somewhat bewildered audiences of the citizens of Geneva. Price and Windham painted the scenes; Price, Tate, and Stillingfleet composed the music; and Stillingfleet also directed the machinery. They could count also on the services of two talented actors who were not regular members of the Common Room. Charles Churchill, a son of the actress Mrs Oldfield by a distinguished General, was the perfect Harlequin. "I question," wrote Aldworth many years later, "if Rich was equal to him, combining grace, action, and agility." For the female parts they availed themselves of George Hervey, the son of Pope's "Sporus" and afterwards second Earl of Bristol. Hervey resembled his father so closely that Horace Walpole, no Hercules himself, always referred to him as "the delicate Lord"; and Aldworth "never saw him equalled as Colombine but by Mademoiselle Clairon." He was also admirable as Lady Macbeth, in a production in which magicians with long beards and black gowns had replaced the three witches. "This alteration," Aldworth wrote, "produced additional awe and horror. Garrick has since approved the idea; but owned he durst not carry it into execution for fear of offending the Gallery."

Long afterwards, when Windham and Price were dead, Aldworth wrote character-sketches of both. As old members of the Common Room were wont to do, he harked back repeatedly to those golden days in Geneva; and although a few details refer to a somewhat later period, his portrait depicts Windham exactly as he must have appeared in his early twenties, in the fullness of his youthful strength and spirits.

Windham, tall, thin, and narrow-chested, would vie with Price in every feat of strength and agility, and so far he succeeded that he was known through London by the name of *Boxing Windham*; whilst few knew his quiet friend Mr Price could box at all. Fewer yet could divine that Mr Windham would have excelled in almost every pursuit but those he was seen to follow; that he possessed Greek, Latin, Spanish, and French, to a high degree; and knew something of Dutch and German. This was, however, the fact; and from those various sources, his amazing parts, equally quick and retentive, had drawn and amassed treasures of science and amusement, which was the more striking from his apparent dissipation: he was besides a mathematician, mechanic, and draughtsman; could and did build vessels, and navigate them himself; in short, he was every thing.

He had an utter abhorrence of restraint, which made him love to associate with those that put him under none at all: here he might throw his legs against the chimney, round himself into a hoop in his elbow chair, and at the same time read one subject, and converse on another;

a method he constantly practised, and with what success the following instance will best illustrate. One day in our Common Room at Geneva (which for an hour or two after dinner was the resort of every odd genius of every country) two sets were at the same time talking on different matters; one in English, the other in Italian. Windham was between them, reading as usual, yet occasionally joining with each in the language that party was speaking, and in a manner that would have made you think him solely attentive to one single subject. I remarked this, made another do so likewise, and we watched him for some time; when our surprize was increased by his shutting his book (which was old Brantôme in French) and telling us an excellent story which he had been reading at the very time he was keeping up the double conversation. Intolerance of the least restraint was a marked part of Windham's character, and serves as the best clue to unravel some seeming inconsistencies. This accounts for a man of nice honour, bright imagination, and extensive knowledge, often throwing away such talents on those who could neither do credit to that honour, entertain that imagination, nor improve that knowledge. . . . The lively beauty of his countenance was most striking, and every feature spoke genius; it was impossible to see and not admire him: to this, when he chose to please, he had an address that could not fail to captivate.

Aldworth's reminiscent eulogies are supported by the verdict of a contemporary observer. Early in 1741 old Patrick St Clair wrote to Ashe Windham about a gentleman staying in the neighbourhood who had lately been in Geneva, and who was sounding William's praises wherever he went.

I hear he gives him a very great character, that he is perfectly free from all vice, highly accomplisht in all sorts of learning becoming his quality, wonderfully obliging to all that are acquainted with him, and which is the infallible consequence of these good qualities, the darling of all men of best sense in the place where he now resides.

II

Throughout his life William Windham was a fervent admirer of women; and whether or not he was at this time perfectly free from all vice, as the gentleman from Geneva assured the Norfolk neighbours, he had already formed one virtuous attachment. On 30 September 1740 he entered into a marriage contract with Elisabeth de Chapeaurouge, the daughter of a prominent citizen and former First Syndic of Geneva, Jacob de Chapeaurouge.

This contract, executed and sworn before Georges Grosjean, notary public, is preserved among the civic archives.[1] Under its terms "*ledit noble William Windham, époux, et ladite Elisabeth de Chapeaurouge, épouse . . . de leur gré ont promis de se prendre pour mari et femme, et de faire benir leur marriage dans l'Eglise de Dieu, après la publication de leurs anonces, le plutôt possible.*" William undertook to settle upon his bride the sum of twenty-seven thousand livres. Her father provided a dowy which included "*un logement meublé pendant sa vie suivant sa condition.*" If, contrary to the hopes of the contracting parties, the marriage could not be celebrated "*soit de la mort prématurée du susdit époux soit autrement,*" William declared that Elisabeth might levy upon his goods the sum of thirty thousand livres. The document was signed by the betrothed, the bride's parents, and certain other witnesses, including the great jurist Jean-Jacques Burlamaqui, who had married Elisabeth's sister Renée.

It was altogether a mysterious affair. Elisabeth was thirty-four years of age, and William was twenty-three. It seems unlikely that Ashe Windham would have approved the marriage of his only son to a foreign lady, however distinguished her family and connections, whose background was so entirely remote from his own. A political and territorial alliance within his own Whig circle was much closer to his ambitions. It is significant that neither Stillingfleet nor any other English friend signed as a witness of the contract. Yet so respectable an alliance could hardly have been kept secret from them; and it would have been Stillingfleet's duty to have reported such an occurrence instantly to his pupil's father. Nor do I think that William's inheritance from his mother would alone have sufficed for a marriage settlement upon this scale.

The very wording of the contract suggests some uncertainty in the minds of the bride's family as to whether the marriage would take place; and their doubts were fully justified. Ashe Windham may have found means, by some exercise of persuasion or authority, to postpone and finally to prevent it; or there may have been other reasons. No violent breach seems to have occurred between the lovers. William continued in Geneva for almost two years after their betrothal. But there was no marriage, and I have not found a single reference to Elisabeth de Chapeaurouge in all the letters which passed between the

[1] A transcript was kindly provided, through the good offices of Sir Gavin de Beer, by Dr Bernard Gagnebin, Keeper of Manuscripts at the Bibliothèque Publique et Universitaire at Geneva.

various members of the Common Room. The contract, however, remained valid; and the reader will learn in due course how its provisions were enforced ten years later, when William married another woman.

In the course of 1741 the Common Room began to break up. The first to go were Tate and Dampier, the stages of whose return to England in the spring were marked by a series of exuberant letters to the "Dear Bloods" who remained. Tate wrote about music, Dampier about pictures, both about their memories of the "never-to-be-forgot Common Room." An immense letter from Amsterdam describes how "last night we drank to the Healths of the seven Bloods of Geneva in Arrack-Punch, one by one, and afterwards a Bumper to them all together. . . . We beseech you all, dear Mathematicians, Philosophers, Beaux and others, not to forget your Travelling Friends."

In June the members of the Common Room embarked on their best-remembered enterprise. At that time no one indulged in mountaineering as a source of enjoyment or a test of physical endurance. But some scientific curiosity was already being felt about the flora and fauna of the Alps, and about the composition and progress of glaciers. Windham himself had explored some of the higher valleys within reach of Geneva, in company with the well-known traveller Richard Pococke. Now the Common Room organised an expedition to survey the Mer de Glace, the glacier now so famous but then virtually unknown, except to occasional parties of peasants in search of crystal. Six of its members took part—Windham, Stillingfleet, Price, Aldworth, Haddington, and Baillie—together with Pococke and another Englishman named Chetwynd. Williamson was given charge of the barometrical and mathematical instruments, but could not face the fatigues of the journey.

The expedition was later described by Windham in a pamphlet, drawn up in the form of a letter addressed to Jacques Arlaud, a painter living in Geneva. The pamphlet was adorned by an engraving after a drawing by Price, a "View of the Ice Valley and Mountains that surround it." The little book is wholly typical of the blend of seriousness and hilarity that characterised the Common Room. The party set out from Geneva on 19 June, "Eight in Company, besides five Servants, all of us well arm'd, and our Baggage-Horses attending us, so that we had very much the Air of a Caravan." On the 21st they reached Chamonix, and encamped for the night at a nearby monastery. "The Prior of the Place was a good old man, who shew'd us many Civilities, and endeavoured to dissuade us." Nevertheless they started on the ascent next day, up a steep and broken mountainside made still more difficult by the havoc of recent avalanches; and after nearly five hours' hard climbing found themselves looking down on the great glacier.

> I own to you that I am extremely at a Loss how to give a right Idea of it; as I know no one thing which I have ever seen that has the least Resemblance to it. The Description which Travellers give of the Seas of *Greenland* seems to come the nearest to it. You must imagine your Lake put in Agitation by a strong Wind, and frozen all at once, perhaps even that would not produce the same Appearance.

They scrambled down the steep descent on to the tumbled ice with its alarming crevasses, explored its surface for half an hour or so, fired without success at some distant chamois, and "drank there in ceremony Admiral Vernon's Health, and Success to the British Arms." Then they set out down the mountainside, and arrived back at Chamonix just at sunset. The expedition had little scientific value, owing to the absence of Williamson and his instruments; but as a piece of English enterprise it had been wholly successful and immensely enjoyable, and played its small part in revealing the wonders of their country to the people of Switzerland and Savoy. In due course a tablet bearing the names of Windham and Pococke was placed at the edge of the Mer de Glace.

The Common Room suffered a further loss when Price set out for England in October. He, too, sent from Paris and London long letters full of enthusiastic talk about painting and music, describing how greatly his landscapes by Busiri had impressed the connoisseurs in Paris, and how he had smuggled them through the customs at Dover in his fiddle-case.

> My dear Bloods [he wrote from London], the greatest pleasure I can receive next to that of being with you, is hearing from you all in a Body. Nay I may say I have one satisfaction in a Letter which I seldom had when I was with you, that of having you all together and being able to keep you so. I read your letter over and over, and think my self among you. I think I see you all in your favourite corners, each Blood enjoying himself and the Company. While I read your letter you all pass before me like the Ghosts in *Macbeth*, only with this difference, that you never entirely vanish.

He and Tate had a project of sharing a house, in the hope that "you Bloods would all follow the same laudable scheme, and bring the Common Room from Geneva to London."

Its few remaining members continued at Geneva for several months.

Aldworth indeed spent much of his time there for several years to come, and eventually married Magdalen Calandrini, the daughter of one of the leading Syndics. It was not until July 1742, more than four years since the beginning of his Grand Tour, that Windham at last set out for home. We shall never know what scenes of farewell passed between him and Elisabeth de Chapeaurouge, and what arrangements for the future they may or may not have made. The mystery of their relationship remains impenetrable.

The course of the journey home can be traced through the pages of a notebook in which Windham jotted down his travelling expenses, together with a few sketches of the scenes through which they passed. He and Stillingfleet set out from Geneva on 19 July and crossed Switzerland by the customary route, spending a few days at Berne and Zürich, then going on to Schaffhausen and down the Rhine to Basle. During the month of August they saw something of Germany—Heidelberg, Mainz, Frankfurt, Coblenz, Bonn, Cologne—and visited the French and German camps on the opposite sides of the Rhine. Early in September they had reached Holland; but at this point the accounts were discontinued, and the date of their passage to England is not recorded.

It is probable, although not certain, that Windham acquired during this stay in Holland the greater part of the Dutch and Flemish pictures which completed his collection. He probably took most pride in two paintings long attributed to Rembrandt, the *Man Cutting a Pen* and the *Old Woman in a White Cap*. Neither of these has survived the learned criticism of the present century; they are competent studio work, and nothing more. But some of Windham's other purchases showed much discrimination. They ranged from a delicate little river landscape by Lucas van Valckenborch, and a beach scene of very high quality by Ecgbert van der Poel, to a series of sea-fights of imposing size. The most remarkable of these was an enormous canvas by Simon de Vlieger, signed and dated 1650, of a battle fought some twenty years earlier between the Dutch and the Chinese, off the coast in the neighbourhood of Amoy. It shows a wide land-locked bay in which five Dutch men-of-war are engaging, and putting to flight, a far larger assemblage of Chinese vessels with unwieldy hulls, great square mat sails, and outlandish flags. On the shore an agitated mandarin spurs his horse, and other spectators watch the unequal contest, while survivors flounder through the shallows, and the smoke of battle rises into a calm cloudscape above.

Windham was a great admirer of the work of the Willem van der Veldes, father and son. He bought two large paintings of the Battle of the Texel, one a general view of the engagement, the other depicting the episode in which Sir Edward Spragg was killed.[1] Both are signed by the elder Willem, but the younger appears to have worked on them also. Windham also acquired five smaller paintings by the son, of ships tossed by squalls or driving before gales; but no example, unfortunately, of the tranquil harbour scenes in which he excelled. Among his other choices were a pair of landscapes with classical figures by the Flemish artist Cornelis Huysman, and a view of the bleaching-ground near Haarlem by Jan van Kessel. Something in the balance and the quality of his collection suggests that when assembling it he had its eventual disposition in the rooms at Felbrigg always in mind.

III

The travellers were back at Felbrigg in October 1742. At last Ashe Windham could embrace his dearly loved son, and judge for himself the accomplishments and graces that he had acquired during the past four years. Stillingfleet likewise received a warm-hearted welcome. He had justified the confidence that his pupil's father reposed in him, and might contentedly resume his botanical studies and his modest excursions into poetry.

Unfortunately this happy state of things did not last very long. The years of travel had not quenched Stillingfleet's love for Anne Barnes. But she was now a married lady, having at last surrendered to one of her most persistent suitors, a very eligible young whalebone merchant named William Russell. They were living at Barningham Hall, which had lately become vacant through the bankruptcy and ruin of the Paston family; and they were valued members of Ashe Windham's circle at Felbrigg. Stillingfleet could not face their visits. He left the house which had been his home for so much of his life, and set out on a round of lengthy visits to his other Common Room friends.

Before long William followed him. It was not to be expected, perhaps, that he would live at Felbrigg with his father indefinitely; and the disagreements between them, which clouded the last years of Ashe Windham's life, had probably not begun at this early date. It was natural that a young man with William's wide interests should be drawn to the life of the town. He and Price took a house together in

[1] The second of these is now in the National Maritime Museum at Greenwich; the first remains at Felbrigg.

Panton Street, and entered full-bloodedly into all the enjoyments that London could offer.

Their love of boxing has already been mentioned. Pugilism was coming much into vogue among fashionable young men of the tougher sort; and the name of "Boxing Windham" probably dates from this time. The famous bruiser John Broughton had lately opened his establishment off Oxford Street known as the Amphitheatre, and the two friends at once became his pupils and patrons. They also hired a hunting-box on the borders of Suffolk and Essex, in order to follow the hounds of their friend Lord Rochford.

Windham's love of the theatre soon brought him into touch with Garrick, then at the outset of his career. He had still been abroad at the time of Garrick's brilliant début in London during the winter of 1741; but now he became his warm admirer and friend, and in time of need a most aggressive partisan. In 1743 the theatrical world was convulsed by the quarrel between Garrick and his rival Macklin, whose sympathisers were vocal enough on the opening night at Drury Lane to bring the play, *The Rehearsal*, to a standstill. They tried to repeat the demonstration at the next performance two nights later, with results described by Garrick's biographer Arthur Murphy.

> Garrick had an eminent and generous friend, who was resolved to protect him; that was Mr Windham, of Norfolk, a gentleman of the most polished manners, and an elegant scholar. It happened that he was an admirer of the athletic art, which at that time was in great vogue; and, having selected thirty of the ablest in that line, he desired that they might be admitted into the house, by a private way, before the doors were regularly opened. This was granted. The bruizers took possession of the middle of the pit. When the last music was playing, one of them stood up, and stopping the band in the orchestra, said, in a loud voice, "Gentlemen, I am told that some persons here are come with an intention not to see the play; I came to hear it; I paid my money for it, and I desire that they who come to interrupt, may all withdraw, and not stay to hinder my diversion." This occasioned a general uproar; but the Broughtonians knew how to deal their blows with irresistible vigour. They fell upon Macklin's party, and drove them out of the pit. The fray was soon over, and peace and good order being restored, Garrick made his appearance; and after bowing respectfully to the audience, went through the character of Bayes without interruption.

Garrick stayed at Windham's hunting-box in Suffolk in 1744, and they were together at Bath in the following year. About the same time

Francis Hayman painted them together in a landscape setting. Only a few traces of Garrick survive among the papers at Felbrigg—a song, the fragment of a letter, a ribald epigram on Kitty Clive. There is also the manuscript of *Ragandjaw*, a little play written by Garrick in 1746. It is an exercise in curiously adolescent indecency, a parody of the scene in Brutus's tent in *Julius Caesar*, with the Roman generals transformed to an English sergeant and corporal, seated at a table with beer, pipes, and tobacco, and lamenting the loss not of a noble wife but of a mastiff bitch. The standard of its humour is perhaps best suggested by the names of the characters—Brutarse, Cassiarse, and the boy Loosearse. The dedication to Windham concludes thus:

> I must declare that the Choicest Flowers which I have added to this Poetical Nosegay, were all gather'd and cull'd from your Private Conversation, Writings and Publick Disputations on the Water, the Roads, in the Streets, at Cuper's Gardens and Mr Broughton's Amphitheatre. I am under no apprehension of putting you to the Blush by this Confession, for Experience has convinced me, that your Countenance (like your Heart) is incapable of Weak and Womanish Impressions; and therefore as it is my Frailty to be too susceptible of Shame, I here make this Just and Publick Transferr of all my Right, Title, and Merit in this Performance to You, and am (with the Greatest Reverence to your Superior Genius and Abilities)
>
> Your Admiring Pupil and most Humble Servant
>
> D: Garrick.

During these London years Windham maintained his more serious interests, was an assiduous buyer and reader of books and pamphlets, and continued his scientific and architectural studies. But by degrees his friends began to feel some misgiving. Was he not in danger of wasting his talents, or of throwing them away on unworthy companions, as Aldworth later asserted was the case? Were pugilism, hunting, and the theatre to be the whole of his life? He would have been an admirable candidate for a Parliamentary seat, and many people in Norfolk hoped that he would stand for the county at the next election. During 1743 a great deal of manoeuvring took place with that end in view;[1] but in that age of septennial Parliaments the election

[1] MS. letters from John Fowle to Horatio Walpole (Wolterton Hall Archives). The Walpole interest was adverse to Windham in this particular matter, e.g. Fowle to Walpole, 6 October 1743: "Mr Fellowes is determined against you, and so deeply engaged in the Windham scheme, as not to be

was not due for five years, and for various reasons the scheme was abandoned. It was probably during these years that Stillingfleet, who often stayed in the house in Panton Street, addressed a set of sonnets to his eight friends of the Common Room. There is a gentle note of reproach in the sonnet to Windham; and at the same time a suggestion, cryptic but unmistakable, that he was prevented from entering upon a more distinguished career in life by circumstances beyond his control.

O born for active life! When shall I see
Thee, Windham, governing the grave debate,
'Midst the few pillars of the falling State
With sense acute and elocution free?
How long wilt thou, as once Pelides, be
Depriv'd of glorious deeds by envious fate,
And forc'd to bear the mock of jealous hate,
As if by choice thou didst the burthen flee?
Go on, like him, to wake thy idle hours
With the sage Muse; give to thy soul her due;
Nor let her handmaid our best hopes beguile;
For she too may benumb her finest powers
With din too coarse; as those, if fame says true,
Grow deaf, who dwell too near the falling Nile.

IV

During all these years Ashe Windham had been consoled for the failure of his marriage by the affection and the brilliant promise of his son. Everyone sang the young man's praises, and the most roseate prospects seemed to lie before him. But something went wrong two or three years after his return from abroad. A mysterious coldness, almost an antagonism, developed between father and son. Ashe Windham was fated to suffer a second disappointment, and the close of his life was lonely and sad.

The causes of their disagreement are uncertain. There is no reason to suspect any political difference, or to associate Ashe Windham with the "envious fate" to which Stillingfleet ascribed the frustration of his pupil's parliamentary ambitions. Nor have I found any confirmation of the legend, already mentioned, that William went abroad again and

taken from it. . . . The Windham scheme is at present in great strength in Norfolk, but many accidents may happen in the course of 5 years to disconcert it."

served as a hussar officer in the army of Maria Theresa.[1] It is far more likely that he first incurred his father's displeasure by associating with unsuitable women, and then by refusing to give them up.

Ashe Windham still hoped that his son would marry an English girl with money and good connections. He was, of course, aware of the contract with Elisabeth de Chapeaurouge, but this difficulty was not unsurmountable. The degree of William's affection for the lady in Geneva at this time remains unknown to us. It did not, at any rate, prevent him from taking as his mistress a woman of obscure origin, Mary Morgan, by whom he had a daughter, Elizabeth. Soon afterwards Mary Morgan died; and he then formed a similar liaison with a handsome widow named Mrs Lukin. In 1746 Robert Price, with whom he shared the house in Panton Street, married the Hon. Anne Barrington. Windham then took a house of his own in Golden Square, Soho, and Mrs Lukin came to live there with him. She was accompanied by the children of her marriage to Mr Lukin, two sons and a daughter. Windham's daughter by Mary Morgan was also included in the *ménage*.

Mrs Lukin was born Sarah Hicks of Tanfield in Essex, and had married Robert Lukin, a gentleman with a small property at Dunmow. It is possible that Windham first met them during his hunting sojourns in Essex. Robert Lukin died in 1744, leaving his widow in decidedly modest circumstances with two sons, Robert aged eleven and George William aged five, and a still younger daughter Dorothy. She was thirty-four at the time of her husband's death, and seven years older than William Windham. From every point of view the relationship was intensely annoying to Ashe Windham, who understandably regarded Mrs Lukin as a designing woman, resolved to maintain herself and her children at his son's expense.

[1] See, for example, *Fifty Years of my Life*, by George Thomas, Earl of Albemarle (1876), where it is stated (i. 106–7) that "he was seized with a chivalrous feeling of devotion towards the young, beautiful, and spirited Empress-Queen . . . and fought for and bled in her cause at the battle of Dettingen." All this is based on a letter from his cousin and namesake William Windham of Earsham (see p. 107), who had been present at the battle as *aide-de-camp* to the Duke of Cumberland.

There is also a paper in Windham's hand, headed *History of my Horses*, which records his purchases and sales of horses in every year between 1742 and 1749. It seems unlikely that the owner of this expensive stable, with its frequent additions and changes, can have been serving abroad at any time during those years.

It does not appear, however, that at this time William had any serious thoughts of marrying her. Her status was that of a kept woman; and if she angered or disobeyed him he was prepared to "discharge her for ever." This phrase occurs in a deplorable exchange of letters which he conducted in the summer of 1747 with his cousin Mary Humphreys, formerly Dobyns, a niece of his mother. He accused her, in almost hysterical terms, of mischief-making and tale-bearing, despite the many kindnesses which she had received from him. She had, he asserted, been "the author and fomenter of the disquiets and uneasiness of my dear poor deceased Molly," his first mistress Mary Morgan; "and in that light I detest and abhor you, and with my last breath shall curse you." Worse still, stories retailed by her were now causing similar distress to Mrs Lukin. Her conduct was "a complication of wickedness, perfidy and ingratitude not to be match't on this side Hell." He renounced for ever all relationship, friendship, and correspondence with her; he would never see or speak to her; he was from the bottom of his soul her mortal enemy. "I have told Mrs Lukin that if ever she speaks or corresponds with you, directly or indirectly, I shall discharge her for ever."

Although her offence is not explicitly mentioned in Windham's letter, Mrs Humphreys had in fact discussed with both his mistresses the subject of Elisabeth de Chapeaurouge. She admitted it in a reply which was not without dignity. She had evidently liked Mary Morgan —"whatever I saw of her was most amiable and praise-worthy"—and had never done anything to give her uneasiness, since she knew all about Elisabeth already from Windham's own lips. "I never heard her say any thing but lament her fate that she must resign you some time to the lady abroad, but this has been frequently spoke of in your presence." As for Mrs Lukin, she had heard rumours about Elisabeth and asked Mrs Humphreys for the truth, which she duly received. "You cannot have any resentment against me, but from a just principle of my telling her of your ingagement abroad, which you know that you have told me most frequently of." It was only at William's request that she had ever made the acquaintance of his two ladies; and "was the time to pass over again, I shoud desire to be a stranger to them you distinguish." She despatched a curt note to the same effect to Mrs Lukin; and then sent copies of the entire correspondence to Ashe Windham, whose displeasure with his son can hardly have lessened by its perusal.

By this time father and son were almost wholly estranged. They may have met sometimes when Ashe Windham visited London or Twickenham, but there can have been little pleasure in their meetings. William's inheritance from his mother, and under certain other Dobyns family trusts, enabled him to live an independent and fairly expensive life. For country pursuits he hired a house in Warwickshire, and for some years he never came to Felbrigg at all. He knew he would inherit the Norfolk estates in due course. Had he not been his father's only child, different arrangements might conceivably have been made. As it was, Ashe Windham made no alterations to his will, but stoically resigned himself to live out his last years alone.

Some light is thrown upon these years in the letters to him from his kinsman Thomas Wyndham, who had inherited Cromer Hall and its estate from an invalid brother in 1745. Thomas Wyndham had long been settled in the West Country through his marriage to an heiress, a Wyndham cousin, who brought him the estates of Clearwell in Gloucestershire and Dunraven in Glamorgan. A second marriage, to a Miss Edwin, had added much further land in South Wales.[1] But he remained much attached to "the small Family Nest" at Cromer, where havoc had been wrought during his brother's long illness by a dishonest steward and a "female Crocodile." He came there for long periods, which sometimes coincided with Ashe Windham's absences from Felbrigg; and letters would then pass between them. "At present the whole of Felbrigg seems to mourn the Absence of a Master, while all the neighbouring Seats daily appear in surprizing Beautys," Thomas wrote in 1745: and again two years later, "all Friends wish to see you at Felbrig, which used to animate all our Neighbours, and now is the only Seat which mourns the absence of its Lord, and appears like a neglected Mistress."

Thomas Wyndham was an enthusiastic amateur architect, and longed to see Felbrigg improved—"to pull down, build, plant &c (in imagination), being ambitious to see this ancient Family Seat outshine the Clumsy Magnificence of Houghton." The situation demanded it: "the fertile Fields on one side, and wild spatious Common on the other, with Hill and Vale commanding a large Prospect of the Ocean, may justifye an Expence to improve a Place which Nature has bless'd with Variety of Beautys." The house might easily be made, in all its parts,

[1] Thomas Wyndham was born in 1686 and died in 1752. His only son by his cousin Jane Wyndham died without issue. Of his two sons by Anne Edwin, the elder, Charles, inherited the West Country properties: the younger, John, succeeded to Cromer, and was my great-great-grandfather.

"Light, Chearfull, *Simplex dumtaxat et unum.*" But its greatest defect was the lack of a really large eating-parlour. If his cousin Ashe would not embark upon "a compleat new plan," would he not at least consider throwing the eastern half of the south front, which then contained the kitchen and the buttery, into a single room in which guests could be worthily entertained? The work could be done for five hundred pounds; and it would not be necessary to "pull down the Noble Front," as he had first suggested. The scheme had the support of Lord Leicester, the great local authority on architectural matters, who was at this time engaged upon his life's task of the building of Holkham.

Ashe Windham had reached his seventy-fifth year without showing any disposition to rebuild or reconstruct his house. He received his kinsman's suggestions with his usual good humour, and quietly laid them aside. In any case his life was nearing its close. Thomas Wyndham wrote to another friend in December 1748 that when he was last at Cromer "Mr Windham did us frequently the favour of a Visit, had been much out of Order, but recover'd soon, not only health but his best looks, and appears the Same Man, within as well as without." But these signs of good health were deceptive. Ashe Windham died at Felbrigg early in the following spring, on 4 April 1749.

Chapter Seven

WILLIAM WINDHAM II

William Windham's marriage to Mrs Lukin, and the birth of his son—extensive alterations to the house—James Paine's new dining-room, staircase and library—redecoration of other rooms—life at Felbrigg and in London—Windham's part in organising the Norfolk Militia—his declining health, and death in 1761

I

ASHE WINDHAM'S ownership of Felbrigg had lasted for sixty years. In all that time he had made no addition or alteration to the house, except for the building of the Orangery. William Windham's ownership was destined to last for no more than twelve years; but during those years he completely reconstructed and redecorated the whole interior, giving almost every room the appearance which it still presents today. He plunged into these activities at once, putting schemes in force which he had planned long before, and driving everyone concerned in them with his accustomed furious energy. It was as if he knew that his time was short.

Thanks to his father's careful management, the estate was in good order; and he had little difficulty in taking over the reins. Some of the outlying portions, however, had latterly been neglected. His man of business, Peter Taylor, wrote plaintively of the troubles that confronted him on a visit of inspection to the Somerset property at Worle. These letters from Taylor also tell us something of Windham's first months at Felbrigg, where he and Mrs Lukin remained throughout the summer of 1749.

Taylor was required to send down by ship to Cley all kinds of requisites—a dozen of old hock, a dozen of Rhenish, two dozen calico shirts at a guinea apiece, Mrs Lukin's stay-buckles, and a small fire-engine. Mrs Taylor tried to match flowered silks for Mrs Lukin, and succeeded in finding a cook for the London house—she would not come for less than £8 a year, but was prepared to clean a room or two besides the kitchen. Some venison was sent up for Taylor to distribute, a haunch apiece for Garrick and himself, and two sides for Mrs Ashe; but she had gone into the country, so "I believe Garrick and I must share it." In this same letter Taylor mentioned that "I have purchased the house in Southampton Street for Garrick, I think cheap." Garrick had lately married Eva-Maria Veigel, and they were to live in this house for twenty-three years.

It appears that Windham had already chosen the architect to whom he would entrust the remodelling of his house. Taylor wrote on 4 June that "I sent you Pain's plan by the coach Monday, am glad any of these Gentry pleases you, I know little of either of them, hope you will take care of being in the house whilest tis repairing." There is nothing to show who the other architect was; but in mid-July "Mr Pain certainly sets out Tuesday, hopes to be with you Thursday," and at the end of the month, "I sent to Mr Pain's as you ordered me, am glad he is liked." The architect thus approved was James Paine, a man of Windham's own age, who had already designed several important country houses and public buildings, more especially in the northern counties.

Windham returned to London in the autumn. There was now no reason why he should not marry Mrs Lukin, a step which it would have been impossible—or at any rate highly inadvisable—to take while his father was still alive. She was, moreover, expecting a child; and it was desirable that a legitimate succession to Felbrigg should be assured. So they were married on 13 February 1750. The child was born at their house in Golden Square less than three months later, on 3 May. He was given his father's name, and became the most remarkable of the many William Windhams who figure in this book.

But Elisabeth de Chapeaurouge, far away in Geneva, was still betrothed to Sarah Lukin's husband: still faithful, at the age of forty-four, to the young Englishman who had impulsively surrendered to her charms ten years before. Much negotiation was required before their bonds could be sundered, and much expense. Nevertheless Elisabeth, and those who advised her, did not wish to make things too difficult. In June 1751 she executed before a notary in Geneva a deed appointing François Duval, a Swiss merchant residing in London, to act as her attorney in the proceedings made necessary by Windham's breach of their marriage contract. But it was specifically stated in the deed that Duval was empowered "*avant toutes contestations et procédures tenter les voies aimables*"; and an amicable compromise was duly reached. Duval brought a formal suit against Windham in the

Court of Common Pleas at Westminster, and Windham by his own attorneys confessed a judgment against him for four thousand pounds. Thereupon Duval announced his willingness to accept on Elisabeth's behalf the sum of two thousand pounds, together with interest at 4 per cent until payment was made, which was not to be later than July 1753.

Much of the credit for this friendly arrangement must have been due to the good-natured Richard Aldworth, whose signature as a witness appears on some of the documents. He had himself married a lady of Geneva; and although she died only two years afterwards, he still no doubt retained connections there which were of use in these negotiations. It was a settlement with which all parties could feel reasonably satisfied: not least Elisabeth de Chapeaurouge, who was married in 1753 to Jean-Daniel Alléon, another member of the same little group of the leading families of Geneva.

II

Windham lost no time in putting Paine's plans into effect. Work was begun in the spring of 1750, and continued for the next three years. The late seventeenth-century staircase designed by Samwell, and adversely criticised by Roger North, was removed; and the new "eating-parlour," which Thomas Wyndham had been so anxious to see, was created in its place, with two bedrooms over it. An entirely new staircase was built in the angle formed by the junction of the south and west fronts, rising to roof-height and with a skylight above. A two-storied bay was thrown out at the northern extremity of the west front. The large room above the great hall was fitted up as a library. And in all the rooms not radically altered a good deal of redecoration took place.

For long periods the house was totally uninhabitable. Windham would pay frequent visits, sleeping in whatever room happened to be available, and dining off mutton roasted by the dairy-maid. Most of the time he lived either in London or in Essex, where he now hunted his own hounds from a house at Rivenhall. From early in 1751 all his activities are reflected in a series of letters which he wrote to Robert Frary, an excellent and reliable man who acted as a sort of local factotum both to him and to his neighbour Mr Doughty of Hanworth. The letters vividly suggest Windham's character—impetuous, excitable, habitually generous and warm-hearted, very unreasonable when thwarted or provoked. They deal with every kind of topic—estate business, justice business, household affairs, the garden, the stable, hunting in Essex, game-preserving in Norfolk, the races at Holt and Swaffham, boats, firearms, fireworks, turning-lathes, all his multifarious interests. But running through each one of them is his urgent pre-occupation with the progress of his house, his attention to every detail of structure and ornament, his impatience with the workmen and with Mr Paine.

The earliest work to be undertaken was the bay of two stories projecting from the northern end of the west front. This was the only point where the outward appearance of the house was altered to any noticeable extent; and Paine harmonised his design with Samwell's by continuing the existing cornice (though not the string-course) round the new bay. He finished this work in 1751. During the following year the structural portion of the new eating-parlour was built, and the walls enclosing the area of the new staircase were also completed.

These were all reasonably straightforward tasks, which could be carried out, under the supervision of a good foreman, by bricklayers and carpenters locally recruited. But now began the far more intricate and troublesome business of decoration. The services of experienced London craftsmen were required, stone-cutters, plasterers, paper-hangers. This in turn necessitated the presence of one of Paine's own foremen, and he sent down a Yorkshireman named Hull, "a very clever workman and capable of directing the others, but he has sometimes a fault of getting loose for a day or two, which he has promised to reform, and you will keep a look out about." Hull did quite well and remained on the job for at least a year; but even so, there were mistakes and delays. Communications were bad, posts were erratic, all heavy goods had to come by ship and were subject to the uncertainties of wind and tide. A certain amount of confusion was inevitable over designs, colours, measurements, and so forth; and between Paine in London, Windham in Essex, and Frary at Felbrigg, it is surprising that there was not more.

The first room to be ready for decoration was the small Drawing Room, henceforward known as the Cabinet, at the end of the west wing. This was the room which Windham had planned to display the pictures collected on his Grand Tour. The windows to the west were blocked in order to afford more wall-space, and its sole light now came from the three tall windows, reaching to ground level, in the new bay. The existing seventeenth-century plasterwork was copied in the ceiling of the bay, and some areas of the older ceiling themselves appear to have been reworked. The magnificent ceiling of the larger Drawing Room was left untouched.

At first there was some trouble about the plasterwork. "It was very absurd sending a plaisterer who could not do Ornaments," Windham wrote to Frary in February 1752, "and Hull must write to Mr Rose for another." Joseph Rose was a particularly able plasterer, much employed by Paine at this time; and it appears from subsequent letters that he came down to Felbrigg himself, and that much of the best plasterwork in the house may be attributed to him. Presumably the additional decoration to the ceiling of the Cabinet was from his hand; and he was certainly responsible for the best work of all, the ceiling and walls of the new Dining Room. He had arrived at Felbrigg by April 1752, by which time Paine—"who seems vastly desirous of clearing himself from neglect, and in some measure (tho not intirely) has done so"—had been goaded into producing acceptable designs for the plasterwork both of the Dining Room and the staircase. His first design for the staircase has survived, and was pronounced by Windham to be "too much ornamented," as indeed it was. A simpler version was executed by Rose and his workmen, and has survived unaltered, except for some portions that were removed owing to later adaptations of the original skylight.

Paine fitted the Dining Room, and the two bedrooms above it, with great ingenuity into the space left by the removal of Samwell's staircase. A little "coaxing"—it was Windham's word—proved necessary to relate these rooms convincingly to the new staircase; but double doors masked the expedients by which this tricky architectural problem was overcome. Above one of the bedroom doorways a space remained which was adapted into a sort of loft; and within it may still be seen a remnant of the rich plaster ceiling which surmounted the older staircase. This small apartment is concealed when the door is closed. It was never intended for secrecy, but later received the name of "the priest's room," although few families are less likely than the Windhams to have harboured a priest at any period of their history.

The ceiling of the Dining Room was the subject of much discussion. Finally Windham accepted a flowing rococo design in which spears, drums, and hunting-horns are linked by foliage round an eagle with wings outspread, from whose talons a chandelier might depend. In the corner panels were heads of the four seasons—spring garlanded with flowers, summer with ears of corn, fruitful autumn, bearded winter.

Windham had chosen casts for these by the end of April, and Rose began the execution of the whole ceiling shortly afterwards.

The plasterwork of the walls was designed to frame, in elegant swags of fruit and flowers, the existing family portraits—William and Katherine Windham and her father Sir Joseph Ashe, all by Lely; Ashe Windham by Kneller, and his wife possibly by Dahl. Over two of the doorways were inserted oval portraits of William Windham the Colonel by Kneller, and his naval son Captain Charles Windham by an unknown painter.[1] Oval mirrors, eight in number, were set beneath the larger portraits, between the windows and on either side of the fireplace. Paine's design for the wall-decoration shows several alternative treatments of these glasses, of which again the simplest was chosen. Above several of them he carried out a design in large slender links of chain, sometimes looped, sometimes interlaced. This unusual motif may possibly have been suggested by the links of the fetterlock which forms part of the Windham crest.

Windham was not so preoccupied by the decoration of his fine new rooms as to overlook the claims of humbler apartments. He had much to say about "the little house near the bleach"—the laundry-ground behind the domestic offices.

I think it the best place imaginable. Should not the inside be stuccoed, or how do you do it? how many holes? there must be one for a child; and I would have it as light as possible. There must be a good broad place to set a candle on, and a place to keep paper. I think the holes should be wide and rather oblong, and the seats broad and not quite level, and rather low before, but rising behind. Tho the better the plainer, it should be neat.

Gradually the rooms took shape. The crimson hangings and gold cord for the Cabinet, which had been sent down at the close of 1751, were in place next spring, soon after the ceilings had been completed. They are still there, the flowered crimson damask little faded by the passing of more than two centuries. "India paper," which in fact came from China, was hung in at least two of the bedrooms above. The

[1] Charles Windham was the youngest of Ashe Windham's three Earsham nephews, and a particular favourite with him. He had a distinguished career at sea; and a painting of an action off Mogadore Bay, in which he and a Captain Towry destroyed some "Sallee rovers," hangs in the Drawing Room. He died in 1747. In *Norfolk Portraits* I mistakenly reproduced his portrait as that of his uncle James Windham, with whom he first went to sea.

bow-room above the Cabinet still retains its Chinese wallpaper, an enchanting display of lotuses and peonies, ducks, silver pheasants, birds of paradise. There was much debate about the staircase. Finally in April "we have agreed for a mahogony rail, and iron ballusters." Windham draws a little sketch of a section of them, a design considerably less attractive than that which was finally carried out. Samwell's chimney-piece from the Drawing Room, a severely plain work in grey marble with a deep bolection moulding, was placed in the Library, and was replaced by another in a more fashionable style.

There was a good deal of frustration and delay over the chimney-pieces, and indeed over all the stone-work. Windham had written in February 1752 that "I wish the scoundrell stone-cutter in Yorkshire was 25 fathom deep in the sea with all the window-sills about his neck." He instructed Frary to have the sills done by an excellent local mason, Robert Page of Norwich, and to send the others back to Yorkshire by the next ship. In June he was again "in the cursedest passion imaginable with all the workmen." On this occasion the culprits were figures of some note in their profession. The chimneypiece and two tables for the Cabinet had been entrusted to a man named Carter, presumably one of the brothers Benjamin and Thomas Carter, who were in great employment at this time. He sent word to Windham that "he could not get the chimney done before the end of next month, upon which I sent to stop all his doings and swore I would not have the chimney at all." Eventually Windham relented, on the understanding that the work would be completed by the beginning of July. The Dining Room chimney-piece—a substantial affair requiring much intricate carving of lions' masks, vine-leaves, oak-leaves, grapes, and acorns—was to be executed from Paine's designs by one of the Biggs family, masons of Bath, who also worked much in London. It was discovered in mid-June that he had not even begun this or certain other commissions; and he "kept out of the way" when Windham sent to demand Paine's drawings back from him. He had previously given dissatisfaction—"there is not any bearing that fellow's carelessness and blunders"—and eventually Windham "put a stop to all kind of work which he had in hand." Paine's drawings were recovered and sent down to Felbrigg, where they were executed in due course by other workmen.

A few days later Windham asked Frary to charter a Wells or Yarmouth vessel to bring down a cargo from London early in July. It was to convey, among many other things, Carter's chimney-piece and tables, the iron-work for the staircase, and most of the pictures; but

THE DINING-ROOM

THE LIBRARY

"my great Van de Velde I cannot trust to the seas, so that alone shall go by land." In his next letter Windham wrote that he would come down to Felbrigg in a day or two, having just heard from Paine's clerk that the architect himself would shortly arrive there, presumably in the course of a tour of inspection of his various undertakings. "If so you must, if you can, contrive to keep him. He may make the drawings for the library, and you must battle with him about Biggs."

It is to be hoped that Windham arrived before Paine had left, and that Frary did not have to fight the battle alone. The strained relations between client and architect could have been eased only by long discussions on the spot. But at this point there is a long gap in the letters, since Windham remained in Norfolk for most of the summer and autumn. When they were resumed in November little more was said about the Cabinet and Drawing Room, which must have been advancing towards completion. The shelves and ceiling of the Library, and the decoration of the Staircase Hall, were now the main preoccupations.

The Library was designed in the Gothic style. It may not have been a very congenial task for so strict a Palladian as Paine, but his drawings show that he devoted much care and thought to it. The large room above the Great Hall was completely fitted with shelves to within two feet of the ceiling, and the shelves were also extended above each of its three doorways. The Gothic ornament on panels and doors was extremely restrained; and even the elaborately crocketed pinnacles, which were to surmount the shelves at intervals, were eventually discarded in favour of a plainer conical form.[1] In design and colouring the apartment was notably less ornate than the most famous Gothic library of the decade, Horace Walpole's at Strawberry Hill, which was undertaken two years later. And whereas Clermont painted for Walpole a ceiling that was a riot of heraldry and charging knights in armour, Paine confined himself to plaster and a sober geometrical design.[2]

This ceiling was executed by a plasterer named George Green, who

[1] Windham told Frary, when Paine was first preparing the drawings, that "I think the library should be nearly as that at Blickling." This may give some indication of the original aspect of the Blickling library, which was totally and irrevocably altered in the nineteenth century.

[2] This has now been replaced by a plain ceiling, except for the portions which have survived undamaged in the bays. The circumstances of the change are explained on p. 283.

replaced Rose at Felbrigg during the summer. A drawing for it, not quite as it was finally carried out, was sent down to him in August by Joseph Rumball, one of Paine's staff, with a letter of instructions which shows that he was also entrusted with the plasterwork on the staircase. The principal feature of the staircase decoration was a series of classical busts, set on pedestals within shallow circular recesses, above each of the seven doorways. The cargo sent down from London in July had included some "medals from Cheere"; and it is evident from one of Paine's drawings that originally these large medallions or plaques—classical heads in profile—were to be placed above the doorways. But in November 1752 Windham wrote that "I have ordered seven bustos for the staircase, so there must be recesses made where the medals were to have been." The bustos are of bronzed plaster; and as the "medals" were presumably original works by the distinguished sculptor Sir Henry Cheere, or by his almost equally talented brother John, Windham's alteration of plan is to be regretted.

In the same month of November 1752 another incident, totally unconnected with Felbrigg, involved Paine in further trouble with Windham, who wrote to Frary:

> On Sunday night my wife returning from a visit was overturned in the Landau by a heap of Rubbish laid in the street, but thank God had no hurt of any consequence. She had all her jewels on, and the mob getting about her was a good deal frightened; but luckily a gentleman came by who being a coachman and a Bruiser knew me and my Landau, and was very assistant to her and put her into a chair and saw her home. The Landau and Servants escaped unhurt. I have ordered a severe prosecution against the people who laid the rubbish, who it seems are workmen of Paine's, and repairing a house of his in Castle Street. His clerk Wolf was with me to intercede; but I have utterly refused to give any ear to them, and will make an example of them.

Owing to a gap in the series of letters, no more is heard of this unfortunate affair.

III

It would be agreeable to quote many passages from Windham's letters to Frary, which grew ever more friendly and confidential as the years went by. He often liked to turn aside from estate business and building details, to describe a spectacular run with his hounds in Essex, or touch upon some chance incident that had occurred in London. For example, "I was up all night with Mr Welch on a grand search last night. Fielding has but slightly painted the scenes of misery and debauchery one meets with." This was Saunders Welch, who succeeded Henry Fielding as a Justice of the Peace for Westminster, and was regarded by Dr Johnson as "one of my best and dearest friends."[1]

At times Windham could be as vehement and uncontrolled as in earlier years. In 1753 there is a tremendous denunciation of some people in Cromer, a father and son named Ellis, who had incurred his displeasure.

There is nothing I would not do, consistent with honour, to mortify the Ellises and make them repent their behaviour to me. For as I think in my conscience I was neither in the wrong originally, nor acted with any heat or passion, but rather with a desire of accomodating matters; and that had I been a little to blame, I might have expected a small degree of compliance from them on account of past benefits; the manner they have acted in, has stirred my resentment to such a degree that nothing can exceed it. And as their behaviour was not just a sudden start, but they had time to cool and reflect, so never can I forgive them, but declare eternal war with them: for no condescension or even submission on their side could ever make me look on Jack Ellis in any other light than that of a meanspirited ungrateful lying scoundrell, and the old man of a wrongheaded old fool.

These outbursts were exceptional; and Windham's more usual line of conduct is shown in his treatment of a footman named John Lubbock, a young man from Norfolk whom he had brought to London, and who unexpectedly lapsed from grace. The episode is not without its humour, and is perhaps worth recounting in full. It shows that Windham, once his initial wrath was over, could behave with tolerance and consideration.

On 14 January 1752 he wrote to Frary:

John Lubbock last night took it into his head (being I believe a little in beer) to be very valiant, and began picking a quarrel with the maids. He first was very rough with the nurse maid, then with Molly Ward whose face he slap'd pretty handsomely, and at last threw her down

[1] For a description of Welch see Boswell, *Life of Johnson* (ed. Hill-Powell), III, 216–19. "Johnson, who had an eager and unceasing curiosity to know human life in all its variety, told me, that he attended Mr Welch in his office for a whole winter, to hear the examinations of the culprits; but that he found an almost uniform tenor of misfortune, wretchedness and profligacy."

chair and all against an iron fender, hurt her side and her neck so much that I was forced to send for a surgeon this morning. Then he got foul of Dolly, whom he would have struck, but she took a box iron, and swore she would split his skull, which she certainly had done, but that he prudently desisted. Of this complaint was made, and this morning I made him the compliment of telling him that I kept no servants that fought women, and that he had nothing to do but to be gone as soon as possible. So I suppose he will set out tomorrow for Norfolk. I desire therefore you will settle his account, as I do not know what is due for wages. Board wages and bills I shall pay, as I know the amount.

Frary was then instructed to send to London another footman named Barna—a contraction, probably, of Barnabas.

Let him bring his dressed Cloaths &c as he shall come into John's room. The post blows his horn, so I can only add that John may take his frock to Felbrigg, which I shall give him, but the Livery he is to leave.

Next day Windham wrote again.

John is set out this morning. I paid him his board wages and bills in full amounting to £7 – 16 – 6, so you have nothing but wages to pay him. His behaviour was vastly unaccountable, as I never heard any thing of him before of that sort, but took him to be a good natur'd fellow, and that he had too great a respect for the sex to beat them; but he showed a kind of unconcern and indifference, at thus losing his place, that I own I cannot account for. He said only that he knew complaints had been made against him; but neither my wife nor I ever heard the least, before this capital one. I told him he must leave his livery, but his frock and working things he might take. As I was out when he went I don't know exactly what he did take, but that you may just enquire into, and settle it as is proper, for he had no cloaths here to go in. We have a notion he is on a scheme for marrying the Laundry Maid; perhaps some love quarrel or disappointment, or falsehood, may have made him angry with the whole sex, and indifferent to what he does.

Five days later:

If you can form any guess at the motives of John Lubbock's strange conduct I should be glad to know, for Thomas told me that the next morning he advised John to begin with making it up with the maids, and asking pardon of me and his mistress; but he did not chuse it, tho' I did not speak to him till 12 o'clock. Indeed when I did I was pretty short and pithy, but he seemed quite easy about it, only made some slight excuse of his being drunk and sorry for it. I believe he looked on himself as too usefull a servant to be parted with, but he did not consider that when provoked, I am devilishly rugged.

Early in February arose the inevitable problem of a character for John Lubbock. Here again Windham showed himself conscientious and fair.

I hate giving a general written character; one does not know what to say, for you cannot mention faults, and if a servant has none, why is he turned away? so that unless in very particular cases they are ridiculous, and indeed are very little minded by any body, as some people and indeed too many make them things of course. But if John will cause application to be made to me in person, if in town, or by letter by any gentleman I will give him a character which will be of more service to him, tho' strictly just. For I think, tho' he was guilty of such a fault as was sufficient reason for discharging him, that he is a good servant, and could safely recommend him to any gentleman.

Finally Windham wrote from London at the beginning of June:

Pray send to John Lubbock and tell him that Mr Bullock will take him as his servant if they can agree, and he has desired me to have you agree for him. He gives his present servant 8 guineas per annum, and 8 shillings a week board wages, cast off cloaths &c. You may see if he will come cheaper, and make as good an agreement as you can. He gives livery and so forth. You may agree with him and send him up directly. I think I have done him a great piece of service by recommending him, so inculcate to him to be sober and behave well.

And so John Lubbock passes from the scene.

IV

Gradually the interior of the house assumed its new appearance, which it substantially preserves to this day. The decoration of the Dining Room was completed, and the older portraits were hung in their intended places. The pictures which Windham himself had acquired were arranged most carefully in the Drawing Room and Cabinet, in accordance with the meticulous diagrams which he had prepared and which still survive. "I must be present at that work," he had told Frary; and so no doubt he was. The Cabinet was entirely filled with the pictures he had acquired on the Grand Tour, the huge de Vlieger occupying the place of honour, and the thirty-two works by Busiri disposed all over the room, in company with most of the Dutch and Flemish paintings. At one end of the Drawing Room he placed his two great Van de Veldes. The opposite wall was adorned by a more recent purchase, a pair of large paintings of contemporary riverside London by Samuel Scott, one depicting the Tower and its surroundings, the other a view of London Bridge with its packed houses and the water thundering through its many arches.

The Library was completed in 1753; and Windham's books, with those of his father and grandfather, took up their stations in the Gothic shelves. Among them were about three hundred volumes of miscellaneous pamphlets, poems, plays, and so forth, bound uniformly in quarter-calf with marbled boards and reddish morocco labels. Windham's practical interests included book-binding; he had acquired in Geneva a manuscript copy of Gauffecourt's *Traité de la reliure*, and he owned a large outfit of binders' tools and materials. I think it is likely that these volumes were bound on the premises and under his supervision.[1] The series of these bound-up volumes stopped short in 1761, the year of Windham's death; and so did the generous inflow of the latest French and English books.

The Staircase Hall was also completed in the course of 1753. Green made an end of the plasterwork, the bustos were set in place, and finally the ironwork of the stairs was put up by a valued employee of Paine's named Mr Wagg. "I just now hear that Wagg setts out for Felbrigg tomorrow," Windham wrote on 9 June. "You must somehow scheme about his living, for he is a top master workman and lives in a very good way."

Work on the house must have proceeded some while yet; indeed a rainwater-head at the rear of the west wing, where new passages were built and the whole refronted in brick, is dated 1756. But there are no more letters to Frary after the summer of 1753, when Windham and his family came down to Felbrigg; and I suspect that Frary died in the following year. His health had not been robust, and Windham made frequent enquiries about it, showing an especial anxiety lest he should be exposed to the risk of smallpox on his journeys to the Essex and Somerset estates. On 17 August 1754 a corn-merchant named William Palgrave wrote from Coltishall recommending the bearer Robert

[1] This theory is treated with sympathy by Mr A. N. L. Munby in his article "Windham and Gauffecourt" in *Transactions of the Cambridge Bibliographical Society*, 1950, pp. 186–90.

Thurston as a suitable steward for Windham. He was duly engaged; he must have been engaged as a successor to Frary; but no letters from Windham to him have survived, and we have no further details about plasterers, or stone-cutters, or the shortcomings of Mr Paine.

V

Henceforward Windham's life was divided between Felbrigg and London. His daily activities, during the next few years, can be traced in his account-books, which form a record of sociability and enjoyment. In London the theatre continued to be his chief delight. There are constant visits to the play, the opera, the burletta; payments at the benefit-nights of actors and actresses, Christmas gifts to the boxkeepers and the housekeeper. Garrick's name appears frequently, both in connection with the theatre and as a private friend. It was probably through him that Windham came in contact at this time with Samuel Johnson. We do not know how close their acquaintance may have been, since only one chance record of it has survived. Many years later, when someone was praising Windham's son, Johnson is described as having turned in his chair and said, "True, Sir, for his father was a noble fellow."

Windham's natural daughter Bess and his step-daughter Dolly Lukin were now growing up; his step-sons Bob and Billy Lukin were at Eton, Bob being destined for the Army and Billy for the Church. Thomas Dampier, once of the Common Room at Geneva, had now become Lower Master, and took much interest in their welfare. The account-books show payments to boxing, fencing, writing, music, dancing, and Italian masters for Windham's various children and step-children. As dancing-masters Garrick's Swiss *protégés* the Noverres were usually employed. In 1756, for instance, Mrs Garrick was paid £15 8*s*. "for Noverre teaching and stockings," and Garrick received four guineas "for Noverre *cadet*." This younger Noverre, Augustin, eventually settled in Norwich and became the city's leading dancing-master, dying there early in the next century.

Windham subscribed for many books and volumes of prints—Stuart and Revett's *Antiquities of Athens*, Thomas Sandby's drawings of the formation of Virginia Water, Miss Sarah Fielding's *Lives of Cleopatra and Octavia*, Franklin's edition of Sophocles, Martinelli's edition of Machiavelli, the Della Crusca Dictionary. He paid £2. 5*s*. for some unspecified purpose to Mr Hogarth. He gave two guineas annually to the Society for the Encouragement of Arts, and five guineas to the Lock

Hospital. There are constant records also of small charitable payments —"given in charity," "a poor casualty," "decay'd musicians," "some seamen whose ship was burnt." He paid seven shillings in vails to the servants "at Mr Walpole's"—Strawberry Hill, where he must have compared Horace's new library with his own. He paid two guineas to Ruspini the tooth-cleaner, and £68. 5*s.* to Mr Ellicott for a repeating watch, and £21 to George Church for the library table, which was designed in conformity with Paine's Gothic shelves and for which Church's drawing still exists.

Every summer he and his wife would go for a long tour in the west of England. There seems already to have been some deterioration in his health, though none in his spirits and outward vitality; and he would spend at least a month drinking the waters at Bristol or Bath. Then they would go sight-seeing—to Tintern Abbey and the Wye valley; a little "scheme" into Wales; a visit to Lichfield, where vails of half a crown were given to Miss Garrick's servant and a guinea to the servants of Peter Garrick; or a more southerly journey to inspect Longleat, Stourhead, Salisbury, Wilton, and Stonehenge. And so back to Felbrigg for the autumn and its varied sport; and to London for the colder months of the winter.

Whatever the true state of Windham's health may have been, his love of hunting and shooting was little diminished. There is much correspondence with his attorney, George Hunt Holley of Aylsham, about sporting boundaries, trespassing after game, and encroachments of neighbouring packs of hounds. Indoors his mechanical ingenuity was constantly employed. One room was fitted up as a turning shop; another was devoted to the making of fireworks, a pursuit which had a particular fascination for him and on which he bought every available treatise. During one of his absences in London the firework shop blew up, to the great alarm of the household but without doing any serious damage. He read incessantly, and wrote a lively pamphlet attacking Smollett's specimen of his proposed translation of *Don Quixote*. "Your criticisms of the translator are so just," wrote Stillingfleet, "that if the world is not as blind as he is impudent, he must be oblig'd to give over."

There is an attractive picture of Windham's family life at Felbrigg in a letter from Dampier, who had stayed with him for the Christmas of 1756. Dampier had lately lost his wife, and the Windhams hoped to arrange a marriage for him with an eligible widow who lived in Norwich. These negotiations were not successful, and Dampier had to wait a year or two longer for his second bride. On his return to Eton he wrote to Windham:

If I owed you a Grudge, I could be well revenged upon you in my first Letter after the first visit to Felbrigg: I could cram you with compliments upon your House, Park &c, the Elegance and convenience, the *Utile Dulci*; the freedom and Ease; just enough Civility without Ceremony; the various Amusements for the Belly and Head from the Library to the Turning Wheel; above all, the Cheerfulness of mine Host and Hostess; the mad Bess and the obliging Dolly, with the pranks of the Etonian [Billy Lukin] and his Pupil [Billy Windham]: I could say a great deal of the Magistrate, how cordially he entertains or damns those that deserve it or not, from the Parson down to the Postilion . . . *Thanks*, dear Windham, which is literally a word to the Wise.

The tone of Dampier's letter was echoed, though with a note of anxiety that was somewhat ominous, by David Garrick in the following autumn. He and his wife stayed at Felbrigg in the course of an East Anglian tour, and he wrote afterwards to his brother Peter: "We were indeed most happy at Windham's. All was Mirth, Joy, Love, Elegance and What Not. He desired his best wishes to you most affectionately. He seems thoughtful; at times greatly so, and I don't absolutely like his looks or cough."

The bonds of the Common Room continued to hold firm, its members foregathering in London and visiting one another in their country homes. Dampier wrote to Windham, when the business of the widow was under consideration, that:

ever since the dispersion of the Common Room and my return into England, I have never lived with comfort, but during the time I was married; for in truth, *Su loved me and I loved Su*: since her death, I have been miserable, forlorn and solitary; and you know, my Business won't suffer me to hunt far from home for Amusements, nor yet for a Wife; therefore I must trust to my friends to get one for me . . . A little while ago Still, Johnny, Dick and Tory[1] came and staid a night with me: you had your health drunk *pro more*. Methought we were an assembly of little Gods. How I shall rejoice to see the Common Room Book at Felbrigg,[2] how often Haddy belched and Dossy farted . . . I pray you, never tell the Widdow the story of the Arve, nor how I used to harangue Italian Postilions from a Bulk.

[1] Stillingfleet, Williamson, Aldworth, and Samuel Torriano, the last not a member of the Common Room but a friend of most of its members.

[2] Regrettably it is no longer to be found at Felbrigg.

In the same way, if in more decorous colours, the various members of the Common Room appear constantly in the long series of letters to Windham from his old tutor. Stillingfleet lived for the greater part of 1754 and 1755 at Stratton Strawless near Norwich, where the squire, Robert Marsham, was an enthusiastic botanist and a most assiduous planter of trees. Subsequently he lived in modest lodgings in London, paying long visits to Robert Price in Herefordshire, to Richard Aldworth in Berkshire, and to other friends all over the kingdom. He and Windham corresponded, with intimacy and affection, on every kind of subject—politics, plays, architecture, music, the coal-porter at Norwich who had become a landscape-painter, the use of certain agarics as styptics for wounds, the demerits of Gray's two *Pindaric Odes*, the precise weight of the golden-crested wren.

My great joy [he wrote on one occasion] is natural history of all sorts, written by men of parts, accuracy and learning. And i must add that i never had so true a relish for the Psalms of David (which now i prefer to all the poetry in the world) as since i have fallen into this tast: for there i find a deeper sense of the beauties of the creation than in any other writer, and that express'd in a more manly, plain and noble manner.

It will be noticed that in his letters, as in his later publications, Stillingfleet adopted the habit of writing the first personal pronoun with a small letter. It was and is, after all, the practice of all European nations except ourselves. Nevertheless it was regarded as a trifle eccentric on Stillingfleet's part; and he began to display other mild peculiarities as the years went by. For example, he used to attend the evening *salons* of certain learned ladies—Mrs Montagu, Mrs Boscawen, Mrs Vesey, and the rest—in the stockings of blue worsted which he habitually wore during the day. They all loved him for his gentle manners, his easy conversation, "his smile indicative of all the benignity of his mind." Their parties were not complete unless he was there. "We can do nothing," they used to say, "without the blue stockings." And presently the expression *Blue Stocking* became attached to the assemblies of those learned ladies, and finally to the ladies themselves.

VI

The year 1756 saw the outbreak of the Seven Years War, into which, as into so many other wars, Great Britain entered ill-prepared and inadequately armed. Far into the next year, defeats and setbacks followed in gloomy succession. Invasion from France seemed imminent. The militia system had fallen into complete disuse, and the country lay virtually unprotected. Large numbers of Hessian and Hanoverian troops were hastily brought over. As Gibbon said in later years, "in the outset of a glorious war, the English people had been defended by the aid of German mercenaries."

It was a humiliating moment for a nation which detested standing armies and foreign mercenaries. Pitt and his followers at once set themselves to revive the militia, as a second line of defence and as a means of releasing regular troops for service overseas. Prominent in this movement was the Hon. George Townshend, one of the Members for Norfolk, who in 1757 succeeded in carrying a Militia Bill through Parliament. It provided for the raising of a large and effective body of men. But its success depended largely on the enthusiasm with which it was carried through in the various counties, by the Lords Lieutenant who were to command the militia, and by the country gentlemen with whom lay the main responsibility of raising and officering the new force. It had met with considerable opposition in its passage through Parliament; and in some counties the indifference or active hostility of their leaders went far to endanger the whole scheme.

George Townshend was passionately resolved to ensure the success of his project in his own county of Norfolk; and he found an eager and capable supporter in William Windham. The two men were related—Townshend's grandfather and Windham's father were first cousins: they were much of the same age, with Windham a few years the elder, and had long been friends. As a young officer Townshend had been in all the actions of the seventeen-forties, and had served for several years as *aide-de-camp* to the Duke of Cumberland. He was hot-tempered and impulsive, prone to violent quarrels, and with an extraordinary gift for drawing disrespectful and wounding caricatures. Politically he lacked the spectacular talents of his younger brother Charles, but he was by no means a negligible figure, and he pursued his militia scheme with formidable resolution.

He had serious obstacles to overcome in Norfolk. His father, the third Viscount, with whom he was on the worst of terms, made everything as difficult as possible. Horace Walpole told a friend that this nobleman, "who is not the least mad of your countrymen, attended by a parson, a barber, and his own servants, and in his own long hair, which he has let grow, raised a mob against the execution of the Bill, and has written a paper against it, which he has pasted up on the door of four churches near him." Another prominent figure of the older generation, the architecturally minded Earl of Leicester, did all he could to bring the militia into discredit and ridicule. He was already at loggerheads with Townshend on questions of game-preserving and the destroying of foxes. Their antagonisms led in due course to a quarrel which reverberated through Norfolk, and a challenge to a duel which Lord Leicester firmly and sensibly declined.[1]

On the other hand, Townshend had some enthusiastic supporters. The Lord Lieutenant, the third Earl of Orford—Horace Walpole's "mad nephew" in years to come, but in abundant possession of his faculties at this time—readily assumed control of the militia, and proved an admirable figurehead. Volunteers came forward in large numbers, and less than half the force had to be recruited by the compulsory ballot which the Bill had introduced. It was divided into two battalions, the Eastern, which was commanded by Sir Armine Wodehouse, Townshend's fellow Member of Parliament for the county, and the Western, which was commanded by Townshend himself. Windham, though resident in the eastern half of the county, became Lieutenant-Colonel of the Western Battalion, and Townshend's second-in-command. Month after month he devoted himself unremittingly to all the details of organisation and administration—the balloting, the equipping, the disciplining and drilling of a wholly inexperienced body of men.

To overcome local opposition and indifference, he wrote a short pamphlet, *A Plain Address to the Farmers, Labourers and Commonalty of the County of Norfolk*, and had it distributed as widely as possible. He depicted the danger of invasion in the plainest colours.

> We are engaged in a War with the French, our old implacable Enemies; they hate us both on account of our Religion; and because we are rich, happy, and Free, while they are poor, miserable, and Slaves; they remember that we have formerly beat them, and gained many and glorious Victories over them; and desire nothing so much as Revenge.

He contrasted the freedom and security of the humblest Englishman with the down-trodden condition of the peasants of continental Europe. He exhorted his Norfolk neighbours to learn to defend their liberties and their families by force of arms. He explained the terms of the Militia Bill, repeated his assurances that no militiaman would be

[1] I have given a full account of this affair in the chapter entitled "The Phantom Duel" in *Norfolk Assembly* (1957), pp. 151–68.

sent abroad, and ended by calling female patriotism to his aid. "I think that those who would at such a Time call upon Substitutes, to defend their Sweethearts, their Wives and Families, deserve richly, that my pretty Countrywomen should find Substitutes to serve for them in a more pleasing Duty."

Windham soon afterwards embarked upon a much more ambitious piece of writing, the manual of drill published in 1759 and entitled *A Plan of Discipline, composed for the use of the Militia of the County of Norfolk*. He had formed the conclusion that the system of drill practised by the regular forces was too complicated to be mastered by a part-time force, and had evolved a simplified method, based largely on the manual exercise introduced by Frederick William of Prussia and perfected by Frederick the Great. The critics of the militia system had proclaimed that such a force could never be brought to any real efficiency. To obviate these objections, as Townshend expressed it in a foreword to the book, "a worthy gentleman of Norfolk, though no regular bred soldier, nor the offspring of the parade, has endeavoured to prove, how easily a healthy robust countryman or a resolute mechanic may be taught the use of arms; and how very attainable that degree of military knowledge is, which will enable a country gentleman to command a platoon."

The volume must be one of the most elaborate and decorative training-manuals ever produced. Windham expended endless pains upon it, and especially upon an introduction which almost amounted to a history of the military art, from the days of the Grecian phalanx down to those of Marshal Saxe. It was packed with learned allusions, and with material which, however interesting to the antiquary, can have had singularly little bearing on the actualities of the Seven Years War. Stillingfleet was frequently consulted during its composition, and contributed an enormous note on the use of music by the ancients in warfare. It was also submitted for revision to Garrick and other friends.

When his introduction reached modern times Windham gave a clear exposition of the Prussian exercise, both in drill and musketry; and he found space also for his views upon those regular officers who endeavoured to decry the militia, although they themselves had "grovelled on for years in the routine of the service, without ever attaining to a greater degree of military knowledge than would constitute a tolerable sergeant." His own system was most carefully explained, with ample directions and diagrams. The firelock and bayonet drills were also illustrated with a long series of beautifully executed plates. The figures in these bear a resemblance to some of Townshend's work, and may have been drawn or at least outlined by him.

The book was advancing towards completion by the spring of 1759. On 11 January of that year Windham addressed a letter to Garrick, hitherto unpublished, which mentions its concluding stages and is otherwise not without interest.

My dear Friend,

I was so taken up last week with our military exercises at Fakenham that I could not answer your two most obliging letters. Indeed I have now only time just to acknowledge them, and thank you for your kindness in taking the trouble I gave you so readily. I shall not fail acknowledging Mr Stanley's civility in a post or two, but my Colonel presses me so much to get the preface finished and the book of exercise ready for the press, that I have no time. I have however almost finished it, and shall send it to you: be so good as to mark for me what you think may be altered or retrenched, and what is ungrammatical in all expressed, for I am sensible there are many parts that are so. I return you your correspondence with Master Robert Dodsley. How could you think of ever remaining in friendship with a man whose vanity you had hurt? Had you ravished his wife, b—g——d his son, and then set fire to his house and shop I should not have thought it impossible but he might have forgiven you; but to refuse his play that he and Mr Melmoth and company read and wept and wept and read, was never to be pardoned. I am delighted with your last letter to him; it treats him just as he deserves to be.[1]

I saw Hogarth's print, which I could not make any meaning out of. You know my sentiments of him, though you and I have often disputed that affair. He is an ignorant conceited puppy, nor has no sure idea of a car*i*cature, which the blockhead writes car*a*cature, not knowing it comes from *caricare*, to overload any part or *outrer* any feature; the French painters call such kind of drawing *des charges*. I always thought him envious, but thought it was only with regard to brother painters. Since he has the impudence to attack my friend the Colonel, I will try at a dinner for him. I think I have materials in my head; you shall be sole confidant, and to your hands shall it be committed to burn or publish.

[1] This refers to Garrick's refusal to produce Dodsley's tragedy *Cleone*, and the resultant quarrel between them. The imbroglio is described in Carola Oman's *David Garrick*, pp. 202–3, where the letter which delighted Windham is printed in full.

Adieu, many happy new years to you and Mrs Garrick, and all blessings attend you. My wife joins in this.

My dear Garrick
Yours ever and affectionately
W. Windham.

I shall soon send you my preface.

Shortly after the date of this letter, Townshend was appointed one of the three Brigadiers who were to serve under Wolfe in his expedition against Quebec. He sailed for Canada with Wolfe in February, and from that time the command of the Western Battalion devolved upon Windham. The general situation was now less grave; the tide of the war had turned, and all over the world the offensive was passing to the British armies and fleets. The threat of invasion was not finally to disappear until the autumn, when Hawke destroyed the French Fleet at Quiberon Bay. It was already clear, however, that the militia would be needed not to defend their own hearths and homes, but to take over the duties of regular troops who had been sent abroad. Contrary to original intention, it was now decided that they might be marched out of their own counties in order to serve at more vital points. The Norfolk Militia had come to be regarded as one of the most efficient corps in the kingdom; and it was the first to be ordered for duty outside its own county boundaries.

Townshend's departure laid a heavy and unexpected burden upon Windham, who was always conscious that, unlike his Colonel, he was "no regular bred soldier, nor the offspring of the parade." To the responsibility of commanding the Western Battalion was now added the duty of marching it across England, to its new quarters at Hillsea Barracks near Portsmouth. This involved a further delay in the publication of his book; and also, a more serious consideration, it meant a further strain upon his declining health. Growing anxiety on this score is noticeable in the letters of Stillingfleet and other friends. In fact his once vigorous physique was already undermined by consumption. In the foreword to the *Plan of Discipline*, dated from Hillsea Barracks on 24 August, he referred to "my own very infirm state of health"; and there can be no doubt that his abnormal exertions at this time helped to shorten his life.

The two battalions of the Norfolk Militia, under the command of Lord Orford, marched down to Hampshire in July in a blaze of publicity and popular enthusiasm. Crowds lined the road everywhere, and a vast concourse of Londoners turned out to see them march through Hyde Park on their way to be reviewed by the King outside Kensington Palace. A delighted ensign recorded that the King "expressed very great satisfaction, for our men had the pleasure of hearing His Majesty often call out 'They are brave fellows,' 'They are noble fellows,' which filled every heart with joy." Horace Walpole, on this occasion at least, had reason to feel proud of his nephew.

> My Lord Orford, their Colonel, I hear, looked gloriously martial and genteel, and I believe it; his person and air have a noble wildness in them; the regimentals, too, are very becoming, scarlet faced with black, buff waistcoats, and gold buttons. How knights of shires, who have never shot anything but woodcocks, like this warfare, I don't know; but the towns through which they pass adore them: everywhere they are treated and regaled.

One of the officers in Windham's battalion caused him some perturbation by saluting a Beefeater, and then marching on past the King "with infinite composure, and without bestowing upon him the slightest notice." Nor was it easy to convince him of his mistake. "Do you think, Colonel Windham, I did not know the King as well as you did? How could I miss him? Had he not the G.R. on his breast?"

There exists at Felbrigg a volume kept for the next two and a half years by a certain Ensign Hicks, in which he entered, with elaborate flourishes of penmanship, copies of the daily battalion orders. Mrs Windham's name had been Hicks, and the Ensign was, I think, her nephew. From his order-book we can follow the routine at Hillsea and the other places where the battalion was later stationed—parades, inspections, exercises, field-days, the guarding of French prisoners, an occasional court-martial. The men were encouraged to help with the Hampshire harvest, and at other times they had opportunities to practise their private trades and callings. After endless delays, partly due to his other preoccupations and partly to a series of difficulties with the printers, Windham was able to get his book published before the year was over. It was well received, and not only in military circles. Johnson quoted several paragraphs, with due acknowledgment to the "ingenious author," in his account of Ascham.

The battalion wintered at Gloucester, where Price and Stillingfleet came over from Foxley to visit Windham. "He seemed to be but very so so," Stillingfleet wrote to Aldworth. "He exercised his militia to entertain us. They do amazingly well." They remained at Gloucester until the following June, when they moved back into East Anglia and were quartered there for several months, first at Bury St Edmunds and subsequently at King's Lynn. By this time the British arms had triumphed, and were continuing to triumph, all over the world, in India and Canada, in the West Indies and on the high seas. "Our bells are worn threadbare with ringing for victories," wrote Horace Walpole. These victories were reflected in the daily pass-words which Ensign Hicks entered in his order-book—Rodney, Hawke, Granby, Boscawen, Belleisle, Wolfe, Quebec. The militia had now served its original purpose, and might well have been disbanded, although it was still doing useful work in liberating regular troops for overseas service. Gibbon, thoroughly bored with his militia duties and longing to return to literary pursuits, grumbled that "after the pretence of an invasion has vanished, the popularity of Mr Pitt gave a sanction to the illegal step of keeping them till the end of the war under arms, in constant pay and duty, and at a distance from their respective homes." His words might well have been echoed by Windham, whose health was growing steadily worse, and who was finding it increasingly difficult to maintain a high standard of discipline and efficiency among his men.[1]

Townshend returned from Canada at the end of 1759. He had fought with gallantry in the battle which formed the climax of that memorable campaign, and it was to him that Quebec had surrendered after the death of Wolfe and the disablement of Monckton, the senior Brigadier. On the other hand, he had made himself consistently disagreeable to Wolfe, by minor pinpricks in the form of caricatures, and

[1] Two extracts from Ensign Hicks's order-book: "The Lieutenant-Colonel was very much surprised on Monday last to find that the Battalion behaved so ill, and show'd so little attention or desire to do better. He knows they can if they will, and therefore since they make so ill a use of the Indulgence that has been shown them of going to work, he declares that if on Monday next they do not go through all the Parts of the Exercises and Evolutions, that shall be commanded them, with the greatest attention and exactness, and do not make full amends for last Monday's neglect, he will not suffer a man of them to go to work, but will have a Field Day of the whole every day next week."

"It has been reported to the Lieutenant-Colonel that Whores have been of late brought into the Guard Room several times, which is so scandalous a Proceeding, and so contrary to Discipline, that he cannot sufficiently express his Indignation at it; and if he can find out the Offenders, he is determined to punish them severely."

by a good deal of criticism and obstruction. He returned to England with the laurels of a victor; but stories of his conduct towards the real victor were spread abroad, and in some cases unjustly.

Windham was delighted to see him back. Their old friendship was renewed, even though Townshend did not spend so much time with his militia as hitherto, and the responsibilities of his Lieutenant-Colonel were consequently not much lightened. For years past Windham had collected his friend's caricatures, sketches probably thrown off after dinner or in any spare moment—drawings of the King and the Duke of Cumberland, Lord Sandwich and Bubb Dodington, foreign ambassadors and eminent lawyers, jockeys, prize-fighters, rustic militiamen.[1] He had pasted these into a large album, sometimes adding identifications of their subjects in shorthand. Now there was added to this collection a fascinating series of drawings in colour of American Indians, of whom Townshend had encountered many during his recent campaign—"an Indian pursuing a wounded enemy with his tomahawk," "an Indian war chief compleatly equipp'd with a scalp in his hand," "an Indian of the Outawas Tribe and his family going to war." These outlandish warriors had a great attraction for Townshend. The poet Gray described in a letter how he had brought back to England an Indian boy, who attacked his master with a scalping-knife and was with difficulty prevented from killing and devouring his dog.

It is likely that Townshend, fresh from active service with regular troops, did not appreciate the problems that confronted Windham and his fellow-officers of the militia. At Bury and Lynn the men were close to their own homes and their own civilian employments. The country was no longer in the slightest danger of invasion, and no amount of exhortation could revive the patriotic fervour which had led many of them to enlist three years before. At heart their officers probably felt much the same. Nevertheless Townshend, on one of his occasional visits to the Western Battalion, attempted during the summer of 1760 to introduce a variety of new regulations which officers and men alike regarded as "whimsical and finical." He expressed strong views upon hats, capes, buttons, linen, the blacking of gaiters, the tying of hair, the selection of men for the grenadier company, the colour of the stocks

[1] Horace Walpole had described, a few years earlier, how Townshend "adorns the shutters, walls and napkins of every tavern in Pall Mall with caricatures of the Duke [of Cumberland] and Sir George Lyttelton, the Duke of Newcastle and Mr Fox."

to be worn by the men so selected, the necessity of a more exacting standard at the next balloting for recruits, and much else besides. The individual reforms were not in themselves vexatious, but cumulatively they appeared excessive, and implied some measure of criticism of existing standards. Moreover Townshend made use of his accustomed strong language. After their years of hard work it cannot have been agreeable for Windham and his subordinates to hear that their men were "cloathed like Slovens," or that they would be better employed "cleaning themselves and taking care of their Dress, than lolling about the Streets, raking about with Bunters, or sleeping upon a Bulk Head."

A disagreeable wrangle ensued. Windham wrote a formal protest on his own behalf and on that of his fellow-officers. Townshend replied that he would not be reduced, on his visits to the battalion, to the status of "an insignificant Titular Colonel and Cypher, ostentatiously affecting a Merit where I have neither Authority or Justice done me . . . upon the footing of Mr Morse [the Quartermaster], with the difference only of two Centries at my Door to command or amuse myself with—a meer Cypher." This and a second letter caused Windham, in terms as unmeasured as anything Townshend ever achieved, to announce his intention of resigning his commission. He spoke of his surprise "that one of the most strenuous advocates for liberty, and who is esteemed one of its firmest friends and patrons, can, when in command, adopt the arbitrary imperious sentiments of a Russian General." He concluded:

However different the degrees of estimation we possess in the world may be, yet my small share is as dear and valuable to me as your large one can be to you. Therefore as I cannot submit to be made a Cypher, I think it is high time for me to quit a service, in which I see very evidently that I must be one, or have continual disputes and be on ill terms with my Commanding Officer.

Further correspondence ensued, in the course of which both men offered to resign; but in the end neither did so. Their disagreements were somehow adjusted, and their long friendship suffered only a brief interruption. The gravity of Windham's illness was now obvious to everyone; and some of Townshend's letters, both in this and in a later dispute, reveal an unexpected kindliness and patience. After all, they both had the same objects at heart, and their differences were only on minor issues. Townshend was on active service abroad again in

1761; and in his last letter, addressed from a camp in Germany only a few weeks before Windham's death, he wrote:

With good and proper discipline, which is our duty to preserve and it is effeminate to depart from, we must, my dear friend, mix much temper and at certain times some forbearance, and even discipline ourselves. I believe we both want this lesson in particular moments in some degree, I am sure I can recollect much so in my own case.

In a codicil to his will Windham wrote:

I leave to my much honoured and valued friend the Honourable George Townshend fifty pounds to purchase a ring or some other memorial of me that may now and then recall to his mind one who was sincerely attached to him and who was so happy as to assist him in the establishing a militia in this county.

A scrap of paper bearing the words of this bequest has been preserved in the archives at Raynham, a witness of the attachment between these strong-willed and fiery-tempered men.

VII

Windham had given much thought to his will, as was natural in a man of declining health whose large property would pass to a young and only son. Eventually the will and its two codicils extended to eighteen closely written sheets. Every possible provision was made for his wife, for her three Lukin children, and for "my natural and reputed daughter Elizabeth Morgan commonly called Elizabeth Windham." There were generous bequests to "my very good friend and cousin Benjamin Stillingfleet," to his several god-children, to his illegitimate sister Mary Phillips, and to other friends. Most of the Common Room were rich men, but all their names appear in his will—Aldworth, Price, Tate, Haddington, Baillie, Williamson, Dampier—as recipients of bequests of various kinds. "He could not die," wrote Aldworth, "without leaving us marks of his latest remembrance and affection." He appointed Price, Garrick, Dampier and Stillingfleet as his executors and the guardians of his son. Price, however, was fated to die a few weeks before him.

In the first codicil, executed just before he set out with his militia for the south of England, he gave directions as to his funeral and his memorial. He desired to be buried as privately as possible; and "if I should die in the service on which I am now called out, I should desire a Military Interment but with as little parade as possible consistent with my Rank." He asked for a short inscription to be carved in the space left under his father's monument in Felbrigg Church, but it was to be entirely factual—names, dates, and nothing more. "As for any Elogiums that the partiality of my friends or family might chuse to add, I hope they will not do it. I hope in the course of my life I have not merited much censure, and certain I am that I have not merited much praise, so the less that is said the better." His wishes were carried out. He had erected to his father a mural monument of grey marble, surmounted by a flattened pyramid of black marble bearing the inscription, and with his parents' arms beautifully carved at the base. Into the space between these two features was inserted a rectangular slab framed in yellow marble, bearing the dates of his own birth and death, the names of his wife and son, and nothing more.

The second codicil, executed on 4 October 1761, was a sadder affair even than most testamentary documents. Windham had made generous provision for his natural daughter Elizabeth; and should his son William die before the age of twenty-one and without issue, Elizabeth and her heirs were to inherit the greater part of his estate. Now all this was suddenly revoked. His daughter had "by her ungrateful and undutiful behaviour rendered herself unworthy my kind disposition." She and her heirs were to receive none of the legacies and reversions hitherto intended for them. However, "in order that she may not be totally destitute of support," she was to receive during her life an allowance of eighty pounds a year.

I do not know what Elizabeth's ungrateful and undutiful behaviour may have been. It is possible that she had married, or desired to marry, against her father's wishes, at a time when she cannot have been more than eighteen and was probably younger. The diarist Farington, reproducing chance-heard gossip forty years later, stated that "she married a writing master or somebody of that kind at Eton, and her father left her only £50 a year."[1] Her husband's name was Guise. Her half-brother, the younger William Windham, continued on friendly terms with her and Mr Guise in the years to come; and it is possible that he found himself able to supplement the contemptuous pittance bequeathed to her.

[1] *The Farington Diary*, ii. 81 (13 February 1803). Farington's informant was William Fellowes, M.P. for Norwich. He was not very accurate in his details, since he stated that Elizabeth was a daughter of Mrs Lukin by Windham before their marriage.

From her father there was to be no forgiveness. Early that summer, in Townshend's absence abroad, he had marched his battalion of militia down to Chatham Barracks. By now he was in an advanced stage of consumption. The effort finally exhausted him, and he returned to London desperately ill. On 30 October, less than a month after the execution of his angry codicil, he died.

Chapter Eight

WILLIAM WINDHAM III

William Windham at Eton, Glasgow, and Oxford—his relations with the Forrest family and love for Mrs Byng—northward voyage and return through Norway—first political speech—stands for Parliament in 1780—the Felbrigg estate at this time—Windham's short period as Chief Secretary for Ireland—elected for Norwich in 1784

I

THIS book has so far dealt entirely with private people leading private lives. I have pieced together the story of four generations of a country family, using material which is almost wholly unpublished, letters and account-books and manuscripts of all kinds, but very seldom a printed source. There have been gaps in the story here and there, stretches of years about which I have been able to discover little. Now the situation alters. A Windham appears who was to become a national celebrity of the first rank. I am confronted not with a lack of material, but with an excess.

Owing to a series of misunderstandings, the intended official biography of William Windham the statesman was never written in the years following his death. Time passed, his fame receded, and no full-length life of him has appeared to this day. I myself published in 1930 a fairly detailed account of his earlier career as far as 1784, incorporating his three hitherto unpublished diaries which remain at Felbrigg. Extracts from his later diaries were printed in 1866; but the originals have apparently vanished, and no one now knows how much remained unprinted.[1] A vast collection of his correspondence is in the British Museum; and from this collection two ill-selected and ill-edited volumes, *The Windham Papers*, were put together by a hack

[1] I imagine a good deal remained unprinted. See *The Greville Memoirs*, ed. Lytton Strachey and Roger Fulford (1938), i. 316–18 (5 September 1829).

writer, and published in 1913 with an introduction by the fifth Earl of Rosebery.[1]

My difficulty, therefore, has been to prevent this one outstanding figure from overweighting the book. I have said comparatively little about his public career, and a good deal about his private life, more particularly that portion of it which was passed at Felbrigg. In this way he falls into relation with the other members of his line, of which he was the most distinguished and the last.

II

At the time of his father's death the younger William Windham was aged eleven, and had already been four years at Eton. From childhood he had shown himself tough, active, and pugnacious. When he was seven years old and had been at Eton only a few weeks his kinsman the Rev. Dobyns Humphreys wrote to his father that "I am rejoyc'd to hear from the Cornet that your Son has been victorious in three engagements. I pray God he may be so in every concern in life. However, he is blooded, and you have enter'd him charmingly. The misery of a private Education is not to be express'd." His father had been known in London as "Boxing Windham," and he now received at Eton the nickname of "Fighting Windham." The love of pugilism remained with both to the end of their lives.

Obituaries and other memorial tributes often tend to exaggerate the early promise of their subjects. Edmund Malone wrote of Windham, shortly after his death, that at Eton "he was very generally acknowledged to surpass all his fellows in whatever he undertook to perform: in addition to his superiority in classical attainments, he was the best cricketer, the best leaper, swimmer, rower, skaiter, the best fencer, the best boxer, the best runner, and the best horseman of his time." However this may have been, he was certainly an outstanding athlete at school, and showed signs of becoming a very proficient scholar. Among his closest associates at Eton were Charles James Fox, who was a year older, and Thomas William Coke, who was two years younger. An enduring personal friendship developed between the three, to be interrupted but never broken by the political storms of the distant future.

[1] The name of the compiler is not given on the title-page, and may be left in obscurity. Augustine Birrell (see p. 275) told me that Lord Rosebery spoke in terms of great resentment about the slovenly workmanship of the volumes to which he had undertaken to furnish an introduction.

Windham's surviving guardians were his mother, Garrick, Stillingfleet, and Dampier, who was still Lower Master at Eton. Quantities of letters survive from Dampier to Mrs Windham; and it is clear that, besides watching over the boy's welfare and progress at school most carefully, he was in all other respects the most assiduous of the guardians. Garrick was a busy actor-manager, Stillingfleet a somewhat eccentric scholar. After a few years Stillingfleet disagreed with his colleagues over the adjustment of some boundaries between the Windham property at Crownthorpe and Sir Armine Wodehouse's estate at Kimberley, and withdrew from the trust altogether. But Dampier was a tower of strength to the widow and her son, both at Eton and in their dealings with lawyers and agents.

He was careful to see that at Eton the boy did not see too much of his half-sister Elizabeth and her unacceptable husband Mr Guise. "Exclusive of other reasons, such company as probably he would meet with at Mr Guise's might give the child a tast for low people." He was able to arrange with William's dame, Mrs Milward, that there were not more than four boys sleeping in his room, and that William should have a bed all to himself. He reassured the anxious mother when there were epidemics in the school, and when her son's eye was hurt in a fencing-match. Almost every letter contained some mention of William's good progress and high promise; and nothing can have prepared her for a note which Dampier found himself obliged to send on 7 March 1766.

There have been great disturbances amongst the boys here, and I am sorry, that your Son is accused of having a large concern in them. In order therefore to cover his retreat, and to prevent a publick Expulsion, which would probably be the Consequence of his longer Stay, I shall send him home to you tomorrow morning. When I am in Town, about a fortnight hence, we must meet and consider how to dispose of him. If I may advise, I would not have you mention to any one the cause of his coming home so soon before the Holidays.

Doctor Edward Barnard had become Provost of Eton in the previous year. He was a delightful man, as his appearances in Boswell's *Life of Johnson* attest; and he had been immensely popular with the whole school. He was succeeded as Head Master by a less agreeable character, Doctor John Foster, whose appointment led to much rioting and indiscipline, culminating in 1768 in the most serious rebellion that had ever occurred at Eton. Windham's hasty departure was due to the part he played in the earliest of these commotions. The details seem to be unknown, and not much importance need be attached to a later story that Doctor Foster was his "declared enemy." Mrs Windham and the guardians consulted together, and decided to make no attempt to procure his return to Eton. As he was still only sixteen years old, it was decided to send him for a year to Glasgow University, after which he was to go to Oxford.

At Eton he had received an excellent grounding in the classics; at Glasgow the emphasis was upon scientific and mathematical studies. He worked hard, and benefited greatly from the lectures and the private tuition of Doctor Robert Simson, the Professor of Mathematics and the editor of Euclid and Pappus, now in the last years of a very long life. He developed at this time the keen interest in mathematical theory which remained with him to the end of his life. Of all his books in the library at Felbrigg, the treatises on mathematics ancient and modern are the most heavily annotated.

At the end of his year at Glasgow he was sent to Oxford, being entered as a gentleman commoner at University College in the Michaelmas Term of 1767. At this time the reputation of the College stood particularly high, with a very distinguished body of Fellows. Windham's tutor was Robert Chambers, also Vinerian Professor of Laws and Principal of New Inn Hall, a man of great learning and much personal charm. He was a friend of Doctor Johnson, who often stayed with him, engaging in cheerful disputation with the other dons, and abetting him on one occasion in tossing snails over the wall into the garden of a neighbouring dissenter. It may have been at Oxford, and through the introduction of his tutor, that Windham was first admitted into Johnson's acquaintance. Equally he may have met him under Garrick's auspices in London.

His closest friend at Oxford, and indeed for the rest of his life, was George James Cholmondeley. This young man was the son of a clergyman, the Hon. and Rev. Robert Cholmondeley, who had married the virtuous younger sister of Peg Woffington. Mrs Cholmondeley was something of a blue-stocking and an acquaintance of Johnson, who once spoke of her as "a very airy lady." George was intelligent, lively, good-looking, irresistible to women—Glenbervie called him, years afterwards, "that prince of *hommes à bonnes fortunes.*" Windham grew very much attached to him, and Johnson looked on approvingly. "George," he said on one occasion, "I am glad that you are a friend of Windham's, and that he is a friend of yours."

Windham's life at Oxford was on the whole studious and uneventful. He did not think much of the diversions available there. It was a bad place for pleasure, he said afterwards, and therefore he determined to work all the harder—"he did not like wine and water, but he liked a glass of wine and a glass of water." So he became a really proficient classical scholar, especially in Greek. His notebooks show with what thoroughness he liked to investigate subtle points of grammar and philology, and also that he continued his mathematical researches. Dampier wrote glowing accounts of him after a visit to Oxford towards the end of 1770.

Twas a great Satisfaction to me to find him in such good health, and still greater to hear the excellent character given of him for sobriety and learning, both in and out of his College. I took not my Accounts of his conduct from the younger part of the University, but from the best judges, and men of the highest reputation, whom I had an opportunity of conversing with there. He is indeed a very extraordinary young Gentleman. If, please God, he enjoys his health, he cannot fail of making a very considerable figure in the World.

Dampier's faithful trusteeship was now drawing to a close. In the same letter he told Mrs Windham how grateful her son ought to be "for the unwearied pains and attention you have paid to the management of his Affairs during his long Minority." A still greater measure of gratitude was due for the part he had himself played in the trust. Early next year William took his degree, and left Oxford. In May he came of age, and entered at once upon a large and unencumbered inheritance.

III

Mrs Windham did not live at Felbrigg a great deal during her son's minority. She was there occasionally for a few months, but most of her time was spent in London. Felbrigg slumbered in the care of the steward Robert Thurston and the housekeeper Mrs Goldstone, two capable and devoted servants with whom she kept in constant touch by letter.

Her elder son, Robert Lukin, continued in the Army, retiring fairly young as a captain in the Second Dragoon Guards. He maintained his connection with Norfolk by marrying Jane Russell, a daughter of William Russell of Barningham and Stillingfleet's old love Anne Barnes. His brother, George William Lukin, was now Rector of

Felbrigg, Metton, and Aylmerton. Careful provision to this end had been made in his step-father's will. After the death of his old friend Timothy Jones, the incumbent of the livings, the elder Windham had presented a clergyman named John Alexander, who undertook by bond to resign as soon as young Lukin was of an age to hold them. Alexander duly resigned in 1764, and his youthful successor entered upon an incumbency which lasted almost fifty years. Soon afterwards he married Catherine Doughty, the daughter of the Windhams' old neighbour and friend Robert Doughty of Hanworth. Three years later Dampier wrote to Mrs Windham: "I beg you will give my affectionate Compliments to Mr William Lukin, who by this time, I imagine, is the Father of many a smiling good tempered Child." He was the father, in due course, of a family of fourteen—eight sons and six daughters—of whom eight survived the perils of an eighteenth-century childhood.

Felbrigg Parsonage will figure a good deal in the ensuing pages. It stood about a quarter of a mile to the east of the Hall, and midway between the church and the village green. No trace of it now remains, but there are paintings and drawings which show its unpretentious charm. William Windham was extremely fond of his step-brother and his wife, and in due course of their children. In his eyes the Parsonage, with its cheerful family life, came to represent companionship and home. It was his solace whenever he visited Felbrigg during the restless and unsatisfying years which lay ahead.

For Windham, almost as soon as he came down from Oxford, found himself involved in an emotional relationship of a strangely frustrating kind. He and George Cholmondeley made the acquaintance of a lady named Juliana Frederica Marina Cecilia Forrest, who lived with an array of beautiful daughters in a large house in Birdcage Walk. Mrs Forrest was the widow of a naval officer of some distinction, and the daughter of a rich plantation-owner in Jamaica. She was extremely hospitable and hopelessly extravagant, and the parties at her houses—she had another beside the Thames in Berkshire—were noisy and gay. Her eldest daughter, Bridget, was married to the Hon. John Byng, later the fifth Viscount Torrington. The other were unmarried; and one of them, Cecilia, was eventually to become Windham's wife. But that was more than a quarter of a century in the future. At this time, most unfortunately, he fell deeply in love with the only married sister, Mrs Byng.

When I wrote my book about Windham's earlier life the personality of John Byng appeared faint and shadowy. A few years afterwards it was revealed with great distinctness by the publication of his journals of travel in the volumes known as *The Torrington Diaries*. He loved to wander about England in search of the picturesque, a solitary horseman attended by a single groom, exploring cathedrals and churches, musing upon the ruins of castles and monasteries, making agreeable little sketches and in the evening writing up these journals. They show him as a diffident and rather melancholy man, disappointed yet never embittered by his lot in life. He had been a soldier from boyhood and remained nominally in the Army until 1780, when he accepted a rather unsatisfactory post at Somerset House. Owing to the unfair dealing of his elder brother, he was permanently short of money, and the prospects of his numerous children gave him constant anxiety.

Windham's infatuation for Mrs Byng was recorded in his own diaries, which he kept at intervals from 1772 onwards. The entries referring to her were brief and cryptic even when written in English; but at more intimate moments he would diverge into Greek, or into English words with Greek characters, or into a jumble of French and Latin. These diaries were printed in full in my book, and I need only repeat here my firm impression that Mrs Byng behaved with honour and good sense in a very difficult series of situations. She was deeply attached to her husband, to whom she bore twelve children. Windham's friendship with Byng remained unimpaired, and he stayed in their house for weeks at a time. Passionate speeches, fervent glances, reproaches and renunciations—the story reads at times like any contemporary novel of sentiment. It is possible to give more than one interpretation to some of the references to Bridget Byng in Windham's diary, but my own belief is that in all its essentials their relationship remained Platonic.

Whatever the truth may be, the main importance of this affair was its obsessive effect upon Windham. He was at times attracted to other women, and occasional brief liaisons seem to have taken place. But for several years his true emotional life was engrossed by Mrs Byng, with the result that his existence became aimless and desultory. Any thought of marriage was obviously precluded. He had at this time little interest in politics: it had been a joke at Oxford that he never knew who was Prime Minister. He did not care particularly for country life, and seldom came to Felbrigg for more than a few days. With every personal advantage—talents, position, wealth, good looks—he seemed uncertain of his future direction.

He refused an invitation to become the private secretary of his father's old friend George Townshend, now Viscount Townshend and Lord Lieutenant of Ireland. It would have been a good start in public life, had his ambitions lain in that direction; but it would also have meant a considerable sacrifice of personal liberty. In any case Townshend was recalled towards the end of 1772. Windham paid him a private visit of a few weeks at Dublin Castle shortly before his return, and kept a diary, mainly consisting of anecdotes and table-talk, during the period of his stay. In Dublin he felt a passing tenderness for a girl named Barbara Montgomery, whose sister Townshend was to marry as his second wife in the following year. The diary becomes sprinkled with Greek letters, which reveal nothing more reprehensible than this: "Let me not forget my having sat next Barbara at supper, my going with her to the door, and the feelings I had then. Bless her! Farewell Dublin: I part with nothing in it that I regret, but that."

He spent most of the winter and the next spring in London, with frequent visits to the Byngs at their house at Ickleford in Hertfordshire. The cryptic and agitated diary-entries are resumed. George Cholmondeley and Cecilia Forrest flit in and out of the picture; so does a rather notorious member of the Forrest circle named Mary Hickey, a sister of the memoir-writer William Hickey, with whom Windham is supposed then or later to have had a love-affair. Eventually the emotional complications that centred round Ickleford became altogether too much for him, and he decided to join an expedition of Arctic discovery which was setting out at the beginning of June. On the opening page of a new diary he wrote this invocation to Mrs Byng.

Secret and separate. This is my confidential book. In this will be contained all those thoughts, memorandums, notes, reflexions &c. which no eye must see but my own. To thee, my ever-adorable friend, do I dedicate it, with whose name it will chiefly be filled. May God grant that we may meet again, and enjoy together the recollection of the times, when these were written!

The expedition was organised by his friend Constantine John Phipps, afterwards Lord Mulgrave, and its principal object was the discovery of a north-east passage into the South Seas. The ships were vessels well adapted to resist the pressure of ice, the *Racehorse* and the *Carcase*. Windham went as a passenger on board the *Racehorse*, accompanied by his servant John Cawston. An inconspicuous figure on the *Carcase* was a fifteen-year-old midshipman named Horatio Nelson. The expedition failed to discover the north-east passage, but returned with credit after making a valuable survey of Spitzbergen. Windham, however, could claim no share in this enterprise. He soon regretted that he had undertaken the voyage; and on 21 June, less than three weeks after they sailed, he was able to take advantage of a chance-met Hamburg vessel, which set him and his servant on shore at Bergen. "A continued sea-sickness of an unusually severe and debilitating kind" was later given as the reason for his abrupt departure, although a note in his diary lends some support to the rumour of a disagreement with Phipps.

A long and troublesome journey now awaited him, from Bergen to Christiania, then down the western coast of Sweden, and back to England by way of Denmark. The new volume of his diary, which he had intended to fill amidst the Polar ice with sentimental reflections for the perusal of Mrs Byng, became instead a severely factual account of dilatory travel and the discomforts of Norwegian inns. His "dearest friend" was never out of his thoughts, and at times he contrasted his forlorn situation with "the enjoyments of Ickleford parlour"; but in general he wrote cheerfully, with a good-humoured interest in the things he saw and the people he met. He crossed to England from Copenhagen in August; and his life between London and Ickleford, with the Byngs and the Forrests and George Cholmondeley, resumed its accustomed course.

In November he went down to Felbrigg, and thought "the place looked rather melancholy." He tried to study—Euripides, Juvenal, Greek criticism and grammar, geometry, trigonometry—but could seldom concentrate fully, and was never satisfied with the day's progress. At last, just after Christmas, John and Bridget Byng and her sister Juliana came to stay. He met them on the London road at Attleborough, showed them the sights of Norwich, and escorted them to Felbrigg:

> the first time of Byng's and Mrs Byng's and Juliana's having been down here. The period which here succeeds, being such as consists of scenes and passages of happiness not capable of being exhibited in a journal, is better committed entirely to my memory and heart, where it is in no danger of being lost, than imperfectly reckoned out here, by an enumeration of trifling occurrences.

IV

Windham's diaries were not published until long after his death; and they then revealed peculiarities of temperament which had been unsuspected, except perhaps by a few intimate friends, during his lifetime. His outward demeanour seems always to have been confident and firm. But inwardly he had to endure, throughout the whole of his life, the torments of indecision, vacillation, self-distrust. A strange nervous inhibition, which he used to describe in the diaries as "feel," seemed at times to paralyse his spirit. At the height of his political career this neurotic anxiety would accompany the preparation and delivery of some important speech, and would overcloud the plaudits with which it was received. Equally it would intrude upon the most ordinary affairs of life. Should he spend the morning studying Euripides or Euclid? Should he walk in the afternoon, or ride, or use the carriage? Hours would be spent in agonised deliberation upon such points as these.

Windham's diary for the next two years, until the autumn of 1775, is largely concerned with his emotions on the subject of Mrs Byng—expressive looks, agitated interviews, momentous conversations. I have the impression that it all amounted to very little. "Mrs B. has told me that in all the answers and all the declarations about feelings &c, nothing had ever any reference to Mr B. What is to become of me?" This is, I think, a significant sentence. Windham came to no harm; but nothing took place that might seriously have disturbed the marital relationship between Mr and Mrs Byng. The diary contains much also about "feel," and many passages of self-reproach for lack of diligence in study. Its most interesting portion describes a riding-tour through Derbyshire and the North Midlands which Windham undertook in the summer of 1774, in company with Cholmondeley and Byng. It was during this tour, in the neighbourhood of Matlock, that they met Doctor Johnson in a carriage with Mr and Mrs Thrale. Windham merely recorded that Johnson "assented to the remark of the extreme beauty of the country, and observed, that it was an object of reasonable curiosity." Mrs Thrale, in her *Anecdotes*, gave a different version of the encounter. Johnson, she related, was deeply engrossed in a book, when

> a gentleman of no small distinction for his birth and elegance, suddenly rode up to the carriage, and paying us all his proper compliments, was desirous not to neglect Dr Johnson; but observing that he did not see him, tapt him gently on the shoulder—"'Tis Mr Ch-lm-ley," says my husband;—"Well, Sir! and what if it is Mr Ch-lm-ley!" says the other sternly, just lifting his eyes a moment from his book, and returning to it again with renewed avidity.

Little is known of Windham's doings for two or three years after the close of his diary in 1775. His passion for Mrs Byng seems gradually to have subsided into a deep and lasting friendship, while her sister Cecilia began to occupy a more prominent place in his affections. But Cecilia, on her part, had now grown deeply in love with the fascinating George Cholmondeley, who did not return her devotion, but would not wholly reject it. Once again Windham's thoughts of marriage were frustrated. He widened the circle of his acquaintances both social and political, and began to think seriously of entering political life. Before long he was drawn into the group of Whigs who acknowledged the leadership of Lord Rockingham and the intellectual guidance of Burke. In 1777 he was invited to stand for the Suffolk borough of Sudbury, where he had some family influence, but this came to nothing. Early in the next year he made his first important public appearance.

Like the other young Whigs who were his friends—Fox, Coke, Sheridan—he was vehemently opposed to the continuance of the war with the American colonies. In the eyes of the Rockingham party the war was disastrously managed, ruinously expensive, and unnatural in its very conception. The recent surrender of Burgoyne at Saratoga appeared to them a final argument in favour of a negotiated peace, but Lord North and his colleagues still seemed obdurate for war. In order to rally local support for the Government, Lord Townshend convened a public meeting in Norwich; and Windham, in spite of "personal affection and hereditary attachment," determined to oppose him. He hurried down to Norfolk, pondering on his coming speech and rehearsing some of it as his chaise rolled across Newmarket Heath. "I never felt so much disposition to exert myself before—I hope from my never having before so fair a prospect of doing it with success," he wrote to Sheridan.

There was no self-distrust on this occasion, no paralysing access of "feel." The meeting took place at the Maid's Head in Norwich on 28 January. Townshend opened the proceedings, and proposed a public subscription as a gesture of support for the Government. Windham answered in a speech full of personal regard, but countering all his arguments with great spirit and conviction. The meeting was immensely impressed. The majority of those present were against Windham and Coke, who acted as his seconder; but everyone felt that a new star had arisen. The Rev. James Woodforde, the diarist, was in the audience, and wrote afterwards of "one Mr Windham who spoke exceedingly well with great Fluency and Oratory, but on the wrong side . . . Most People admired the manner of Windham's speaking, so much Elegance, Fluency and Action in it." When the subscription was opened, after further speeches, Windham and Coke withdrew with their supporters to the Swan, and drew up a spirited protest against "the continuance of an unnatural War, into which, by various Deceits and Impositions, we have been betrayed."

A few months later came the declaration of war by France. Once again there were rumours of invasion; and Windham, a major in the Norfolk Militia, found himself engaged in army life—which he enjoyed, and for which, as he told Cholmondeley, "he conceived himself to be particularly fitted." That summer, unluckily, during manoeuvres in Suffolk, he rode through a river "in a sort of frolic," and was obliged to remain in his wet clothes for several hours. A violent fever resulted. He lay desperately ill for months, attended night and day by the faithful Cawston, who kept a detailed and harrowing journal of his symptoms and his slow recovery. His friends thought that his constitution never recovered its former strength. Most of 1779 was spent in a gradual convalescence. In the autumn he travelled to Italy, where he remained almost a year.

Horace Walpole knew and approved of Windham, both for his own qualities and as the friend of George Cholmondeley, who was his great-nephew. His friend and correspondent Sir Horace Mann, now nearing the close of his long life, was still Minister at Florence. Walpole commended Windham to Mann's notice in the warmest terms.

He is young, but full of virtues, knowledge and good sense; and, in one word, of the old rock—of which so few gems are left in this wretched country! . . . I do not beg attentions for him; these you have even for the least deserving, from your own good nature: but I entreat and advise you to get acquainted with Mr Windham as fast as you can: your friendship will soon follow, and then he can want nothing in my power to ask . . . My unlimited expressions will tell you how confident I am that your goodness will not be misplaced, as it has often been on travelling boys, and their more unlicked governors. Mr Windham is not so young as to want to be formed, nor so old as to be insensible to the merit of others; and, therefore, I trust you will both be mutually pleased with each other.

In a second letter he wrote:

I am not so much acquainted with him as with his character, which is excellent; and then he is a Whig of the stamp which was current in our country in my father's time . . . He is a particular friend of my great-nephew, Lord Cholmondeley's cousin; but one I should have liked for my own friend, if the disparity of our ages would have allowed it; or if it were a time for me to make friends, when I could only leave them behind me.

Unfortunately, and to Walpole's disappointment, Windham and Mann did not get on well together. A divergence of political outlook, the difference between an enthusiastic young man and a disillusioned old one, seems to have been at the root of the trouble. "I am sorry my *recommandé* is so unwise as not to cultivate you more," Walpole wrote after receiving the first reports from his friend. "I am satisfied of his virtues, but am not so clear that he knows much of the world. I doubt his patriotism is a little of Spartan hue, that is, morose." And again: "I am peevish with him for having looked on you through our ill-humoured foggy eyes." Finally, after Windham's return to England, he wrote: "Mr Windham I have seen. He is wonderfully recovered, and looks robust again. He said ten thousand fine things in your praise. Oh! thought I; but said nothing."

Windham arrived back in England in September 1780. A few weeks earlier, North had appealed to the country on the issue of the American war; and the resultant general election was now in full swing. During the previous session one of the Members for Norwich, Edward Bacon, had gone over to the Court party, while his colleague, Sir Harbord Harbord, had remained faithful to the Whig cause. When he reached Norwich, two days before the opening of the poll, Windham was surprised to learn that in his absence, and without any expectation of his immediate return, his friends had nominated him as the other Whig candidate. He plunged at once into a last-minute canvass; but he was still comparatively unknown to most of the electorate, and found himself at the bottom of the poll. The two former members, Harbord and Bacon, retained their seats in spite of the divergence of their views. The other Tory candidate, John Thurlow, was third, with Windham less than forty votes behind him.

In all the circumstances he was thought to have done well. He had made a decided impression on the Norwich voters; and his address after the election left them in no doubt that he intended to seek their favours again on some future occasion. As soon as the turmoil was over he retired to Felbrigg, where his solitude was presently cheered by a long visit from Mr and Mrs Byng, and her sisters Cecilia and Juliana Forrest.

V

What was the appearance of Felbrigg at this time? There are two more or less contemporary engravings, after drawings by Humphry Repton, and they show a landscape remarkably similar to that of the present day. The parkland extended in an unbroken sward right up to the house, in the approved eighteenth-century manner. The forecourt and outbuildings, indicated in a ground-plan drawn earlier in the century, had vanished entirely; and it must be assumed that the alteration was made by Windham's father during the seventeen-fifties. There is also reason to suppose that he formed the existing lake by damming two little streams, whose accumulated waters covered the site of the "stews" in which his grandparents had cherished their carp and tench. But no professional "improver" or landscape-gardener appears to have been brought into consultation at any time.

One feature of the Felbrigg landscape, much remarked upon in the eighteenth century, is now no longer visible from any point. The approach for carriages was from the direction of Norwich, through the Marble Hill lodges and along a disused drive, now a farm road. At that time much of Felbrigg Heath was still unenclosed; and the visitor, as he emerged from the belt of trees at Marble Hill, gazed across the area of the present Great Wood to the limitless expanses of the sea. There was already some woodland to the north of the house; but there was also a great extent of barren heath, impossible to convert into arable land but entirely suitable for forest trees. Windham and his successors gradually enclosed and planted the whole of this area, until the "unlimited prospect of the German ocean," so enthusiastically praised by the guide-books, was only a memory.

The impressions of one traveller may perhaps be quoted—those of Lady Beauchamp Proctor of Langley Park, who visited Felbrigg in the course of a tour of Norfolk in 1764.

'Tis a very grand looking old house [she wrote] with three elegant modern rooms added above and below, hung with crimson and India papers, and some good pictures, chiefly landscapes. There are a great number of rooms fitted up very neatly. There is not much garden, but a very good greenhouse [the Orangery], out of which the gardener gave each of us a fine nosegay of orange-flowers, geraniums, &c., which travelled with us the rest of our tour, and are safely arrived at Langley, a little fatigued as you may imagine. The park is walled round, and capable of great improvements; but the owner being a minor, nothing can be yet done. There is a good view of the sea, great variety of ground, and the situation, in my opinion, is as good, if not better than any of the seats in Norfolk.

Windham had placed the management of his estate in the capable hands of Nathaniel Kent, a professional agent and agricultural improver well known at that time. Kent was a friend of Stillingfleet and Marsham, who no doubt recommended him to Windham; and during many years of his supervision of Felbrigg he lived in Marsham's neighbourhood at Rippon Hall. As an enthusiastic disciple of Marsham, he was concerned that owners should take full advantage of the timber-growing potentialities of their estates, and bring their woods into a proper rotation of planting and felling. He had much to say on this subject in his *Hints to Gentlemen of Landed Property*, published in 1775, shortly after he had undertaken the management of Felbrigg.

The true way of managing a timbered estate is, to make use of what Nature has brought to perfection, and to keep up a regular, uniform succession; so that at the time we take one egg from the nest, for our own use, we may leave another, as a nest-egg, for the benefit of posterity. Sensible of the importance of this plan, Mr Windham of Felbrigg in Norfolk has done me the honour of approving, and adopting it in its full extent; and has impowered me to carry it on upon such a vigorous scale, as will gradually swell the quantity, and value of his timber, notwithstanding his falls will be considerable every year.

In 1796, when he published his *General View of the Agriculture of Norfolk*, Kent wrote with pride of the growth of the plantations established at Felbrigg under his supervision two decades before. They had been designed, he explained,

to ornament and belt round Mr Windham's park, and to extend his great woodland scene nearer the sea, towards which, at two miles distance, it forms a grand bulwark . . . Most of his plantations have been raised from seed; and there is one that stands unrivalled; it was sown with acorns, Spanish chesnut, and beech-mast, seventeen years since; has been already twice thinned for hurdle wood; the trees, most of which are thirty feet high, being at the regular distance of twelve feet, with a valuable underwood at four feet distance. This plantation was taken out of the park, was well fallowed the preceding summer to its being sown, and, during this state, there was a flock of sheep in the park, which were continually lying on the fallows, to which, in a great measure, I attribute its astonishing floridity, as it surpasses every thing of the kind I ever saw.

I can no longer identify this remarkable plantation: it has become merged in the general mass of the Great Wood. But another important eighteenth-century feature, the Oval, may still be clearly traced. This was described in a contemporary guide-book as

an irregular oval of about four acres, surrounded by a broad belt of lofty silver firs: on entering this oval, the eye is wonderfully pleased, without at first perceiving why it is so; probably it must be from the contrast which this sameness of green makes to the various tints of the other forest-trees, every where mixed in the rest of the grove, and which the lofty evergreens entirely exclude.

This ring of great silver firs has wholly vanished; but at some time they were encircled in their turn by a belt of beeches, and many of these beeches still survive. Their oval formation has been broken in places by gales and other accidents, and it is now scarcely perceptible on the ground; but from the air the original design can still be distinctly made out.

In his *Hints to Gentlemen of Landed Property* Kent showed an exceptionally enlightened attitude towards the human problems of land-ownership. He had given much thought to the design of cottages, the condition and welfare of the poor, and the difficult but urgent question of common rights and enclosures. By his advice and through his mediation, Windham was able greatly to improve the general organisation of the parish of Felbrigg, by the acquisition of the only portion of it which did not already belong to him, "one small farm, of seventy pounds a year, belonging to a young man, a yeoman, just come of age." Parts of this farm were intermixed with the heath and the former common field, which Windham desired to enclose, in order to convert the more tractable portions to arable land and to plant the remainder. The resultant transaction was described, admiringly and in full detail, in Marshall's *Rural Economy of Norfolk*.

Steps were taken towards obtaining the desired possession; not, however, by threats and subterfuges, too commonly but very impoliticly made use of upon such occasions; but by open and liberal proposals to the young man, who was made fully acquainted with the intention; and frankly told, that nothing could be done without his estate. He was, therefore, offered, at once, a specific and considerable sum, over and above its full value to any other person: and, to ensure the object in view, he had, at the same time, an offer made him of a considerable farm, on advantageous terms.

The young man, whose name was Priest, and who was of an enterprising spirit, agreed to sell his estate and accept the tenancy of the farm. Marshall gives the agreement in detail, and the terms certainly appear very generous. In fact the transaction benefited both parties, for Windham was now able to "set out the least fertile part of the heath as a common for the poor to collect firing from," and to parcel out the remainder, both of heath and common field, to various tenants in enclosures of eight to twelve acres each. Since it would appear that all the strips in the common field had already belonged either to himself or to Priest, no injustice was done to anyone. As Marshall expressed it, he had "done away a nuisance, and planted industry and plenty upon an almost useless waste: and this, too, without rendering himself odious, or his tenants miserable."

Of the servants employed by Windham's parents, Robert Thurston had continued to supervise affairs at Felbrigg, and Mrs Goldstone to act as housekeeper. But in 1777 Thurston either retired or died, and Windham engaged a man named William Cobb as his successor. Cobb served him as steward and general factotum for the next fifteen years, kept his accounts in an exemplary fashion, filed and docketed all correspondence most accurately, and in general seems to have been diligent and methodical. The letters from his relations and friends, of which a large number have survived, also show him in an agreeable light. Yet Windham seems never really to have liked him, and never wrote to him in the easy confidential manner in which his parents used to address Frary and Thurston. Cobb undoubtedly made mistakes, and could be obstinate and opinionated. But Windham, in his dealings with subordinates, had his father's peremptory temper without his father's compensating generosity and warmth of heart. He was not an easy master. His letters to Cobb consist mainly of curt instructions, varied by an occasional severe reproof. They are very different from his father's long and delightful letters to Frary, or those which his mother wrote to Thurston about venison and asparagus and the behaviour of the younger maids.

Windham's long absences from home inevitably led to difficulties, especially in the relations between Cobb and Nathaniel Kent, although Cobb was engaged in the first place on Kent's recommendation. When disagreements arose Windham supported Kent, and no doubt with good reason. On one occasion he wrote to Cobb:

Your letter to me was foolish, that to Mr Kent was not only absurd but in the highest degree impertinent. You seem totally to have forgot the distinctions due to the different ranks of life. Mr Kent has always done you justice. He gives you full credit for your good qualities; but knows, what I could not fail to perceive, that you have a most unbounded share of vanity, together with as great or greater a degree of obstinacy. In the original dispute I shall not at all interfere except to express my hope, if I am asked, that the woman will proceed in her prosecution.

History does not relate who this woman was, or whom she was prosecuting, or why.

Cobb also had a passing disagreement with a newcomer to the neighbourhood, Humphry Repton, a young man of artistic tastes who had lately settled with his wife and an increasing family at Sustead. In this little village Repton found himself, in his own words, "obliged to enact the various parts of churchwarden, overseer, surveyor, and esquire of the parish." As overseer he interested himself in the welfare of a Sustead man who was intermittently employed by Windham, and threatened Cobb with Windham's displeasure when there was a question of the man being discharged. But the matter was adjusted in due course, and thereafter his notes to Cobb, usually concerned with the borrowing of books from the Felbrigg library, were always cordial. It was at this time that he made the drawings of Felbrigg which were afterwards engraved; and although he had not yet begun his career as a landscape-gardener, it has been suggested that the layout of the park at Felbrigg may owe something to his hand. I do not think this is at all likely. He was at pains to record every place where he had been employed; and since, as will presently be seen, he owed the first steps in his professional advancement to Windham, he would certainly have referred somewhere in his writings to any "improvements" he had carried out upon Windham's domain.

Any such work, moreover, would be reflected in the accounts or other estate papers. But there is nothing of the kind. All the planting done under Kent's supervision was strictly utilitarian. There was no money to spare at that time for ornamental clumps or elaborate redispositions of parkland. In fact no possible economy was overlooked. When Windham went abroad in 1779 the greater part of the kitchen garden was sown with turnips, with a view to reducing labour. About the same time, in order to save the wages of a park-keeper, the herd of deer was gradually sold off or killed. There have been no deer at Felbrigg since.

VI

Early in 1782 the resignation of Lord North, and the formation of a new Government under Lord Rockingham, at last brought into power the group of Whigs with whom Windham had long been associated. They were anxious to have him with them in Parliament, and there was a suggestion that he should stand when the next vacancy occurred in the borough of Westminster. But his chances seemed brighter at Norwich, where he now had a strong body of supporters, and he preferred to wait. A few months later Rockingham's death threw the Whig ranks into confusion. Windham, together with Fox and Burke and others of his closest friends, refused to support Lord Shelburne, the King's choice as Rockingham's successor. Next year Shelburne's Government was overthrown by a coalition formed between North and Fox, who suddenly joined forces after years of the keenest political hostility.

The new ministry was headed by the Duke of Portland, who appointed Windham to the office of Chief Secretary to the Lord Lieutenant of Ireland. This was an important and responsible post, since the Chief Secretary became the leader of the Irish House of Commons and introduced all government legislation. Windham accepted it after much hesitation, and expressed to Dr Johnson "some modest and virtuous doubts, whether he could bring himself to practise those arts which it is supposed a person in that situation has occasion to employ." The words are Boswell's, the scruples were typically Windham's; but they were blown away by great gusts of Johnsonian commonsense.

> I have no great timidity in my own disposition, and am no encourager of it in others. Never be afraid to think yourself fit for anything for which your friends think you fit. You will become an able negotiator; a very pretty rascal. No one in Ireland wears even the mask of incorruption. No one professes to do for sixpence what he can get a shilling for doing. Set sail; and see where the winds and the waves will carry you.

As his private secretary Windham took with him his neighbour Humphry Repton. "From the moment this business was determined," he wrote, "having got myself into a scrape, my first thought was, how I might bring my friends in with me; and in that light I had very early designs upon you." But his experience of office in Ireland proved unhappy and brief, another false start in his career. He got on well enough with the Lord Lieutenant, the second Earl of Northington. Owing to a dissolution of the Irish Parliament, however, he had no chance to display his abilities as an orator or negotiator. The office work proved heavy and distasteful; he hated the damp and gloom of Dublin Castle, and his health began to suffer. He was in Ireland barely five weeks, after which Northington sent him to London for consultations. When in London he told the Duke of Portland that he intended to resign, on the grounds of ill-health, and wrote Northington a long letter of explanation to the same effect. On his way back to Dublin, to await the appointment of a successor, he did in fact become seriously ill. George Cholmondeley hurried to his rescue, and prevailed upon him not to return to Ireland at all.

Repton stayed a few weeks longer in Dublin, to settle Windham's affairs and give some help to his successor.

> And now, my dearest Mary [he wrote to his wife], what have I been doing? I have learned to love my own home; I have gained some knowledge of the world; some of public business, and some of hopeless expectancies; I have made some very valuable acquaintances; I have formed some connexions with the great; I have seen a fine country, in passing through Wales, and have made some sketches; I have lost very little money; I shall have got the brogue; and you will have got a tabinet gown. So ends my Irish expedition.

He returned to the seclusion of his house at Sustead; but he did not lose sight of those valuable acquaintances, or the connections which he had formed with the great. For a few years he continued in Norfolk, sketching, gardening, spending much time in looking after Windham's political interest in Norwich and Coke's in the county. But soon he embarked upon a new career, and before his death in 1818 he had become the foremost landscape-gardener in England: the acknowledged successor of "Capability" Brown, the creator or improver of hundreds of parks and pleasure-grounds over the whole length and breadth of the land.

During the latter months of 1783 political events moved swiftly. The King, who detested the coalition ministers and Fox above all, found a pretext to dismiss them in December; and William Pitt, at the age of twenty-four, formed his first Government. No one believed that it could last. "Pitt may do what he likes during the holidays, but it will only be a mincepie administration," said Mrs Crewe, the wit and hostess of the Whigs, and a great friend of Windham's. Windham himself, spending Christmas at Felbrigg with the Byngs and Cecilia and Juliana Forrest, no doubt felt the same.

But the country was soon watching Pitt's leadership in Parliament with very different feelings, admiring his courage and skill, contrasting his youthful integrity with the cynicism that had brought about the coalition between Fox and North. His popularity soared, while Fox's prestige sank lower every day. And when in March 1784 the King dissolved Parliament, the young Prime Minister and his followers won an overwhelming victory in the election. The supporters and friends of Fox fared especially badly, and became known as "Fox's Martyrs." Even Coke was obliged to retire from the contest for the county of Norfolk, and give up the seat which he had held for eight years, and was later to recover and retain for forty-two years more.

At Norwich, however, Windham was able to withstand the popular tide. At the moment when so many of his friends were defeated, he won his first victory. Of the two retiring Members for the city, Sir Harbord Harbord was almost certain to be re-elected, while Edward Bacon was ill and would not stand again. A tremendous battle for the second seat was fought out between Windham and the Hon. Henry Hobart, an enthusiastic supporter of Pitt. Harbord headed the poll with 2305 votes: Windham was next, a long way behind, with 1297, narrowly beating Hobart, who polled 1233. It was a small ray of cheer for the Foxites—"the only very satisfactory event," wrote the Duke of Portland, "that has happened since this cursed Dissolution has taken place." Windham took his seat in the ranks of a reduced and dispirited Opposition; but his political career had begun at last.

Chapter Nine

WILLIAM WINDHAM III

The last days of Samuel Johnson—Windham's ascent in a balloon—his unhappiness and irresolution—projected alterations to Felbrigg by James Wyatt—early years in Parliament—he joins Pitt's coalition Government, and becomes Secretary at War in 1794—his marriage to Cecilia Forrest

I

THE year 1784 was the last of Johnson's life. Throughout its course his health steadily declined. A long summer visit to Dr Taylor at Ashbourne, and a further month in his native town of Lichfield, brought no real improvement. In November he returned to London, and on 13 December he died.

Windham did everything he could to support him through these months of weakness and depression. He sat with him, took him for airings in his carriage, was punctilious in his attendances at the Club, showed himself considerate and kind in all ways. In August Johnson wrote to him from Ashbourne:

> The tenderness with which you have been pleased to treat me through my long illness, neither health nor sickness can, I hope, make me forget; and you are not to suppose that after we parted, you were no longer in my mind. But what can a sick man say, but that he is sick, his thoughts are necessarily concentred in himself, he neither receives nor can give delight; his enquiries are after alleviations of pain, and his efforts are to catch some momentary comfort.

Soon after receiving this sad letter Windham appeared at Ashbourne, making a very considerable detour on a journey from Norfolk to Oxford. Dr Taylor was an indifferent host, preoccupied with his own concerns, and engaged at this time in rebuilding most of his house. Ill, lonely, and uncomfortable, Johnson was deeply grateful for this timely visit. He wrote afterwards to Dr Brocklesby:

Mr Windham has been to see me, he came I think, forty miles out of his way, and staid about a day and a half, perhaps I make the time shorter than it was. Such conversation I shall not have again till I come back to the regions of literature, and even there Windham is—*inter stellas Luna minores.*

The talk of that day and a half, recorded by Windham in his diary under the heading *Johnsonian Memorandum of Conversation*, had ranged over many fields, from Homer to the ballad of Chevy Chase, from Virgil and Ovid to Baretti and Joseph Warton: grammatical questions, the art of translation, the meaning of a passage in Lucan, Johnson's reminiscences of his Oxford days, the advantages of a university, the effects of turnpike roads. Then Windham went on to Oxford, characteristically reproaching himself for not having stayed with Johnson another day.

Windham was back in London late in November, and by that time it was evident that Johnson's life was nearing its end. One of their last conversations took place on 7 December.

After waiting some short time in the adjoining room [Windham wrote in his diary], I was admitted to Dr Johnson in his bed-chamber, where, after placing him next me on the chair, he sitting in his usual place on the east side of the room (and I on his right hand), he put into my hands two small volumes (an edition of the New Testament), as he afterwards told me, saying, "*Extremum hoc munus morientis habeto.*"

He then spoke of Windham's recent entrance into political life, "which would lead me deeply into all the business of the world"; and begged him "that I would set apart every seventh day for the care of my soul." He asked Windham to allow his negro servant Frank Barber to look up to him "as his friend, adviser and protector," and to help him in any difficulties that he might encounter. Windham of course agreed; whereupon Frank was called in, and Windham took him by the hand in token of the promise.

A long discussion on religious matters, and especially on the evidences for Christian belief, concluded this interview. Windham repeated his visit almost every day, and made further notes of what was said. On the evening of the 12th he saw Johnson for the last time. On this occasion he added his persuasions to those of the doctors and others in the room, who were trying to persuade the dying man to take some nourishment, but was no more successful than the rest.

I then said that I hoped he would forgive my earnestness—or something to that effect; when he replied eagerly, "that from me nothing would be necessary by way of apology"; adding with great fervour, in words which I shall (I hope) never forget—"God bless you, my dear Windham, through Jesus Christ"; and concluding with a wish that we might meet in some humble portion of that happiness which God might finally vouchsafe to repentant sinners. These were the last words I ever heard him speak. I hurried out of the room with tears in my eyes, and more affected than I had been on any former occasion.

Windham left behind his servant John Cawston to sit up with Johnson; and Cawston remained in the room until ten o'clock next morning, when the dying man said, "You should not detain Mr Windham's servant:—I thank you; bear my remembrance to your master." John Byng had a long talk with Cawston soon afterwards, which he described in a letter to Malone, subsequently printed by Boswell. He reported Cawston as saying that "no man could appear more collected, more devout, or less terrified at the thoughts of the approaching minute."

Windham called again next day, the 13th. He found Johnson asleep, and heard a version of the events of the night which was oddly at variance with Cawston's narrative. The same evening he "received the fatal account, so long dreaded, that Dr Johnson was no more."

To the end of his life he cherished the memory of Johnson's virtue, wisdom, and learning. How meagre his own scholarship appeared to him, how trifling his studies, by contrast with that illustrious example. Had Johnson lived longer, he told Fanny Burney a few years afterwards,

I am satisfied I should have taken to him almost wholly. I should have taken him to my heart! have looked up to him, applied to him, advised with him in all the most essential occurrences of my life! I am sure, too—though it is a proud assertion,—he would have liked me better, also, had we mingled more. I felt a mixed fondness and reverence growing so strong upon me, that I am satisfied the closest union would have followed his longer life.

And again: "There is nothing for which I look back upon myself with severer discipline, than the time I have thrown away in other pursuits, that might else have been devoted to that wonderful man!"

Among the bequests of books in Johnson's will is the entry "To Mr Windham, *Poetae Graeci Heroici per Henricum Stephanum.*" In the library at Felbrigg is a copy of this work, rebound in three volumes—the *Iliad*, the *Odyssey*, and the minor poets. The binding is sumptuous Russia leather of the early nineteenth century. A volume in a closely similar binding, lettered *Novum Testamentum Graece ac Romaice*, contains, in parallel columns, the Greek text of the New Testament and a translation into modern Greek dialect by Maximus of Calliopolis. The book was printed at Geneva in 1638, the earliest rendering of the New Testament into modern Greek. It was issued in two volumes, the first containing the Gospels and the Acts, the second the remainder of the Testament; and they have been rebound as a single volume. I believe—although I shall never be able to prove it—that these books were respectively the bequest and the dying gift of Johnson to Windham. I think that after Windham's death his successor, Admiral Lukin, must have felt that some special reverence should be paid to Johnson's last gifts, and had them rebound in the grandest style. Unfortunately new end-papers were provided, and any inscriptions or other means of identification have therefore disappeared.

The library also contains a number of books which had belonged to Johnson, eighteen volumes in all, Greek or Latin works without exception. They include Eustathius's commentary on Homer, the works of Pico della Mirandola, the *Fax Artium Liberalium* of Gruterus, and Bentley's edition of Horace. All were bought on Windham's instructions at the sale of Johnson's library in 1785, through the agency of the bookselling firm of Nourse. They can be identified by inscriptions in Windham's hand: for example, *fuit e libris viri reverendissimi Sam. Johnson nuper defuncti. W. W.* 1785. I like to keep them in their original state, as tattered and shabby as when they received their last buffeting from their master in his hedger's gloves. They are the only tangible relics that remain of Windham's association with Johnson, that association which meant so much to both.

II

"Did not rise till past nine; from that time till eleven, did little more than indulge in idle reveries about balloons." So Windham wrote apologetically in his diary on 7 February 1784. Everyone was talking about balloons that year. They were the great novelty, and they even appear in the letters of observers so diverse as Samuel Johnson and Horace Walpole. The first ascents in the British Isles were made during the summer; and Windham, during his stay at Oxford in the autumn, encountered James Sadler, who was then making a series of spectacular flights. He was fired with the ambition to make an ascent himself, and on Christmas Day he sat meditating whether to join Sadler in an attempt to cross the Channel. He decided against this; but in the spring he made up his mind to undertake a flight, partly from scientific curiosity and partly as a test of his own courage.

Before the ascent he settled his affairs and made a very curious will. He left the greater part of his estates to George Cholmondeley, and after his death to Cholmondeley's eldest son by Cecilia Forrest; in remainder to their other children; and in default of such issue to the Right Honourable Edmund Burke. There were annuities to Bridget Byng and all the unmarried Forrest sisters, the largest to Cecilia and Juliana. There were settlements also on the Lukin family at the Parsonage; but fond though he was of them, he did nothing at this stage to bring them into the line of succession.

He also wrote a long letter to Cholmondeley, to be delivered only in the event of his own death. He told his "ever dear Friend" that he hoped it would never have to be read. "Something however must be said in case of the worst, that I may not leave the world without one affectionate farewell to him, who in the final evanescence of all worldly objects must be the last to remain upon my sight." First he explained why he had not told Cholmondeley of his coming adventure, and gave his reasons for undertaking it. He then reproached his friend, lengthily and sternly, for having trifled with Cecilia's affections.

Let me now speak of another matter of infinitely greater importance to me, as it affects my opinion of your virtues; in itself, as it relates to the happiness of one, with whose character neither yours nor mine would stand in any advantageous comparison . . . The subject I mean is the history of your conduct to *Cecy*. You have in that instance, done an injury to a fellow-creature, which no means, now left you, can probably ever repair, and for which hardly any degree of contrition and humiliation, which you can feel, can ever atone. You have undone a great and noble mind, whose only weakness has been too fond an attachment to you, by a course of conduct utterly irreconcileable to justice and duty: and as little creditable in the motives as justifiable in the act . . . I forbear to push this matter any further than to say, that her original, fatal attachment to you, has, I have reason to be assured, notwithstanding the most heroic efforts to lock the secret from her nearest connexions, continued with so unhappy a force, as to have destroyed the very spring and power of happiness; and, after a struggle supported with a degree of constancy which redeems the weakness of the occasion, to have proved in the end too hard for her bodily strength, and to be now drawing her apace towards the grave.

There is much more in the same vein, but enough has been quoted to show the strength of Windham's feelings on this matter. In the end none of his plans or his forebodings came to anything. Instead of sinking into her grave, Cecilia lived for forty more years, and was to become his own wife in 1798. Cholmondeley said farewell to his "life of vanity and voluptuousness" when he married Marcia Pitt, the first of his three wives, in 1790. And the Felbrigg property finally passed neither to him nor to Burke, but to the descendants of Windham's mother, those Lukin kindred who now figured so modestly in his will.

The ascent took place on the morning of 5 May. Sadler had made the preparations at Moulsey Hurst in Surrey, where a friend of Windham's had a house, as secretly as possible; but they rose into the air from the midst of a large and excited crowd. Their balloon was carried in an easterly direction over London, and came down early in the afternoon near the Kentish coast, uncomfortably close to the sea. Horace Walpole watched it pass over Strawberry Hill, "so high, that though the sun shone, I could scarce discern it, and not bigger than my snuff-box." It was a flight full of incident, especially in its concluding stages, when they were uncertain whether it would end on land or sea. Windham's notes of their progress, scribbled hastily on thin sheets of cardboard, still survive. In his diary he described not the flight, but only his reactions after it was over.

Much satisfied with myself; and in consequence of that satisfaction, dissatisfied rather with my adventure. Could I have foreseen that danger or apprehension would have made so little impression upon me, I would have deferred going till we had a wind favourable for crossing the Channel. I begin to suspect, in all cases, the effort by which fear is surmounted is more easily made than I have been apt to suppose. Certainly the experience I have had on this occasion will warrant a degree of confidence more than I have ever hitherto indulged. I would not wish a degree of confidence more than I enjoyed at every moment of the time.

III

The balloon adventure may well have reaffirmed Windham's confidence in his own physical courage, of which no one else can have entertained the smallest doubt. But it had no lasting effect on the vacillation, the inward diffidence, the haunting anxieties about the proper use of time, which he confided only to his diary:

> This habit of indecision, if some means are not found to stop its progress and abate its malignity, will corrupt and eat away my understanding to the very core; it wastes my time, consumes my strength, converts comfort into vexation and distress, deprives me of various pleasures, and involves me in innumerable difficulties.

Was he right to refuse to dine with the Warden of All Souls, in order to spend some extra hours in study? Had he chosen wisely the books he was reading, and were his studies directed to the most profitable ends? Why had he neglected to go through his father's papers, or to get by heart some portions of Johnson's writings, or to write in his journal for three months past? And should he not have taken a stronger line about the insolence of that innkeeper at Windsor?

He was especially liable to the assaults of "feel" during his occasional visits to Felbrigg. In the abstract he loved his home, and took great pride in the park, the woods, the prosperity and good order of the estate. He looked forward to days of healthy exercise among his plantations and farms, to evenings of serious reading in the seclusion of his library. Yet he came to Felbrigg only for a few weeks in every year, and even then he soon found himself longing for conversation and social life. He considered a visit to Brighton, where he stayed in Fox's house and dined with the Prince of Wales, much to be preferred to "the solitude and languor of Felbrigg." And a stroll with Edmund Malone in Oxford was "more productive of pleasant images than a walk in Felbrigg woods."

In 1783 he had embarked upon a formidable literary enterprise. Encouraged by Johnson, he set out to translate from the original Latin the history of his own times by Jacques Auguste de Thou, otherwise known as Thuanus. This task was at first reserved for his visits to Felbrigg; and the seven huge folio volumes, still preserved in the library, became something of a nightmare to him. Thuanus figures largely in his catalogues of self-reproach. One of these, drawn up after a fortnight's stay, ends with the sad words: "To Thuanus only a single sentence was added." He would reproach himself also for neglect of his mathematical studies. In spare half-hours before dinner, or during journeys on horseback or in his chaise, he would try to concentrate upon quadratic equations, conic sections, the increments of logarithms; or he would test his mental powers by multiplying four figures by three in his head, and carefully timing the process. Once, exhilarated by the success of a particular line of reasoning, he wrote: "What encouragement this to proceed, even now! What cause of regret that, in years and years, I should have proceeded so little hitherto! Why might not I, at this moment, have been among first-rate mathematicians?" But whether the subject was mathematics, or translation, or questions of grammar and philology, he eventually broke off dissatisfied. "What a life has mine been, that has afforded time for neither business, pleasure, nor study!"

There were happier days at Felbrigg. Now and then he would record that the weather was most pleasant and his spirits uncommonly good; that George Wyndham from Cromer Hall rode through the park with all his horses, and he thought it made a gay scene; that he "walked before breakfast near the house, taking with me Horace, and reading and repeating an ode, *Mercuri nam te*"; that he had been looking over his plantations, "led on by vernal delight and joy, the weather being delicious." On one occasion "after tea I grew into spirits more than ordinary, so as to make me dance and sing about the room, effects now very rare."

He continued to spend much time at the Parsonage whenever he came to Felbrigg. His step-brother's children were growing into spirited boys, with whom he would go shooting and coursing, and attractive girls, in whose reading and other accomplishments he felt an avuncular interest. He was especially pleased with William, the eldest son, who went to sea and was soon a promising naval officer. Most important of all to him was the development of his friendship with Mrs Lukin. The company of this kindly and intelligent woman, always at Felbrigg and sometimes in London, proved a great consolation throughout his lonely middle years, when his passion for Bridget Byng had cooled and Cecilia Forrest still seemed despairingly in love with George Cholmondeley. "Where," he wrote, "shall I ever find one so amiable, so worthy, of understanding so acute, of integrity so confirmed, of disposition so pure, and attached to me from feelings of such genuine affection?" So evening after evening he would leave the solitude of his house, the library where he could not settle down to work, the winter cold which made him "restless and uncomfortable," and walk across to the warm and welcoming Parsonage, with its talk and music and merry card-games, and all the family life which he had missed.

IV

In the middle years of the eighteenth century a great deal of work was done in Norfolk, and a certain amount in London, by the Norwich architect Matthew Brettingham. He completed the building of Holkham, where he was originally clerk of the works, after the death of William Kent; and later he claimed much more credit for Holkham than was rightly his due, even going so far as to publish the plans and elevations of the house with his own signature on the plates, and no mention of Kent at all. His son of the same name was also an architect; and his daughter, Mrs Furze, had a son Robert who assumed the name of Brettingham and followed the family profession. Windham recorded in his diary on 7 June 1787 that he had summoned Robert Brettingham to Felbrigg to advise on some alterations in the house.

The connection he has with places and times which I reflect on with pleasure, might well occasion some satisfaction in his arrival; yet there was an effect from his company of putting one's mind into a state of cheerfulness and activity, above its ordinary rate in this place, which seems to show that the solitude here is more than is salutary.

I do not know what Brettingham's previous connection with Windham may have been; but he now initiated a considerable programme of work, and carried it out over the next three years. The great west window of the library, hitherto open to the setting sun, was filled with bookshelves exactly similar to those designed by Paine for the rest of the room. The corresponding west window in the Hall below appears to have been blocked at the same time, because Windham wished to "get rid of the idea of an end room." (It was unblocked again a couple of generations later.) Some repairs were done in the Drawing Room and Cabinet. A new chimney-piece for the latter room was commissioned from a Norwich stone-mason named John Blackburn. This did not give satisfaction; and if I have rightly interpreted some rather incoherent correspondence between Blackburn and Cobb, the mason was obliged to take it back to Norwich and offer it for sale in his shop.

Windham's diary mentions another visit from Brettingham in the spring of 1789, since when "I have hardly had any regular employment, or thought of anything, but cornices, colours, stained glass, &c." The stained glass consisted, I think, of some floral designs which were placed in the upper part of the library windows, and which were found to be too damaged for replacement when the glazing was renewed. There are some drawings, probably Brettingham's, of cornices, one of which was carried out in the south bedroom; and a drawing in the same hand of a Gothic fireplace, which survives in the south-east bedroom. There is no evidence, either in Windham's diary or in his letters to Cobb, that he found Brettingham's work anything but satisfactory. Nevertheless he had some further scheme in mind; and for some reason he entrusted this not to Brettingham, but to the most fashionable and the most casual architect of the day, James Wyatt.

There is not a word about Wyatt anywhere in Windham's diary; there is nothing to show when he visited Felbrigg, as presumably he must have done; and in the letters to Cobb there is only one passage that may perhaps refer to him, written on 18 March 1791.

As I have been unable to get the inclosed drawing revised by the person from whom I received it, I must leave it to Lambourn [the foreman employed at Felbrigg] to see, whether he can work from it in its present state; and if he can, to try the effect with one window.

Cobb, with all his faults, was an admirable preserver and docketer of letters. But in 1792 he was given, on Windham's recommendation, a small post of some kind in the public service; and thereafter we know much less of the day-to-day history of Felbrigg. So there is nothing to prepare us for the indignant letter of remonstrance which Windham found himself compelled to address to Wyatt on 23 November 1793.

Sir,

I shall no longer insist upon a right, which I have no means of enforcing, nor complain of injuries, which it is not in my power to redress. It is near two years since you undertook a business for me neither requiring, nor admitting of delay; and which you have not done yet: I have written to you no less than five letters desiring to know, whether you meant to do this, or not; and you have returned no answer.

You may think perhaps that this is a mark of genius, and the privilege of a man, eminent in his profession: But you must give me leave to say, that it must be a profession, higher than that of an Architect, and eminence greater than that of Mr Wyatt, that can make me see in this proceeding anything but great impertinence, and a degree of neglect, that may well be called dishonest.

It is dishonest to make engagements which you are either not able or not willing to fullfil: It is in the highest degree uncivil to receive letter after letter, containing a question, which the writer is entitled to ask; and to send no answer.

Pray, Sir, who are you, upon whom engagements are to be of no force; and who are to set aside all the forms of civility, established between man and man? Had the most private gentleman of the country written to the first minister of the country, he would have received an answer in a quarter of the time. And what is this privilege denied to persons in that station, which you suppose to be possessed by you? A privilege not allowed to a man's betters, may be suspected to be one, of which he has no great reason to boast. But of this I leave you to judge. There is one privilege which you shall not posses, that of acting with rudeness and contumely without being told of your conduct. If you are fond of placing yourself in a situation, in which you must hear these charges without the power of refuting them, I wish you joy of your choice, and with that reflexion shall take my leave of you.

I am, Sir,
Your Obedient
Humble Servant
W. Windham

P.S. Am I to expect, that the metal-frames, which you ordered at Sheffield, will come at last, when they are no longer wanted: or am I to understand only, that what you told me, is not true, and no such order was given?

Most architects would have wilted under such a letter; but Wyatt was perfectly indifferent to the displeasure of his clients. In the words of his most recent biographer, "a man of method might just have managed to keep pace with the demands of his enormous practice. But an erratic cycle of intensive application, preoccupation with particular works, and complete inactivity could not but produce a grand muddle." He was engaged on great schemes of construction and alteration all over the land—cathedrals, colleges, the grandest houses in town and country; and at Felbrigg he was only being asked to carry out some minor internal adjustments to a remote house of secondary importance. It seems extraordinary that Windham did not break off negotiations with him at this stage and turn to some other architect. Indeed, Brettingham had not ceased work at Felbrigg altogether, since he provided an elegant design in colour for a water-closet, signed and dated 4 June 1794. Yet Windham, incredible though it may seem, was still hoping to secure Wyatt's services ten years later. On 12 January 1804 he wrote:

Dear Sir,

I do not like even yet to quit the stile of friendly communication, though I must confess that my patience is nearly exhausted: A person has some right to feel impatient, who at the end of some seven or eight years (I believe I might say ten) is going into the country with the certainty of finding the principal rooms in his house, nearly uninhabitable, because he has not been able to obtain from you what would not be the work of a couple of hours. The dissatisfaction may reasonably be stronger, because my late applications have been, not that you would at all events do what was required, but that you would either complete the design or tell me at once that you would not do so. This application I must now renew, suggesting to your consideration, that the plea of this being your way, and that you treat every one else so, is really not sufficient to justify a mode of proceeding so remote from all that is expected and all that is observed by the rest of the world.

If I receive a letter from you, saying that you will without delay complete the design, I will repeat to you more in detail what I have before stated of the manner in which I would wish to have it done. If you say that you cannot do it, I shall then apply to some one else, but a letter I must beg to receive.

I am Dear Sir
Your Obedient Humble Servant
W. Windham

I do not know if this appeal, so much milder in tone than the earlier letter, had the slightest effect on Wyatt. Nor is there anything to show the nature of the work that Windham had asked him to undertake. The reference to metal frames does not give any clue at all. There was in fact only one alteration at Felbrigg, presumably dating somewhere between 1790 and 1810, that could possibly have justified the employment of an architect of Wyatt's standing. Hitherto the eastern portion of the south front still, I think, contained the kitchen and buttery, from which all the food and liquor used in old days to be brought through the screens into the Great Hall, and were now brought into the Dining Parlour. Above the porch was still the little solar or "metzinino," as Thomas Wyndham had called it in 1745—"the Master's Room," he then wrote, "which commanded the Kitchen and Hall . . . where meat was both dress'd and devour'd." This space was now converted into a Morning Room, sunny and airy, with painted panelling and a decorative cornice: and a new window (of which an unsigned drawing survives) was opened in the eastern wall. Certain adjustments were also made to the solar and the mezzanine floor with which it communicated.

These alterations much improved the general amenity of the house; but they could have been planned by any competent architect, and there is no evidence that Wyatt had any hand in them. By 1804 Brettingham had married a rich widow and virtually retired from practice. If, as seems probable, Windham continued to be ignored by Wyatt and had to entrust the work to someone else, the identity of that architect is likely to remain unknown.

On one point, and on one only, Windham sought the advice of his old friend Humphry Repton. Paine's staircase of 1752 had been surmounted by a coved ceiling, and all its light was furnished by a large semicircular window to the north. By 1806 this ceiling had begun to exert too much pressure on the side-walls. In the Norwich Public Library is a drawing of the staircase, signed by Repton and his son and partner John Adey Repton, with their customary hinged flap showing the proposed new work superimposed on the old. In the words of the Reptons, "a hint is here given for a flat ceiling supported by cross girders, with a double skylight to prevent the noise of hail &c." Either at this time or at some later date their suggestion was carried out. Paine's coved ceiling was removed, and replaced by a flat ceiling with a new central skylight. It was found possible, however, to endure the noise of hail, and the Reptonian refinement of a double skylight was not adopted.

V

Windham did not figure with any great prominence during the first few years of his parliamentary life. He spoke occasionally, and always with effect; but the Whig Opposition, despite its reduced numbers, was rich in orators, and he was content to be outshone by Fox, Burke, and Sheridan, his leaders and his friends. His most important public appearance was as one of the managers of the impeachment of Warren Hastings, which opened in 1788. It was his particular task to deal with the alleged breach by Hastings of his treaty with Faizullah Khan.

In the opening days of the trial, which was conducted with inconceivable leisureliness, Windham found time for a good deal of conversation with Fanny Burney, who wrote it all down in her diary. She was herself a strong partisan of Hastings; but she could not resist making the better acquaintance of "one of the most agreeable, spirited, well-bred, and brilliant conversers I have ever spoken with." Windham was, moreover, "a man of family and fortune, with a very pleasing though not handsome face, a very elegant figure, and an air of fashion and vivacity." On the other hand, his remarks on Hastings were so harsh that she could not listen to them without shuddering. When he passed from the misdeeds of Hastings to an examination of his countenance, and observed, "'Tis surely an unpleasant one," she could hardly resist telling him that it was generally thought to be very like his own. During some of the later stages of these interminable proceedings, in 1790 and 1792, they indulged in similar conversations. Miss Burney's accounts of them are far too long to be included in this book; but they are well worth reading, whatever view one may take of the unflagging archness of her style and the possible inaccuracy of her reporting.

The developments of the French Revolution greatly perturbed Windham. Early in 1790, in a speech on Parliamentary Reform, he uttered a warning against the "swarms of these strange impracticable notions that have lately been wafted over to us from the Continent, to prey like locusts on the fairest flowers of our soil, to destroy the boasted beauty and verdure of our Constitution." In this, as in his political opinions as a whole, he was following the lead of Burke; and when Burke's *Reflections on the French Revolution* came out at the end of the same year he wrote in his diary that "never was there, I suppose, a work so valuable in its kind, or that displayed powers of so extraordinary a nature." He did not, however, take any immediate action at the time of Burke's breach with Fox in May 1791. His personal attachment to Fox, his boyhood friend, was still very strong, and he felt in all the circumstances that Burke had gone too far. He visited Paris that same autumn, and was present at the meeting of the National Assembly when the King accepted the constitution. Whig though he was, and deeply though he disapproved in theory of absolute monarchy, he watched that ceremony with misgiving. His Whig principles did not envisage the smallest interference with privilege, order, and the rights of property. If the forces of revolution prevailed in France, he wrote next year, "Farewell, for a long time to come, to all good government throughout Europe. All establishments at least will be overset and everything changed, down to the minutest article of manners. I cannot help having great apprehensions."

When the revolutionary French declared war against England early in 1793 Windham's attitude was no longer in doubt. He advocated the prosecution of the war with the utmost vigour, and found himself opposed in bitter debate to Fox, Sheridan, Grey, Coke, the men with whom he had sat and voted for almost ten years. He became the leader of a group of Whigs, including Burke, Lord Spencer, and Sir Gilbert Elliot, who were now prepared to give their general support to the Government. "Much against my will," he wrote, "I have been obliged to act as a sort of head of a party." They used to meet at his house; they had interviews with Pitt and other ministers; and it was only a matter of time before a coalition was formed.

Although his life had hitherto been passed in an era of almost unbroken peace, Windham had always felt the attractions of a life of arms. He once wrote to Mrs Crewe that "there seems to me to be but two modes of life to be followed with any satisfaction, military and literary." In July he visited the Duke of York's army in Flanders, where he had the satisfaction of coming under fire at the siege of Valenciennes. Afterwards he filled his diary with characteristic regrets that he had not exposed himself to a greater degree of danger. Month by month the toll of massacre and bloodshed mounted in France. In October he wrote to Mrs Crewe, "my hostility to Jacobinism and all its works, and all its supporters, weak or wicked, is more steady and strong than ever. If Pitt is the man by whom this must be opposed, Pitt is the man whom I shall stand by."

For some months longer he and his friends refused to enter the Government, thinking that they could more usefully support its measures against the French from a position of independence.[1] But in July 1794 they agreed to join Pitt in a reconstructed administration, in which four of their leading figures received office. Windham became Secretary at War, with a seat in the Cabinet.

VI

After the dissolution of his first Parliament in 1790, Windham had no difficulty in retaining his seat at Norwich. His former colleague, Sir Harbord Harbord, had been created Lord Suffield in 1786; and his former opponent, Henry Hobart, had been elected in Harbord's place. At the general election Hobart and Windham each received more than double the votes polled by the third candidate, Sir Thomas Beevor.

But Windham was obliged to present himself for re-election after his acceptance of office in 1794; and on this occasion he had a much rougher

[1] There were, of course, other reasons for their hesitation. See the long letter written by the Duke of Portland to Windham on 11 January 1794 (*Burke–Windham Correspondence*, pp. 95–104).

passage. Norwich was still in population the third city in the land. All its freemen were entitled to vote, and by eighteenth-century standards they formed an exceptionally large and independent electorate. And the people as a whole, although still excluded from the suffrage, were beginning to take an active and sometimes a militant interest in politics. With most of them, and with many of the voters too, the war was by no means popular; and Windham's change of front, from a liberal-minded Whig to a furious anti-Jacobin, had not pleased them at all.

So the election, held on 12 July, proved unusually noisy. The Opposition had nominated a lawyer named James Mingay, who lived at Thetford. Apparently this was done without Mingay's knowledge, and he took no part in the proceedings; but he received 770 votes to Windham's 1236. This poll, a comparatively small one, as is generally the case at by-elections, did not reflect the feelings of the populace as a whole. There was a great deal of shouting and abuse. Mingay's supporters carried about a loom wreathed in mourning to signify the decay of Norwich trade. The partisans of Windham retaliated by displaying a toy guillotine, which decapitated a female figure, and was labelled "This is French Liberty." When Windham was chaired in the evening a stone was thrown at him; but he "avoided the blow, jumped down from his chair, seized the culprit, and delivered him over into the hands of an officer."

Mob rowdyism of this kind did not perturb Windham unduly. But he was well aware that Norwich had its Jacobin clubs and its flourishing branch of the Corresponding Society, that the advocates of sedition and republicanism were active in his constituency. He felt so intensely about the horrors in France that his speeches grew violent and extreme; and he began to figure in the public mind, in Norwich and in London alike, as the embodiment of reaction. When a group of prominent "democrats"—Hardy, Holcroft, Thelwall, Horne Tooke—were acquitted of treason at the end of 1794 he referred to them as "acquitted felons." Holcroft promptly retorted in an able pamphlet, *A Letter to the Right Honourable William Windham, on the Intemperance and Dangerous Tendency of his Public Conduct.* And at the next dissolution of Parliament, which took place in 1796, Thelwall went down to Norwich and assailed Windham with all his power, haranguing in the Market Place day after day. On this occasion Bartlett Gurney, a much-respected local banker, was his opponent, and exploited to the full the depression and war-weariness of the Norwich citizens. Hobart was well at the head of the poll, but Windham only defeated Gurney by the disquietingly small margin of eighty-three votes.

Windham had no doubt whatever of the righteousness of his cause, and the iniquity of all those who did not share his own crusading fervour. He now associated his old friends Fox and Sheridan with such figures as Horne Tooke, as "the long dynasty of murderous democrats and proconsuls of France." He had little doubt that rich and self-indulgent Whigs like Coke, who refused to take part in the war against Jacobinism, would end their lives in exile and beggary. He told Mrs Crewe that "my mind gets so soured by all that passes and that has long passed, that I can image to myself no pleasure but in the prospect of the vengeance that will be taken on all those who, by their baseness, their selfishness, their wickedness, or their folly, have contributed to bring on the ruin that awaits us." During the early years of the war such moods of despondency often beset him.

The feelings of his former associates are well depicted by his old friend Dr Samuel Parr, who had remained faithful to Fox and Coke.

> With Mr Windham [he wrote about 1795], though I lament his violence and abhor his apostasy, I am very unwilling to come to an open rupture. I remember with delight those earlier days, when he sustained a better part, with better men; when the charms of his conversation were not counteracted by the errors of his politics; when he was animated, but not ferocious; and when his refinements, instead of being dangerous in practice, were, in theory, only amusing. But I know well, as I long have known, the peculiarities which have lately burst upon the public eye; nor can I assign any limits to the fury of his passions, or the stubbornness of his prepossessions. He is proud by nature; he is visionary by habit; by accident he was made treacherous; and, by situation, he will be made imperious, intolerant, and inexorable.

There had, of course, been no apostasy on Windham's part, no treachery whether accidental or designed. At a time of grave national peril, when England was confronted with war overseas and subversion at home, he had joined a coalition Government pledged to repel the forces of evil. That was his view of the situation in 1794 and the years which followed, and it was both more realistic and more honourable than the line adopted by Fox and his adherents. In retrospect his fear and hatred of Jacobin influences may seem exaggerated; but they did not appear so when Europe was crumbling before the onset of revolutionary France, and England stood alone. In the words of one of Fox's biographers, Christopher Hobhouse, a young man destined before long to give his own life for his country:

> The risk of mutiny and disaffection was too great a price to pay for the right of Englishmen to pass resolutions and to read the works of Thomas Paine. Those who rend the air with lamentations over Pitt's bloodless precautions against Jacobinism, are the very people who pass over with averted glance the carnage with which Jacobinism, in its native home, was enforced.

For seven years Windham remained in office as Secretary at War, in circumstances of difficulty and discouragement. In matters of army administration—pay, pensions, welfare—his record was highly creditable. He did everything in his power, in the words of the epitaph on his monument in Felbrigg Church, "to exalt the courage, to improve the comforts, and ennoble the profession of a Soldier." But as a strategist he was less successful. Even before he came into office, he had been an active sympathiser with the *émigrés*, and with their fellow-Royalists who were fighting a guerrilla warfare in western France. From his place at the Cabinet table he advocated their cause still more warmly. He shared Burke's romantic vision of the war, writing to Mrs Crewe that she must "count upon me as your Reddecrosse Knight to the end of the adventure," dreaming of Royalist armies marching with British support upon the blood-stained fanatics of Paris, and a triumphant restoration of the Bourbons to their throne.

Pitt, severely practical, was never in full sympathy with Windham's belligerence. Nevertheless he listened to his arguments for equipping and despatching a large *émigré* force to support the Royalists fighting in La Vendée. This expedition sailed in the early summer of 1795, and landed on the Quiberon peninsula. The various Royalist elements were hopelessly disunited, and the attempt ended in defeat and massacre. Its failure was a bitter disappointment to Windham, who keenly felt his personal responsibility. But he never wavered in his conviction that the war must be ended by the invasion of France and a Bourbon restoration; and he opposed every suggestion of a negotiated peace. When Wilberforce, normally a steadfast supporter of the Government, attempted to influence Pitt in that direction, Windham wrote of him as "a wicked little fanatical imp."

This belligerence arose not from over-confidence, but rather from a sense of growing disaster. British arms met with reverses in Europe, in the Mediterranean, in the West Indies; and only the might of the Fleet secured the country from invasion. At the end of 1797 he wrote to William Lukin, now in command of his first ship:

I can only state to you in general, that my opinion of the state of things is not more favourable than at the worst period of any at which you have ever heard it . . . unless some fortunate shift of wind should happen, we are so beset with dangers on all sides, so completely embayed, that it is impossible we can weather the breakers upon either tack.

It was hardly an encouraging letter for a Cabinet Minister to address to a young naval officer at a critical stage of the war. But it was written in one of the recurring moods of depression caused by the death of Burke earlier in the year. "Oh! how much we rue that his counsels were not followed! Oh! how exactly do we see verified all that he had predicted!" It had been altogether a black year, with Bonaparte victorious in Europe, mutiny in the Fleet, unrest in Ireland and at home. It seemed as if the tide would never turn.

VII

Windham's diary takes on a different tone after the events of 1793. Until that time his moods of anxiety and indecision had steadily increased. He was haunted by fears that he was losing his memory—"sudden suspensions of the power of recollection"—or that his mental powers were beginning to fail, or that a paralytic stroke was imminent. But now he was shaken out of his hypochondria by the stress of events—the French Revolution, the outbreak of war, the pressure of his own ministerial duties. The entries in his diary naturally become briefer and fewer, but everywhere they indicate a newly achieved decision and firmness of mind.

In 1792 his mother died. Their relations had not invariably been happy, and a good deal of acrimonious correspondence between them has survived. Her husband's will had given her a certain amount of power over the estate, which she was always ready to employ in the interests of her Lukin children. But their disputes were never prolonged, and Windham recorded her death in his diary in an entry full of affection and remorse. On the day of her funeral at Felbrigg he wrote:

Should some thoughts which passed in my mind during the period spent in church, be the happy foundation of a system of belief, less liable to doubt and uncertainty than any I have hitherto formed, I shall have reason to number this occasion among the happiest of my life, and to add this to what I already owe my mother for early habits of piety and devotion.

Despite the cares of office, Windham maintained his contacts with his literary friends. He once described himself as "a scholar among politicians and a politician among scholars." His closest friend in these circles was Edmund Malone, with whom he had much in common. He managed to keep on terms with the learned but cantankerous George Steevens, who bequeathed to him an unrivalled collection of Hogarth's prints and scarcer pieces. He saw a good deal of Boswell, and was often consulted by him during the writing of the *Life of Johnson*. And he retained his interest in contemporary poetry. In earlier years he had first introduced Fox to the excellences of Cowper. Late in life he was able to admire the works of that notorious young democrat Robert Southey.

Yet although he mixed so freely in the social and literary worlds, Windham was at heart a very lonely man. In 1790 he had described in his diary his "strong sense of the unhappiness of my own celibacy"; and his mother's death enhanced this feeling of solitude. His fine looks and his charm of address won the hearts of many women, and some of them made no secret of the fact. One of these was Lady Anne Lindsay, the daughter of the fifth Earl of Balcarres, and author—although few people knew it at the time—of the ballad of *Auld Robin Gray*. Her love for Windham was common knowledge, and it was with some difficulty that he eluded her advances.[1] Finally, in 1793, at the age of forty-three, she married a young man named Andrew Barnard, and went to live with him at the Cape of Good Hope, where he had been appointed colonial secretary to the Governor.

Occasionally some woman made a passing impression upon him. In 1793 a Miss Hayman "this year hit my fancy very much"; and at the Sessions Ball in Norwich that autumn he was greatly attracted by a Miss Welham—"her looks, her manners, the circumstances under

[1] See the frank and amusing letter in which she solicited preferment for her husband in 1806 (*The Windham Papers*, ii. 288–90). Fanny Burney wrote to a friend in November 1790: "I hear Lady Anne Lindsay is going to be married to Mr Windham, the Member for Norwich, the excentric Mr Windham. His choice suits that character." (Reginald Blunt, *Mrs Montagu*, ii. p. 250.)

which we met, all gave me a degree of interest which was well calculated to lay the foundation of great attachment." But his most intimate ties were still with the Forrest family. The years had modified his old passion for Bridget Byng into an affectionate regard, such as he had long entertained for her sister Cecilia. In 1787 he met Cecilia and another of the sisters, Augusta, unexpectedly in London. He had not seen Augusta for some while—they all spent much of their time with their mother at Binfield—and on this occasion she was "to my eyes and taste so attractive, that it was with great difficulty I could forbear to mix in my conversation more of softness than would become the relation in which we stand."

Augusta in due course became Mrs Disney. Cecilia remained unmarried—eternally faithful, it seemed, to the faithless George Cholmondeley. Her love for him, and his unkind treatment of her, were generally known.[1] Windham still regarded Cholmondeley with the same affection as in earlier days, but he grew ever more impressed by Cecilia's fortitude and constancy. Their "long and intimate acquaintance," as he described it in a letter to Mrs Lukin, proved a stronger bond between them than either had realised. They were exactly the same age; they had moved in the same close circle for more than twenty years; they shared the same memories and the same disappointments; they had much in common—tastes, interests, friends. In the early summer of 1798 Windham asked Cecilia to marry him, and "she honoured me by giving me her hand."

They were married on 10 July in the parish church at Binfield—"the solemn ceremony performed, the impression of which, and the vows made during the time, will never, I hope, be effaced from my mind." Only Mrs Forrest and a few other members of her family were present; Bridget Byng attended her sister, and John Byng accompanied the bridegroom. There were a few days of honeymoon at Reigate, and then Windham returned to his labours at the War Office.

The marriage had been kept a secret, and came as a surprise to Windham's political associates, and indeed to his private friends. Pitt, the most resolute of bachelors, was much amused, and circulated a story that Windham had forgotten the wedding-ring on the day and lost the way to Reigate on the night. Malone, a bachelor somewhat against his will, sent warm congratulations:

[1] Cf. Lord Glenbervie, *Diaries*, ii. p. 130. "Cholmondeley, who, among many others, jilted unhandsomely Mrs Windham, many years before Windham married her."

> The object of your choice is one of the most amiable and engaging of women, and whom, ever since I first knew her, I have admired as the most perfect and attractive of her sex: one, with whom you have not merely a *prospect*, but a *certainty* of the greatest happiness this world has to bestow.

Sir Gilbert Elliot told his wife that Windham was "as odd, I think, as most people. However I have great hopes of the marriage improving him, for he will not now be dodging with the world and playing at whoop with all his friends." A few days later he wrote again:

> I have seen Windham and his bride, and am quite delighted with her. She is a tall showy woman, something in the Siddons style of figure and dimensions, with a remarkably sensible as well as pleasing countenance and an engaging manner. He seems the most delighted bridegroom that ever was. I met them yesterday evening, taking a conjugal walk round St James's Park after dinner.

In September they went down to Felbrigg, and it was there that Windham received a letter from Pitt announcing Nelson's victory at Aboukir Bay. He spent a happy hour in the library with William and Robert Lukin, examining travel-books and maps of that distant region. Presently the Byngs came to Felbrigg; and George Cholmondeley, apparently without his wife, was also of the party. The entries in Windham's diary had become more and more laconic during the anxious years of the war, and we learn little about these happy weeks. "Rode to Cromer with Cholmondeley and Cecilia." "Went into Byng's room and wrote long letter to Canning." "Rode with Cecy through Aylmerton Field, and back through south gate. Greenhouse to gather nosegay." The little group of friends and lovers had stayed together at Felbrigg often before; but now they had taken up different positions in the dance of life.

Chapter Ten

WILLIAM WINDHAM III

Windham resigns office in 1801—the Peace of Amiens—the Lukin family—war resumed—preparations against invasion—the death of Pitt—Windham joins the Ministry of All the Talents—his last visits to Felbrigg—his death in 1810

I

THROUGHOUT 1799 and 1800 the war swayed to and fro across Europe, with the greater and the lesser powers now joined in uneasy alliance against France. Bonaparte became First Consul, and broke the Austrian Army at Marengo. In the spring of 1800, on Windham's advice, small expeditions to various points on the French coast were again projected. Some of these were abandoned: those which were attempted met with failure. It was a lamentable dispersal of forces which, concentrated on a single objective, would have compelled the French to fight on two fronts and might well have averted the Austrian defeat.

The mischances of 1800 were the climax of Windham's career as Secretary at War. For his strategic mistakes he must be held to blame; but it is doubtful whether, in the desperately difficult circumstances of the war, another man would have had greater success. He should at least receive some credit for the sole British victory at this time, the battle outside Alexandria on 21 March 1801, in which General Abercromby defeated a superior French force, dying of his wounds a few days later. But on the day of the battle Windham had been out of office for just a week.

His resignation was in no way connected with his record at the War Office. On 1 January 1801 the Act of Union between Great Britain and Ireland came into effect. Pitt and the majority of his Cabinet felt that this measure should be accompanied by emancipation for Catholics, enabling them to sit in Parliament and hold high office. But several ministers were not in favour of Catholic Emancipation; and the King, invoking his Coronation oath, opposed the project with obstinacy and passion. Pitt determined to resign, and Windham was one of several ministers who resigned with him.

Although these resignations did not take effect until 14 March, they had been under discussion for several weeks past. The strain and anxiety had told on the King; and in February he once more became insane—the first attack for many years, but the first also of the series of attacks which developed into the complete madness in which his life ended. Shortly before his illness, on 9 February, he addressed this note to Windham:

However the King may feel hurt at losing so valuable a man as Mr Windham from His Service, He cannot but admit that He believes it arises from the purest intentions, though He may not think them well founded; and, as the former ought first to be looked at, He certainly with great truth assures Mr Windham that his Retiring shall in no ways diminish in His Majesty the real value He entertains for the upright Character Mr Windham has ever borne.

The new Government was headed by the late Speaker, Henry Addington. Pitt supported most of its measures, and was in sympathy with the negotiations for peace which were opened later in the year. Windham, on the other hand, continued to oppose all peace proposals as vehemently as ever. In the previous year he had written to Mrs Crewe:

The aspect of affairs is not good; but there does not appear any immediate prospect of peace—the blessings of peace—and that being the case there is still hope. In war a thousand things may happen; but peace once made, the power of Bonaparte seems certainly fixed, and I know not then how we are to escape.

He had urged the same point of view on Pitt for years past; and he held unwaveringly to it when the blood-stained welter of Jacobinism was replaced by the military dictatorship of Bonaparte. There could be no security for Britain while France remained undefeated.

The preliminaries of a peace treaty were signed on 1 October. Addington courteously wrote to inform Windham of the fact, and received a reply which began:

I must not omit to thank you for your note, however dreadful the intelligence which it contains. I can have no idea of the measure in question but as the commencement of a career which, by an easy descent, and step by step, but at no very distant period, will conduct the Country to a situation where, when it looks at last for its independence, it will find that it is already gone. I have no idea how the effect of this measure is ever to be recover'd. Chance may do much, but, according to any conception I can form, the Country has received its death blow . . . I lament that you should have been reserved for the instrument of this work.

When the terms of the Peace of Amiens were debated in the House of Commons on 3 and 4 November, Windham attacked them in a lengthy, eloquent, and emotional speech. To the older men in the House it recalled the great orations of Burke; and only his most persistent critics suggested that it showed "Burke's insanity without his inspiration." But he could make little headway. The government speakers were supported by Pitt, representing the former ministry, and by Fox on behalf of the Opposition; and the address was carried on both nights without a division. Windham published his speech soon afterwards as a pamphlet, with notes of considerable length. His printer was a young man whose acquaintance he had lately made, William Cobbett, then in the full tide of the Anti-Jacobinism of his early years. He was indeed Cobbett's first patron, and was closely associated with Cobbett's publications, *The Porcupine* and *The Political Register*.

When the treaty was ratified a few months later Windham moved an address against its terms in the same vehement strain, but found himself in a hopeless minority. His motion was rejected by 278 votes to 22. Many people admired his persistence and his conviction, and a few still felt that he was absolutely right; but he was more generally regarded as crack-brained and quixotic. Lord Guilford in fact compared him to Don Quixote, and said that he never saw him without thinking he had a barber's basin on his head.

The Peace of Amiens was welcomed throughout the war-weary country, and nowhere more enthusiastically than in Norwich. The trade and manufactures of the city had declined seriously during the past few years, and there was much poverty and unemployment. All this was blamed upon the war, and upon those who had opposed an earlier peace. Windham had long been in trouble on this score with his constituents, and several prominent supporters had lately deserted him. When Parliament was dissolved in the early summer of 1802 he knew that a hard struggle awaited him.

His former colleague at Norwich, Henry Hobart, had died in 1799.

In the ensuing by-election the seat was held by a Tory, John Frere of Roydon, who defeated the Whig candidate, Robert Fellowes of Shotesham. Windham and Frere were now opposed by Fellowes and an extreme Whig named William Smith, an ardent supporter of Fox, who had previously sat for Sudbury. A bitter contest followed, weeks of strenuous canvassing, floods of printed handbills and squibs. The Whig candidates extolled the blessings of peace, the iniquities of war, the glories of constitutional liberty. Windham put it differently in a letter to a friend: "All that system and organization and malice and activity and Jacobinism and puritanism can do against us here, it is doing, but I think upon the whole that we shall prevail against it." He and Frere issued statements condemning the "Jacobin Politics" of their opponents, "those low and flagitious Arts, which are now systematically employed to poison the minds of the people."

Polling took place on 5 July: Fellowes 1532, Smith 1439, Windham 1356, Frere 1328. The Whigs had won both seats, and Windham had been rejected by the Norwich electors after representing them continuously for eighteen years. But he was not thereby excluded from Parliament. One of his late Cabinet colleagues, and the most consistent supporter of his campaign against a negotiated peace, had been Lord Grenville; and the Grenville family had offered him a safe retreat, in the event of disaster at Norwich, at their Cornish pocket-borough of St Mawes. There was some talk that he might stand for the county of Norfolk, or for some other seat; but in the end he gladly accepted St Mawes, with its handful of docile electors. The Marquess of Buckingham, the proprietor of the borough, wrote to him:

> If I did not always feel sorry for everything that could disturb you, I should be almost tempted to rejoice at your delivery from the eternal hot water in which your Norwich pursuits have kept you for so long. The only political tenet to which your St Mawes electors will bind you is the belief that the pilchard is the best of all possible fish, which, as long as you are not obliged to taste it, you may undertake for their sake to believe.

II

The marriage of Windham and Cecilia proved a very happy one. The laconic style of his later diaries does not conceal his affection and pride. "Cecilia in white, with gold and fur; head-dress very becoming; looking well." When in 1800 they paid a visit to Weymouth, where the Royal Family were spending the summer months, he wrote to Mrs

Byng that "our stay is uncertain, owing partly to Cecy's being such a favourite with both Queen and Princesses, that she cannot be parted with."

They visited Felbrigg occasionally; but more often they went to Bath, to drink the waters and to see their friends, and especially the Lukin family, for in 1799 the Rev. George William Lukin had been appointed Dean of Wells. Windham had previously obtained a prebend of Westminster for his half-brother; and on 4 February 1799 he mentioned in his diary that he "wrote to Mr Pitt about deanery at Wells, vacant by the death of the Dean on Saturday night." Lukin retained his Norfolk livings until his death, but the migration of the family to Somerset made a great alteration in the pattern of Felbrigg life. The Parsonage was occupied, when he was not at sea, by the Dean's eldest son Captain William Lukin, who in 1801 married Anne Thellusson, a daughter of the banker Peter Thellusson. The parochial duties were undertaken by a succession of curates, one of whom was the Dean's youngest son John.

To this period belongs the painting by William Redmore Bigg of William Lukin and his three brothers outside Felbrigg Parsonage, with the church in its grove of trees at a distance. The landscape and trees are touched with autumn, and the brothers, surrounded by excited spaniels, are going out shooting. William stands in the middle, ramming down the charge of his gun, while Cawston the keeper—a relation of Windham's servant John Cawston—kneels down to fasten one of his gaiters. Robert and George are also holding guns; and the youngest brother John, black-coated as befits a future clergyman, is on horseback at the rear of the group. The picture was exhibited at the Royal Academy in 1803, and must have been painted at Felbrigg in the autumn of 1802. Bigg was a minor painter in the excellent rural tradition of George Morland and Henry Walton. This is one of his best works, a calm and happy portrayal of life in the Norfolk countryside during that spell of deceptive peace.

The same air of tranquillity pervades the account of a visit to Felbrigg by a party of Quaker girls a few years earlier, in the summer of 1797. The writer of the artless narrative was Louisa Gurney, one of the seven Gurney sisters of Earlham, the most famous of whom was Elizabeth Fry. Louisa (subsequently Mrs Samuel Hoare) was then aged thirteen, and was staying with her uncle Richard Gurney at Northrepps Hall. On a June morning she and some of her sisters, refusing the offer of Uncle Richard's chaise, walked towards Felbrigg "down some most sweet lanes" and seem to have found their way to the farm-premises attached to the Parsonage.

At last when we got close to the park we asked the way to get in at a barn. A genteel young gentleman of an agreeable appearance was coming out of the stables and told us he would show us the way. We thanked him and followed him rather suspecting he was leading us wrong because he laughed *so*. However we were mistaken for he led us to the *most* delightful park I ever saw in my life. He took us to the house and knocked at the door for a servant to show us over it. After waiting some time *she* came and *he* left us. We then looked all over the house. I never saw such a place, nor such fine rooms. They were full of the most beautiful pictures. I enjoy to see the fine arts in perfection. After we had satisfied ourselves with the sight of the house, we went into the park. We had two or three hours to ramble about in it. We went wherever we liked, it was so delightful to be so entirely at our liberty. At any particularly sweet spot we sat down, and ate some of the bread and cheese which we had brought in our basket. We went into a sweet church situated in the park surrounded by a little grove of trees, and then by palings which we clambered over and got into the churchyard which was very sweet. We then went and rambled at the other side of the park which was most delightful. After we had spent as much time as we could spare in the park, and compleatly walked round it we went back. We were *so* thirsty we called for some water at a poor cottage. A nice poor woman said she would not give us water but she hoped we would have a little of her beer. She got a mug and having filled it out of a pitcher that seemed the only one in her house we drank it with great pleasure, for hunger and thirst give a relish to most things. After we had offered her a shilling which with difficulty we made her accept we went away. . . . I never saw so sweet a place. It is delightful to look back to pleasant times. I don't think I shall ever forget this walk it was so *truly* pleasant. The young gentleman who showed us the house was Master Lukin.

This was John Lukin, the only one of the brothers young enough to be described as "Master" at this time, and a year older than Louisa Gurney.

Windham's interest in all the Lukin children continued, and he was deeply grieved when the eldest daughter Mary, who had married a Mr Foy, died in childbirth in 1800. "I really loved her as a daughter," he wrote to Mrs Crewe, "and not every father has had a daughter attached to him so much, as I believe she was to me." He took great pride in William's naval career, which he was able to assist through his friendship with Lord Spencer, the First Lord of the Admiralty. He was also much pleased by William's marriage into the opulent Thellusson family.[1] Although he had been able to advance his Lukin kinsmen in their professions during his years of office, "his own emoluments"—to quote his secretary, Thomas Amyot—"were of a very trifling amount, totally inadequate indeed to the rank and station of a Cabinet Minister; nor was his retirement accompanied by pension or advantage of any kind." But it seems likely that he had already resolved to make William his eventual heir, and Miss Thellusson's substantial prospects further encouraged him to do so.

III

In 1787, on a journey from London to Felbrigg, Windham's thoughts "were employed drawing up resolutions for a society which Sheridan and I had projected, for the encouragement of ancient games." The society was never formed, and his friendship with Sheridan had not many more years to run; but his interest in ancient games was lifelong. He seldom hunted, and, I think, hardly ever went shooting: the woods and stubble-fields at Felbrigg were the preserve of the younger Lukins from their boyhood. But he had inherited all his father's love of pugilism, and would travel miles to see a prize-fight: his diary is full of descriptions of them. When the Prince of Wales witnessed the death of a man in a boxing-match, and publicly declared that he would never be present at another, Windham hastened to London in order to insert a letter in the newspapers "to take off, as far as could be, the effect of the accident." At Felbrigg he was a great patron of the traditional Norfolk game of "camping," a ferocious kind of footfall in which no holds were barred and no form of violence was forbidden. It was his view that camping "combined all athletic excellence; that to excel in it, a man must be a good boxer, runner and wrestler: in short, a sort of *pancratiast*." Camping-matches were often held in the park at Felbrigg, with prizes of a hat apiece to the winning side and a pair of stockings to each of the losers.

Few people criticised Windham's taste for prize-fighting and camping. After all, both pastimes survive in a modified form to this day.

[1] Mrs Lukin's father, Peter Thellusson, was already dead by the time of her marriage. He had left an extraordinary will, famous in legal history, by which the greater part of his wealth was to accumulate until the third generation of his descendants in the male line. So his daughters were not as rich as they would otherwise have been; but William Lukin's marriage was a good one nevertheless.

But even some of his admirers were disconcerted by the violence with which he resisted any attempt to abolish the ancient sport of bull-baiting. Bills to this effect were brought before Parliament in 1800 and again in 1802. On both occasions Windham opposed them in long and eloquent speeches, and his arguments prevailed. He was not himself a patron of bull-baiting—he had only twice witnessed the sport, when he was a schoolboy. But he resisted these Bills on the ground that they were an unwarrantable interference with the liberty of the subject. "This petty, meddling, legislative spirit cannot be productive of good: it serves only to multiply the laws, which are already too numerous, and to furnish mankind with additional means of vexing and harassing one another." It was, in fact, an attempt by the rich to take away the pleasures of the poor. If the promoters of the Bill abolished bull-baiting they would soon legislate against boxing and cudgel-playing. And was bull-baiting more cruel, if viewed dispassionately, than hunting or shooting? "It is mere solemn mockery in gentlemen to talk of cruelty, when they themselves indulge in sports equally cruel." No: the promoters were interfering and insincere, and at the same time they were playing into the hands of the Jacobins, part of whose exertions were "directed to the destruction of the old English character, by the abolition of all rural sports." But his main argument was the injustice that would be done to the poor. He pictured them as saying:

> Why interfere with the few sports that we have, while you leave to the rich so great a variety? You have your carriages, your town-houses, and your country-houses; your balls, your plays, your operas, your masquerades, your card-parties, your books, your dogs, and your horses to amuse you—On yourselves you lay no restraint—But from us you wish to take the little we have.

Windham was attacked on this issue in at least one pamphlet, and the question of bull-baiting was loudly raised by his opponents at Norwich during the election of 1802. His arguments, for all their wit and force, were in support of an indefensible cause. They enhanced the impression, already widely current, that he was growing wrong-headed and perverse: that his love of abstract reasoning, his hair-splitting habits of thought, were loosening his grasp of the practical affairs of life.

IV

During the years of peace a large number of English people, including several leading Whig politicians, crossed over to France. They were a good deal disconcerted by what they saw. English progressives in all centuries tend to applaud certain forms of totalitarianism from afar, but a closer contact generally disillusions them. The interviews between Fox and the First Consul were not very successful. In particular, Bonaparte thought fit to abuse Windham, declaring him to be unfeeling and unprincipled. Despite their years of estrangement Fox replied that "*il n'y a sur la terre un être plus noble, plus humain, plus rempli d'honneur et de talents que M. Windham, intègre jusqu'au scrupule . . . J'ai le malheur de ne pas m'accorder avec lui sur tous les points, mais je l'estime et je le revère.*" Bonaparte then accused Pitt and Windham of being concerned in the plot to assassinate him by means of an infernal machine, a notion which Fox rejected with even greater vehemence.

Before long it became evident that the peace would not last. The dictator was not appeased, and aggression was not checked. French domination was consolidated or extended in Holland, Switzerland, and Italy; and this policy of expansion was obviously to continue. Finally, as the result of innumerable acts of provocation, Britain declared war in May 1803.

Windham did not rejoice in the reopening of hostilities. He felt that after the interlude of peace it would be harder than ever to rouse the country to a sense of its peril. "This only I feel certain of, that we must soon have perished in peace; and this effect at least may result from war begun even as this seems likely to be, that it may stop the progress of the ruin which was before coming fast upon us." Bonaparte began to assemble his armies across the Channel, and invasion seemed probable, if not certain, within a few months. After seven years as Secretary at War, immersed in problems of world-wide strategy, Windham now found himself without responsibilities other than those felt by any private gentleman towards his own immediate neighbourhood. Instead of despatching expeditions to Belleisle and Minorca and the West Indies, he began to concern himself with the unprotected state of the Norfolk coast, and the defence of the gap in the cliffs at Cromer.

A month after the declaration of war the Secretary at War in Addington's Government, the Hon. Charles Philip Yorke, introduced a Bill to increase the Armed Forces. Its principal feature was the raising by ballot of an Army of Reserve of 50,000 men. Windham felt that a force of this kind would be little more effective than the existing Militia, and would hinder recruitment into the regular Army, which alone could give its officers and men the necessary training to withstand Bonaparte's formidable troops. In a remarkable speech he urged the ministry to make a vast increase in the regular Army, and to organise the rest of the male population into lightly armed guerrilla forces which could operate in their own districts. His plans were curiously similar to the first conception of the Home Guard in the summer months of 1940.

It would never enter into my idea to introduce into bands of this sort any of the foppery of dress, or any distinctive dress at all; a ribband, or even a handkerchief round the arm to distinguish them, is all that would be necessary. Firing at a mark, learning indeed to fire at all, which (thanks to the Game Laws) few of our peasantry are acquainted with; some instruction in the manner of cleaning arms, much instruction in the methods of lining hedges, firing from behind trees, retiring upon call, and resuming a new station; these are all the heads upon which I should propose them to be exercised . . . The greatest, possibly, of all the advantages which I should be inclined to hope from this plan is, that it will produce that most important of all preparations, the preparation of the mind. Both a sense of the danger, and a knowledge of the means necessary to be employed against it, will be carried into every farmhouse and every cottage. It will be the conversation of the village green, of the church porch, and what is not least perhaps, of the alehouse.

He lost no time in putting these ideas into effect in his own neighbourhood. William Lukin had not yet been recalled to duty at sea, and he was entrusted with the raising of a local force. Windham sent him letter after letter of instructions, and also sent down a consignment of firelocks which he had purchased himself. On the back of one letter Lukin scribbled a muster-roll for a village parade on Sunday 31 July 1803. It vividly recalls similar Sundays in the same village in the summer of 1940. Very few men were noted as absentees; and almost every name survives in the immediate neighbourhood today.

Later in the summer Windham came down to Norfolk himself, made a personal inspection of the coastline, and tried to infuse his own enthusiasm into certain of his less enterprising neighbours. "Your country gentleman of the present day is apt to be a very stupid and spiritless creature," he wrote to Cobbett. He wrote also at great length, pointing out the defects of everyone and everything, to his harassed successor Yorke.

> You have been in office in very difficult times [Yorke replied] and know the embarrassment of Government upon many of these points. Certainly they were never greater than at present . . . Arms are much wanted, but I hope everything is doing and will be done to fill up the void; in the mean time the people must be encouraged to take pikes, and to bring forward their fowling-pieces and other arms in aid.

He had now succumbed to "the foppery of dress," and wrote to Lukin after his return to London about the uniform he had evolved for his little corps—green, with black or tan leather buttons, and gaiters of dark grey or brown. "The great difficulty is then the head; and I am amazingly inclined to a Scotch bonnet, with green instead of the tartan. I want to learn from some who have served with Highland regiments what the inconveniences are." But later in the year, as the organisation of the country's defences got under way, these private and unorthodox little forces were merged into larger units; and Windham was invited by the Lord Lieutenant—Lord Townshend, his father's old friend of many years ago—to take command of the 4th (Cromer and District) Battalion of Norfolk Volunteer Infantry. He said farewell to his green uniform and Scotch bonnets with regret, but wrote to Lukin that "I suppose, if I have this corps, I may make them exercise in the way I like, notwithstanding their red coats and feathers." In the course of 1804, however, he handed over the command of his battalion to George Wyndham of Cromer Hall.

Addington resigned in May 1804, and Pitt was called to the head of affairs once more, and for the last time. He wished his administration to be as comprehensive as possible, a real Government of national unity, which would include Fox, Grenville, and Windham, as well as his own supporters. The King, however, could not forget the long years during which Fox had opposed the war in every possible way, and strongly resisted his inclusion in the new Government. But the Grenville party, during their period of opposition to Addington, had made common cause with Fox; and they now refused to enter the Government without him. Windham followed the same line. He had written in February suggesting a meeting with his long-estranged friend, and the draft of his letter still survives.

> After an interval of twelve years or more, for such I am afraid it is, there must be thus much of ceremony before former habits can be resumed; but in all that relates to personal regards and feelings, things will be found, I trust, as exactly in their places, as in the case of the Prince who had dipped his head in water in the Arabian tale.

So, in the words of his secretary Amyot, "he was now once more the ally of Mr Fox, and the adversary of Mr Pitt—a situation which unjustly exposed him to the charge of inconsistency." The justice or injustice of the charge cannot be discussed here. Windham had good reasons to offer for his action, and a number of highly respected Whigs had done precisely the same. Nevertheless, it was a drastic change of front, and the name of "Weathercock Windham" clung to him henceforward.

Great events followed fast during the next two years. On the European mainland Napoleon set all the efforts of the Allies at defiance, and eventually won his overwhelming victory at Austerlitz. Britain was finally liberated from the fear of invasion by Nelson's equally momentous victory at Trafalgar. And Pitt, worn out by all those years of struggle and disappointment, died on 23 January 1806.

Four days after Pitt's death, an address was moved in the House of Commons that he should receive a public funeral and a monument in Westminster Abbey. To the general surprise, Windham opposed this motion, in a speech full of subtle intellectual refinements but curiously lacking in magnanimity. The two men had never been in full sympathy. They had frequently differed in Cabinet, especially when Pitt wished to consider peace terms and Windham was urgent for the continuance of the war. Nevertheless they had been colleagues for seven momentous years; and although one must accept Windham's words about the painful situation in which he stood, and the duty he felt bound to discharge, one still wishes that he had kept silence. He observed that a public funeral had not been granted to Burke: why, then, should Pitt be accorded that honour?

> With the fullest acknowledgment both of the talents and virtues of the eminent man in question, I do not think, from whatever cause it has proceeded, that his life has been beneficial to his country. For the earlier part of it, including the commencement of his power, I must contradict every principle, that I ever maintained, if I said that it was so. For the succeeding period, the greatest in which a statesman was ever called to act, I cannot say, that he acted his part greatly.

So much for the Pilot who Weathered the Storm. Windham was back in the Foxite ranks with a vengeance.

The motion for the funeral and the monument was carried by a large majority. A few days later Windham made some amends when the question of paying Pitt's debts came before the House. On this occasion he felt able to support a motion that a sum not exceeding £40,000 should be applied to this end.

He considered that, in the part the House were now called upon to act, they were not indulging themselves in an improper sentiment of liberality, nor catching at any transient reputation of magnanimity, nor wasting the public money; nor should he think that the case, even were they to make some provision for those who were most near and dear to the deceased.

The King now invited Grenville to form a Government, and at last withdrew his objection to the inclusion of Fox. Grenville assembled what was known as the Ministry of All the Talents, with Fox as Foreign Secretary and Windham as Secretary for War and the Colonies. It lasted little more than a year; and Fox, who was one of its mainstays, was already in ill-health, and died after only six months of office. Windham introduced in April, in a four-hour speech which Fox considered one of the most eloquent ever delivered in Parliament, a new scheme of recruitment for the Army. Its provisions included increased pay, shorter periods of service, the abolition of the existing system of volunteers, and an attempt at compulsory short-time training for all. Few of them were carried into effect; but the improvements in pay, and the seven years' period of enlistment, were long and gratefully remembered. His strategic conceptions were not more successful than during his earlier term of office. A contemporary satirist described him, not without justification, as "plan-mad, and amorous of th'unfruitful moon." The Spanish dominions in South America had now been drawn within the field of operations; and one of his less practicable schemes, fortunately not carried out, was the subjugation of Chile by a force of 4000 men.

Shortly after Fox's death the ministry had decided to appeal to the country, and a general election was held in November. The seat at St Mawes was not available for Windham on this occasion, and he felt it was useless to attempt to regain his former seat at Norwich. But he and Thomas William Coke, who had been on the most distant terms ever since the cleavage in the Whig party, were now completely reconciled; and Coke suggested that they should stand together for the two county seats, as his colleague Sir Jacob Astley did not intend to stand again. He himself was certain to be elected. His political consistency had been absolute, his prestige in the county was enormous, and there was a good chance that he could persuade the electors to accept Windham in Astley's place.

They were opposed by the Hon. John Wodehouse, a man considerably younger than themselves, who had stood as a Pittite Tory in the election of 1802, but had offered to withdraw in Windham's favour after his defeat at Norwich. Windham had then likewise been regarded as a supporter of Pitt; now he was a Whig once more, and he was not allowed to forget it throughout the election. But the Whig ballad-writers turned even his unfortunate nickname to good account.

Let fools, who without sense or reason will bawl,
With their jeers try our feelings to shock;
O come to the poll, Norfolk freeholders all!
We'll vote for the old Weathercock.

Let peer-courting sycophants promise or rail,
For their flummery we care not a feather;
When their turn is once serv'd, all their promises fail—
Our Windham's a Cock for all Weather.

After a long and strenuous contest the two Whigs were returned, with Coke well at the head of the poll, and Windham some 350 votes ahead of Wodehouse. "Nothing but the irresistible influence of Mr Coke could have secured him success," wrote Bishop Bathurst, who although a Whig could not forget Windham's attack in Parliament upon "the greatest man whom this country ever produced, and that man then no more." But there was trouble still to come.

Two ladies, Mrs Berney of Bracon Hall and Mrs Atkyns of Ketteringham Hall, had made themselves conspicuous throughout the election by driving everywhere in a carriage bedecked with Tory favours, canvassing, cajoling, and shouting "Vote for Wodehouse." Some of the younger Whigs had dressed up two local prostitutes in imitation of them, and had escorted them all over Norwich in a carriage similarly arrayed. The insult rankled in the breast of Mrs Berney's son, a rich and keen young Tory. He swore vengeance on the Whigs, and seems genuinely to have believed that Coke and Windham had some responsibility for the affair. He set on foot a petition alleging treating, bribery, corruption, and many other irregularities on the part of the Whigs. Such things were not difficult to uncover, with a little persistence and persuasion, in most eighteenth-century elections; and in this particular contest the expenses of the three candidates were said to have amounted to £70,000. After a long hearing the petition was declared successful, and Coke and Windham were unseated.

It was a vexatious business, but not irreparable. Windham had already been elected for another of those convenient pocket-boroughs, New Romney in Kent; and he duly took his seat in Parliament for that place. Coke's brother Edward resigned in his favour his own seat in Derbyshire, and stood unopposed for one of the vacant seats for Norfolk, while Sir Jacob Astley, unopposed likewise, returned to the other. But the new Parliament had not lasted long when the Ministry of All the Talents came to an end. There were disagreements with the King on the old issue of Catholic Emancipation; and a new Government, of Tory complexion, was formed under the Duke of Portland at the end of March 1807.

V

Windham did not hold office again during the three remaining years of his life. He had more than once been offered a peerage, on the first occasion in 1799; but he preferred to remain in the House of Commons, as an independent-minded and outspoken member of the Opposition. At the next general election, in the spring of 1807, he was once more provided with a seat for a pocket-borough—this time at Higham Ferrers in Northamptonshire, through the good offices of yet another Whig magnate, Lord Fitzwilliam.

He visited Felbrigg more often than he had done for many years past, and for longer periods. His letters speak, almost for the first time in his life, of the pleasures of retirement and the attraction of country pursuits. His diary tells of days spent in his woods, inspections of his farms, visits to neighbours and tenants. Attendance at Quarter Sessions in Norwich revealed, even after the lapse of a few years, "the decrease of people whom I remember, or who remember me." Cecilia sometimes accompanied him to Felbrigg; but he was alone there in September 1808 when he suffered a violent attack of nose-bleeding, losing a quantity of blood which Mr Earle, the surgeon from Cromer, estimated at 32 ounces. The diarist Farington, on a visit to Cromer a few years later, indulged in long gossips about this affair both with Earle and with Windham's housekeeper. Earle told him that this great loss of blood must certainly have impoverished Windham's constitution.

In other ways Windham's health was declining at this time. He suffered from a pain in the hip-joint which his doctors diagnosed as ischias, a form of arthritis. Cecilia was the victim of severe headaches, and together they spent much time at Bath for their respective complaints. They were there when Parliament opened at the beginning of

WILLIAM WINDHAM III
By Sir Joshua Reynolds
(Reproduced by permission of The National Portrait Gallery)

Vice-Admiral WILLIAM LUKIN (afterwards WINDHAM)

By George Clint

1809. Windham wrote to Mrs Crewe: "Till the battle was actually begun and the sound had reached us, I felt very composed, and perhaps even comfortable, at being exempt from the necessity of taking any part. . . . Today I feel a little uneasy and restless, like an old dragoon horse at the sound of a trumpet."

On 8 July of the same year Windham was walking home from an evening party when he saw a house in Conduit Street on fire. This house was close to that of his friend the Hon. Frederick North, which contained a large and valuable library. Knowing that North was then abroad, Windham collected a party of volunteers among the bystanders, and rescued four-fifths of the books before the flames engulfed the house. It was a dangerous business: two of the volunteers were badly injured, and one died soon afterwards. Windham himself slipped and fell when removing some heavy volumes, and received a severe bruise on the hip. He made light of the matter in his diary, and was at first more inconvenienced by a protracted cold, caught from these exertions on a night of heavy rain, than by the injury to his hip.

Later in the summer he went down to Felbrigg for several weeks, and once more occupied himself in estate business—marking plantations for thinning, deciding to replant Swift's Grove, settling the site of some new cottages. William Lukin and his wife were at the Parsonage, and their eldest boy, yet another William, went off to school for the first time. The Dean of Wells was there too, and together they looked through the accumulations of old papers at the Hall. In September, after the resignations which followed the expedition to Walcheren, it seemed that a new coalition might be formed, which Windham and other leading Whigs would be invited to join. He was far from eager to return to office. "It is one of the things that one neither knows how to accept or decline," he told Amyot. "If I could always be as well as I am here—if Downing Street were in Felbrigg Park, or a dozen miles from London—I should think much less about it . . . my hope must be that the intelligence is unfounded, or that the question will not arise." In the end the ministry carried on, and no coalition was attempted.

The year 1810 began sadly for Windham with the death of George Wyndham of Cromer Hall, his kinsman and neighbour. He had died suddenly in the night while staying with Sir Jacob Astley at Melton Constable.

He was a friendly, well-disposed man, who never offended and often pleased [he wrote to William Lukin]. In all cases where liking and preference were alone concerned, he was always disposed to side with me, and would have done, I dare say, for me as much as he would for anyone. How much in any case that might have been I have no means of knowing, but whether it was more or less, one owes something to the preference, and it is always pleasant to have as a neighbour a person so disposed; and whether the feeling was that of pure, unmixed kindness, or from his interest and consideration, in virtue of the name and family connection, as in some degree united with mine, I shall feel that a great blank is left by his death in the system of Felbrigg life.

George Wyndham had married a Suffolk lady, Marianne Bacon, and left a young son and four daughters, the eldest of whom was my great-grandmother.

In the same month of January he also lost his natural sister Mrs Guise, who had been disinherited by their father for marrying the writing-master at Eton half a century before. Latterly she had been living at Bath, where he and Cecilia used to visit her. He wrote in his diary: "How one feels now that the opportunity one had of seeing and being with her were not turned to the best account. It is satisfactory, however, to have seen her so recently, and to have parted with such marks of kindness."

To outward appearance he was himself full of vigour and activity. His old friend Lord Glenbervie had met him and Cecilia in Bath during the Christmas season, and recorded in his diary that "Windham is in excellent looks and great spirits." His own diary speaks of politics, social activities, the opera, the Academy banquet. Between January and May he made at least nine speeches in Parliament, some of considerable length. But all the time he was worried by a swelling near his hip-joint, the result of the injury sustained the summer before at the fire in Conduit Street. In May he consulted several surgeons, of whom the majority, seven out of nine, advised an immediate operation.

He said nothing to Cecilia, but arranged for the operation to take place at his house in Pall Mall while she was spending a few days with Mrs Burke at Beaconsfield. He was under no illusions as to his danger, or the severity of the pain that he was to undergo. On 13 May he received the Sacrament from an old Oxford friend, Dr Fisher, the Master of the Charterhouse, privately in his library. The operation took place on the 17th, and lasted two hours, during which a large and possibly malignant tumour was removed. As might have been expected, he bore the long agony with extraordinary courage. When Cecilia returned next day it seemed that he might make a successful recovery.

But this hope was short-lived. The reader shall be spared further medical details, which are lavishly furnished in contemporary records, and more particularly by Farington. Windham proved unable to rally from the operation. "Mr Lynn," he said to the surgeon in attendance, "you fight the battle well, but all won't do." One of the surgeons who had discouraged the operation told Farington that "the endurance of exquisite pain for so long as he felt it must have had a great effect upon his constitution, that severe pain does and will kill persons . . . Human constitution cannot support it. Mr Windham felt overcome by it." Gradually he drifted into complete exhaustion, and died on the morning of 4 June 1810.

VI

Many men and women of Windham's own generation, and of the generation that came after, have left their impressions of him, in letters, in diaries, in carefully considered estimates of his character. These impressions vary between admiration and exasperation, warm affection and deep dislike. They often end upon a note of perplexity. None of them, I think, were as close to the mark as Windham's own definition of himself—a scholar among politicians, and a politician among scholars.

He was in fact a distinguished example of the intellectual who engages in politics. He went with the wayward current of his ideas, wherever it bore him. It is perhaps too much to say, as Brougham did, that he was "the dupe of his own ingenuity." But it is easy to see how his reputation for inconstancy grew in the popular mind, by contrast with the unwavering concentration upon his objectives of such a man as Pitt—how, for all the power of his oratory and the dignity of his bearing, his public image gradually became that of "Weathercock Windham."

There are two splendid portraits which depict him as a statesman, authoritative and composed—the Hoppner at Norwich and the Lawrence at Oxford. But it is the head by Reynolds in the National Portrait Gallery, painted at a time when he had scarcely entered public life, that reveals the essential Windham. These sensitive and introspective features, together with certain passages scattered through the diaries, do much to explain the personality which seemed so enigmatic to his friends and his enemies alike. Such a man could go far towards success, as the world counts success; but the ultimate prizes would always elude him. He will always rank high among the illustrious failures of English political life.

Chapter Eleven

VICE-ADMIRAL WILLIAM LUKIN, afterwards WINDHAM

William Lukin's naval career—life at Felbrigg Cottage—the Cremer family and their friendship with the Lukins—Admiral Lukin succeeds to the Felbrigg estate in 1824, and assumes the name of Windham—his alterations and improvements at Felbrigg—his death in 1833

I

WILLIAM WINDHAM was the last of his line. His death in 1810 ended the hereditary succession to the Felbrigg estate which had continued for the past three hundred and fifty years. William Lukin, whom he made his heir, was the grandson of his mother by her first marriage, and had no Windham blood. Nor had any subsequent owner of Felbrigg until my father came into possession of the property in 1924.

Subject to various legacies, Windham bequeathed Felbrigg and all his other possessions to his widow for her life. After her death it was to pass to William Lukin and his male heirs; in default of these, to George Cholmondeley and his male heirs; and in default of these, to George Wyndham, third Earl of Egremont, the representative of the senior branch of the Wyndham family. Since Lukin had five vigorous sons, there was little likelihood of the inheritance passing to Cholmondeley or to Lord Egremont. Nevertheless the latter's inclusion in the will incurred the displeasure of that eminent busybody Lady Holland. She pronounced it "a curious instance of weakness in Windham, and one that probably never would have been drawn forth, but for the feelings stirred up by the French Revolution. . . . During his life the relationship was never claimed, and certainly not admitted, either by him or by Lord Egremont." She then went on to criticise Cecilia for having "most indecorously exposed to sale" the books and pamphlets in Windham's house in Pall Mall.

Cecilia Windham did not live at Felbrigg after her husband's death. I am not certain whether she ever went there at all. But from her residences in Bath and elsewhere, until her death in 1824, she kept the affairs of the estate firmly in her hands. Relations between her and the Lukins were not always easy. William Lukin's brother Robert, who lived in London and kept in close touch with Mrs Windham, told him frankly that she had been hurt by the manner and conduct of her eventual successor. "There is clearly a dread of your getting any power," he wrote. "You do so much without power, that with it, there is no knowing what lengths you might go." But on the whole there was good feeling and good sense on both sides, and no lasting disagreement took place.

II

William Lukin was born on 20 October 1768, and first went to sea at the age of thirteen. He had become a Lieutenant by 1793, was in command of the *Hornet* sloop in 1795, and was promoted to Post-Captain in the same year. Shortly afterwards he was given command of the *Thames*, a vessel of thirty-two guns. It has been mentioned that William Windham had always watched over his prospects, and occasionally put in a word for him with the First Lord of the Admiralty. But his successful career in the Navy was due mainly to his own abilities. After the mutiny at Spithead in 1797 the *Thames*, "owing to Captain Lukin's judicious management of her crew," was the first ship that put out to sea after its suppression, although she was bound for the dreaded West Indies station. Later she cruised in the Channel and the Bay of Biscay, and took a number of prizes.

When the war was resumed after the termination of the Peace of Amiens, Lukin commanded several other vessels, and finally the *Mars*, a ship of the line of seventy-four guns. The *Mars* distinguished herself greatly in the action off Rochefort on 25 September 1806, when a squadron of six ships under Sir Samuel Hood attacked a French squadron bound for the West Indies with troops, and captured the four largest troopships. One of these, *L'Infatigable* of forty-four guns, surrendered to the *Mars*, and she played a leading part in securing a second ship, *La Gloire* of forty-six guns.[1]

[1] There is a good deal of correspondence at Felbrigg relating to the share of the prize-money of *La Gloire* to which the *Mars* was entitled. Lukin retained the order-book of *L'Infatigable* and a large number of documents

Two log-books of the *Mars* have survived. The first begins in December 1806, just too late to record this action; but thereafter they provide a continuous narrative of life on board until almost the end of 1809. The principal event recorded in the first volume was the expedition to Copenhagen in the summer and autumn of 1807. It was an act of aggression on a virtually unresisting nation, justifiable perhaps as a strategic precaution, forgotten by most Englishmen today, but vividly remembered by the Danes. A great part of Copenhagen was set on fire, and the Danish fleet was taken over and eventually brought back to England. The log of the *Mars* records the conflagration in the city, the fall of the spire of the great church, and much moving to and fro of prisoners and stores. She was responsible for the provisioning and the escorting to England of the *Fyen*, a Danish ship of seventy-four guns. Captain Lukin brought back with him six small Danish cannon, which bear inscriptions showing that they were cast at the royal foundry in the middle of the eighteenth century. These figure in an early drawing of the Parsonage, and they still remain at Felbrigg.

Next year the *Mars* was in northern waters again, when Sir John Moore was despatched with a large force to Sweden, at this time Britain's sole ally in Europe except for the faithful Portuguese. He made the voyage in the *Mars*, and was landed at Gothenburg on 22 May. But the vagaries of King Gustavus prevented any effective action, and the expedition was withdrawn. Most of the troops were transferred to Spain, where Moore died heroically at Corunna early next year. The *Mars* continued to cruise in the Baltic, in Danish waters, or off the Texel for the rest of the period covered by the log, on one occasion sailing as far as the Gulf of Finland, and only once returning for a period to Spithead.

These logs were kept by the ship's master, and few personal details about William Lukin can be obtained from them. The punishment records suggest that he was a firm but not a harsh disciplinarian. Sometimes months would pass without a single flogging; then there would be several. By far the most frequent offence was drunkenness, sometimes accompanied by riotous conduct, and two or three names reappear several times on this charge. There was a good deal of theft, punished more severely than any offence except the very rare cases of gross insubordination or attempted desertion. There were occasional

captured with her. These have now been transferred to the National Maritime Museum.

charges of insolence, neglect of duty, fighting, uncleanness, bringing spirits into the ship. One feels rather sympathetic towards Francis Carroll, who received eighteen lashes for giving spirits to a prisoner.

During her northward voyages the *Mars* several times passed close to the Norfolk coast; and on 31 July 1807, in squally weather, she anchored within sight of Cromer. A young artist from Norwich, John Sell Cotman, was staying in Cromer that summer, courting Ann Miles, the daughter of a farmer at Felbrigg. It must have been on this occasion that he made one of his finest water-colours, *The Mars off Cromer*, which now forms part of the Colman bequest in the Castle Museum at Norwich. It is a splendid and dramatic drawing, with the *Mars* and other ships close to shore, the beach with its familiar boats, and the sweep of sombre cloud advancing across a clear pale sky. It cannot have been an exact reproduction of the scene: no ship of the line could conceivably have anchored so close inshore, and it is evident from the log that her position that night was some way east of Cromer. But the *Mars* and her captain, no doubt well known to the girl whom Cotman hoped to marry, must have appealed to his imagination, and inspired this superlative drawing.

I am not certain which of the farms in Felbrigg was occupied by the parents of Ann Miles. But on 6th January 1809 she and Cotman were married in Felbrigg Church by Captain Lukin's youngest brother John, by now a clergyman and acting as curate for his father the Dean. One of her sisters married another Norwich artist, John Thirtle. A third married a certain Captain Hicks, the son, I think, of the Ensign Hicks who was mentioned earlier in this book, and therefore a connection of William Windham and Dean Lukin through their mother. Cotman was often again at Felbrigg. He drew the Hall for the *Excursions in Norfolk*, and the brasses in the church for Dawson Turner's *Norfolk Monumental Brasses*. Years later, when touring with Turner in Normandy, he wrote to his wife that he had observed "three pretty farmers' daughters, well dressed and arm-in-arm; and I thought on Felbrigg and old times."

Captain Lukin's last ship was the *Chatham*, of seventy-four guns: and in 1814, when he left the service, he was advanced to the rank of Vice-Admiral. The death of William Windham did not make much immediate difference to his prospects. For some years past he had been looking about for a small estate in Norfolk, where he could retire and farm while awaiting the Felbrigg inheritance. There was much correspondence about neighbouring properties that might be for sale,

Mr Flower's at Sheringham, the widowed Mrs Cremer's at Beeston Regis. In the end he bought some property in Metton which adjoined the Windham estate. It was a step that greatly assisted another plan which he had in contemplation.

In 1812 his father the Dean died at Wells. For almost fifty years Felbrigg Parsonage had been the Lukins' home, linked with the Hall in the closest intimacy. It seemed almost unbearable to the whole family that some strange clergyman should now replace them. Mrs Windham had already presented a successor to the Dean's four livings —Felbrigg, Metton, Aylmerton, Runton. He was the Reverend Geoffrey Hornby, the husband of her niece Georgiana, one of the daughters of John and Bridget Byng. Normally he would have lived at Felbrigg Parsonage, the best of the various houses which went with the livings. But Lukin now offered to improve the old parsonage at Metton to the same standard as that at Felbrigg, provided that Mr Hornby would undertake, on his own behalf and that of his successors, to reside there. He would exchange the Felbrigg glebe for an equivalent acreage of his recently acquired land at Metton. Felbrigg Parsonage would become Felbrigg Cottage; and future incumbents would live at Metton Parsonage, as they do to this day.

Mrs Windham was not enthusiastic about the scheme. She might want to come and live at the Hall one day, and would not care to have her successor watching her every movement from the Cottage a few hundred yards away. Mr Hornby was not enthusiastic either. He would have to live uncomfortably in the parsonage at Aylmerton while the improvements at Metton were going on. But eventually both gave their consent, and the transaction went forward. Mr Hornby proved a watchful and tenacious bargainer. A stream of letters shows that he was determined not to be done down over the smallest detail of the garret windows or the sink in the back kitchen. His tone grew more and more acrimonious: so, no doubt, did the Admiral's. But all was settled at last; and the rector expressed his hope "that every unpleasing remembrance on both sides may be extinguished by the termination of the business which gave rise to them, and that Felbrigg Cottage and Metton Parsonage may not stand and frown at each other."

One note from Mr Hornby to Admiral Lukin, unconnected with their personal differences, is of some interest. A monument to William Windham had been commissioned from Joseph Nollekens, a plain marble sarcophagus on eagles' feet, bearing a long inscription and surmounted by a version of the noble bust which the sculptor had first executed in 1793. Hornby wrote:

A man is come down from Nollekens to put up Mr Windham's monument, which he expects here today. I am desired to consult with you as to the best place in the Chancel for its situation, and shall be obliged to you for your opinion on the subject. It strikes me that it will stand best opposite to the large monument which is at the north side of the Communion Table. I am going down to the Church in ten minutes with the man.

The Admiral evidently agreed with the rector's suggestion. It was, however, a most unfortunate one. The monument was intended to stand in isolation against a plain wall, or else in some alcove specially suited to the purpose. Instead, it was embedded deep in the beautiful medieval sedilia, which it has irreparably ruined.

Time passed, and Admiral Lukin settled down at Felbrigg Cottage, farming his lands and planning the improvements he would make when the whole estate should at last be his own. He could not help being impatient for that day. He was a man full of vigour and enterprise, accustomed to the quick decisions and the constant activity of the quarter-deck. But now he was condemned to vegetate year after year, while all around him the Hall and its gardens, the farms and the woods were subject to the remote control of an elderly lady who never came near them. He was not a rich man, and his family continued to increase. He and Anne Thellusson had thirteen children, only one of whom died in infancy. Six sons and six daughters grew and flourished; and despite his wife's comfortable income, they were a strain on his resources.

Like many families in the same situation, the Lukins decided to economise by travelling abroad. During much of 1820 and 1821 they were living in Brussels. It was probably at this time that the Admiral acquired the sea-piece by Bakhuysen and the three small paintings by Abraham Storck, two Italian harbour-scenes and a picture of shipping, which he later added to the collection at Felbrigg. Various Norfolk friends stayed with them in Brussels from time to time. One of these was a young clergyman named Cremer Cremer, whose home was at Beeston Regis, in the immediate neighbourhood of Felbrigg and close to the sea.

III

My own family, the Cremers, will appear in all the ensuing chapters; and it is necessary that I should give a brief account of their earlier history. Although the name occurs more frequently in the Netherlands than in England, it was in fact developed from the English name of Skryme, which occurs in King's Lynn and its neighbourhood as early as the fourteenth century. During the sixteenth century a yeoman family, described in various records as "Cremer alias Skryme," began to prosper in west Norfolk; and one of its members, John Cremer, became a considerable buyer of land. He and his wife were commemorated, after his death in 1610, by an elaborate brass in Snettisham Church. Its design includes the effigies of his six sons, whom he settled in properties of their own in various parishes south and east of the Wash.

Most of these sons prospered likewise. Their memorials, or those of their descendants, are to be seen in many west Norfolk churches—Ingoldisthorpe, North Runcton, West Winch, Grimston, Fring, both the great churches in King's Lynn. Others, still visible in Blomefield's day, have now disappeared. By the middle of the seventeenth century the family had acquired a modest local position and a coat of arms. Their sympathies during the Civil War and the Commonwealth were strongly Puritan. But they knew how to trim their sails: in fact one of them, a second John Cremer, was High Sheriff of Norfolk both in 1659 and in 1660, and was knighted at the Restoration.

Sir John Cremer's property, and that of his equally wealthy brother George, which lay south of King's Lynn in such parishes as North Runcton and Setch, became the inheritance of the latter's daughter Anne, who married the second Lord Fitzwilliam.[1] The principal remaining Cremer property was now at Ingoldisthorpe in north-west Norfolk; and a younger son of this branch, Francis Cremer, was married in 1714 to Mary, the daughter and heiress of Robert Greene of Beeston Regis, a small estate which adjoined Felbrigg on the north. He settled at Beeston, and henceforward appears now and then in the Felbrigg papers, paying rent for small pieces of land intermixed with his own, playing backgammon with Ashe Windham and sharing with him a special brand of tea.

Francis Cremer and Mary Greene had two daughters. The elder, Mary, married her cousin, Edmund Cremer of Ingoldisthorpe; and he became the owner of Beeston after her death. The younger, Lucy, married Thomas Woodrow, of a yeoman family long established in the

[1] She and her husband are portrayed in the fine statues which form part of their monument by James Fisher in the church of Marholm near Peterborough.

adjoining parish of Runton. Edmund Cremer considerably enlarged the Beeston estate by purchases of land in Runton and Sheringham. As he had no children, he adopted and brought up his great-nephew Cremer Woodrow, the grandson of Thomas Woodrow and Lucy Cremer. Shortly before his death, which occurred in 1786, he arranged that the boy should assume by royal licence the name and arms of Cremer.

I find it difficult to trace the characters of the Cremer family, or of my more direct forebears the Woodrows, who now succeeded them and assumed their name. Sadly little correspondence was preserved at Beeston, and the surviving letters relate mainly to business affairs. But they seem, Cremers and Woodrows alike, to have been quiet country people, good farmers, fond of sport, wholly without pretension or ambition of any kind; content, generation after generation, with their small house, their large garden, their thousand acres or so of farmland and clifftop-grazing and sparsely wooded heath. Their portraits, by Norwich painters such as Heins and Catton, bear out the impression. And we shall see that they altered little in type during the century which lay ahead.

Cremer Woodrow, now Cremer, came of age and into the possession of Beeston in 1789. Glimpses of him occur now and then in letters from the Rev. George William Lukin to his mother in London. Their young neighbour would often ask the Lukin boys to go shooting or coursing with him. He was intending "to make great alterations at Beeston, and I believe settle as they call it—another term for being married." He was married in 1794 to Ann Buckle, the only child of Thrower Buckle of Cringleford, just across the river from Norwich. The Buckles owned land in the Cringleford and Hethersett neighbourhood, and Thrower's younger brother was John Buckle, a merchant who was Mayor of Norwich in 1793, and a leading political supporter of William Windham.

The bride and bridegroom were painted by an unknown artist, small oval portraits showing a burly young man, in black hat and red waistcoat, and a gentle dark-eyed girl. She was destined to live to a great age, indeed into the era of photography; so that a yellowing photograph of the eighteen-sixties shows this nymph of the seventeen-nineties transformed into a most formidable old lady, gazing like an ancient eagle from a complicated apparatus of lace cap and vast gauze hood. But her husband died in 1808 at the age of forty, leaving her with two sons and a daughter, and in not very affluent circumstances.

It has already been mentioned that at this time William Lukin was on the lookout for a convenient small estate. Beeston lay attractively close at hand; and in 1809 he wrote to William Windham:

> I have just been acquainted that Mr Cremer's Estate at Beeston is to be sold, and that Mrs Cremer in whose possession it is at present (the Son not being of age) is desirous *not* to sell it to Mr Hoare who bought Beeston Abbey. . . . No actual *legal* Title to this property can be given during the young man's minority, but ample security can be had for the money advanced, and a promise obtained that the Title shall be made good when he comes of age. . . . I suppose the price that will be asked will rather exceed £24,000.

The suggested sale did not take place, probably owing to Mrs Cremer's reluctance to part with her son's inheritance except in case of absolute necessity. Once or twice during the next few years her laconic diaries record "great anxiety about Beeston." The place had to be let, and she and her children lived—as indeed she had done during part of her married life—in the house at Cringleford which she had inherited from her father. But in 1817 they all moved back to Beeston, a happy event which was marred by the death of the daughter, Ann Lucy, a year later.

The elder son was named Cremer as his father had been; the younger was christened John Buckle; both were sent to Norwich School and then to St John's College, Cambridge; and both entered the Church. Until suitable livings fell vacant, there were plenty of local curacies to be served by active young men who did not mind long rides in all weathers. There was plenty of hunting and shooting also: John, in particular, was an extraordinarily good shot, as the Felbrigg game-books show. On one occasion he killed forty-eight snipe in one day, no mean achievement in the age of muzzle-loaders and black powder.

Beeston was a hospitable house in a hospitable neighbourhood, and Mrs Cremer's diaries record a constant round of visits and tea-drinkings, dinners and an occasional dance. Of all their neighbours, the Lukins at Felbrigg Cottage became their closest friends. The elder Lukin boys were only a few years younger than the two Cremer sons, and they spent much time together, shooting day after day at Felbrigg or Beeston. Mrs Cremer was beloved by the smaller Lukin children, and became almost a second mother to them. It was soon after Cremer's visit to the Lukins in Brussels that the Admiral wrote him a letter which I shall quote almost in full, since it gives so pleasant an impression of his relationship with his young neighbour.

Brussels, November 29th 1820

My dear Cremer

I am very sure you need have no scruples about the little claret, after the numerous and great friendship you and your Mother have shown for my children, but what that d——d blundering fellow Carbonell could mean by sending you the *Receipt* I am at a loss to conjecture, unless it was to show you the unreasonableness of his own price. Of the Trees I beg you will not only take one score but at least 10 score of the largest plants, and there are too I think five score pretty large ash stands six foot high behind the Garden which I beg you will take without scruple as they will suit you. I am greatly pleased to find that you have come to the resolution of planting your Sheringham Heath. It is the best thing that you as a young man can possibly do, it will attach you to the place more than anything and will in the end add to your strength. My natural object as having an eventual stake in the neighbourhood is to keep all my old neighbours together. I really, my dear Cremer, want no man's land; but what I want, though I should not like *publicly* to hold that language, is to keep such men as Hoare away if possible, and there is no reasonable sacrifice that I would not make to effect that object. This you may say savours of feudality, but if it does, it has a due regard to old proprietors and to the names. I like and always have liked what may be termed I hope without arrogance native consequency, and I am always tenacious of its invasion, and hence my dislike of Cromer. There is certainly in the human mind a natural desire to level every body above us to our own standard, coupled as it always is with a proportionate desire of not lowering ourselves or of elevating others up to us; and it is from this natural propensity of our minds that I dislike such men as Hoare and others, under the mask of a watering-place come among us. Enough of this. . . . Brussels is gaiety itself. I am tired to death of it, but Mrs L. and Cecy like it as you well know. Poor little Bob will be eager enough to get to your Mother, and he is so placed now that I have no power other than troubling you with him. I should hope we may get him to Eton at Easter. . . . Be kind enough as a friend to ride over my wheat and see what you think of the plant, and if the quicks you mention *be alive*, which I fear they are not. Openly find fault with it, and give me a line. I wonder how my bullocks look, and sheep? Remember me most kindly to your Mother and John, and believe me

Your sincere friend

W. Lukin.

IV

Cecilia Windham died on 5 May 1824. Her epitaph, on a plain marble tablet above the Nollekens bust of her husband, records that "the affections of her heart shone forth in her manners and conversation: cheerful, courteous, kind, unassuming, liberal, denying herself and living unto God, she cared for others." The little that is known about her, and such of her letters as have survived, give the impression that every word of the epitaph was justified.

She was almost the last of the group of friends who had figured so much in William Windham's early life. John Byng, who had succeeded his brother as the fifth Lord Torrington, died a few months afterwards in 1813. His wife Bridget followed him ten years later. Only George Cholmondeley lived on until 1831. Long before his death he had become a shadow of his former self. On one occasion he had remarked sadly to Glenbervie, "I am in body and mind become like an empty egg-shell."

Admiral Lukin duly assumed the name and arms of Windham, and entered joyfully upon his inheritance. He was now fifty-six years of age, and he lost no time in starting on the alterations and improvements which he had been planning so long. He employed a London architect named W. J. Donthorn, a former pupil of Sir Jeffrey Wyatville, who had a considerable clientèle in East Anglia at this time.[1] Designs were made for a reconstruction of Felbrigg which would almost have doubled the size of the house. The exterior of the south and west fronts, and most of the existing rooms, were to remain unaltered; but a vast north dining-room was planned, and a grandiose double staircase would lead to the first floor with its gallery and its range of new bedrooms. The offices in the east wing were to receive a new front, whose windows and gables would repeat the Jacobean themes of the oldest part of the house. A new stable block was to be built still farther to the east; but here the general aspect was more or less classical, with a screen of Ionic columns.

Fortunately most of this scheme remained in the realm of fantasy. In 1825 the stable block was carried out in red brick, not in a Grecian style but in an unspectacular form of castellated Gothic, with square towers at the four corners, and a simple archway and flanking screens at the entrance. The treatment of the east wing was also greatly modified, and an oddly proportioned but rather attractive jumble of Gothic

[1] Donthorn signed all plans and letters with his initials only, and no one has yet ascertained his Christian names. For his other works see H. M. Colvin, *Dictionary of English Architects*, p. 183; supplemented by A. Paget Baggs, *Norfolk Archaeology*, xxxii. p. 241. Some other houses by Donthorn are discussed by Christopher Hussey in *Country Life* (1958), pp. 714–16.

features was the result. "For the two windows which are two stories high," wrote Donthorn to his clerk of the works Robert Oliver, "I have united the windows and made them into one large one, which is much more in character with the old front and will look much better, so that the upper part will light the bedrooms, and the lower part the passage." The two windows present a very ecclesiastical appearance, and are often mistaken by the uninitiated for the terminal windows of twin chapels. Nothing whatever was done to the interior of the house, which remained as it had been at the close of the eighteenth century. In 1831 a large corridor was added on the north to ensure better access between the kitchen and dining-room—a spacious and airy corridor, but a sad decline from the immense new dining-hall which Donthorn had proposed for that situation.

Evidently the Admiral's funds had proved unequal to his ambitions; and even the building actually undertaken was carried out in a cheap and shoddy manner. The general appearance of the stable block is pleasant enough. It is well designed and well proportioned, and is not out of harmony with the older buildings. But either Mr Oliver was a bad supervisor or the Admiral was over-economical: for the construction of all this work is exceedingly poor—thin walls, weak timbers, "pie-crust battlements." The brickwork of Samwell's west wing, completed in 1686, is still in superb condition, with scarcely a brick or a moulding eroded. The brickwork of Donthorn's stables of 1825 is soft and crumbling; the plaster renderings of the battlements and screens have mostly fallen away; and so have several of the hood-moulds above the windows, which were carried out in inferior Roman cement. But Samwell's wing was not completed until at least ten years after he had made his designs; whereas Donthorn's stables were finished in the year of their inception, and there is evidence in his letters to Oliver that the Admiral was urging him to hurry all the time.

There was much else to be done. The old stables were demolished, and there is now no trace of them among the trees on what is still known as the Stable Hill. The east and west walls enclosing the kitchen garden were rebuilt, and a Latin inscription above the doorway records that this also was done in 1825, by William Windham, *classis praefectus*. There is reason to think that Cecilia Windham had been as good a landlord as an absentee can ever be; nevertheless repairs to farms and cottages were needed all over the estate. But the main reason for the abandonment of Admiral Windham's ambitious plans for the house was the necessity of providing for his large family.

The eldest son, William Howe Windham, would succeed to the estate. Of the others George and Henry were destined for the Navy, Charles for the Army, Robert for the Law, Joseph for the Church. Their establishment in these professions would be an expensive matter. Then there had to be portions for the daughters. In 1825 the eldest, Cecilia Anne, became the second wife of a man much older than herself, a banker and former Member of Parliament named Henry Baring. Next year the second, Maria Augusta, married George Thomas Wyndham of Cromer Hall.

This young man's father, George Wyndham, had died in 1810. When he and Maria Lukin first became engaged they were both nineteen. It was love at first sight, for Cromer Hall had been let for years, and George and his sisters had lived elsewhere. He was revisiting his Norfolk home and was invited to Felbrigg Cottage. His guardians vehemently objected to his marriage at this early age, and on so short an acquaintance, to one of the many daughters of a retired Admiral. They petitioned the Lord Chancellor, pointing out that George was heir not only to the Cromer estate but to large properties in other counties, whereas Maria "had small fortune, and that only at her mother's death." So the marriage was forbidden, and the lovers were directed not to meet or correspond. In 1826 George Wyndham came of age; Maria's prospects had improved through her father's succession to Felbrigg; and they were duly married. They at once instructed Donthorn to rebuild Cromer Hall in the most baronial Gothic manner. Two months after completion it was burned to the ground. He was then ordered to rebuild it all over again; and so it remains to this day.

V

In 1818 the Rev. Geoffrey Hornby had accepted preferment elsewhere, and Mrs Windham appointed to his livings a young clergyman named Philip Hudson. He died early and unexpectedly in the autumn of 1826. Shortly afterwards the diary of Mrs Cremer of Beeston Regis contains the entry: "Confabulation with the Admiral." The outcome of this confabulation was an offer by the Admiral to her elder son of the same livings, Felbrigg with Metton and Aylmerton with Runton.

The offer was not unconditional. The Admiral had a sister who was married to a clergyman named Berry, and who at once demanded this piece of preferment for her husband. But he did not want the Berrys so close at hand. By one of those tacit and somewhat simoniacal understandings which were not infrequent at the time, he offered the livings to Mrs Cremer for her son on condition that the sum of £200 a year was paid to Mrs Berry. It is clear from his letter of confirmation that no other conditions were attached. I must quote this letter in full, since the Admiral's sons later maintained that Cremer had promised to resign the livings if one of them should decide to take orders.

January 12th 1827

My dear Mrs Cremer,

I enclose to you *open* my offer of the Livings to Cremer, of course without any stipulation or condition whatever, the understanding between you and I remaining unaltered, namely that *you* pay to my sister Mrs Sarah Berry two hundred Pounds annually so long as Cremer holds the Livings. Previous to the Presentation this little agreement between you and I should not be mentioned, and even afterwards it should be kept generally as secret as possible, for I have agreed personally to pay my sister the £200 a year without mentioning even your name, but subsequently and after the induction and taking possession, there will I find upon enquiry be no kind of harm in your mentioning it to Cremer, and of making such an arrangement with him as you may think proper. For all reasons I make you the Bearer of this pleasing intelligence to your Son, which gives me as much satisfaction as I hope it will both to you and him.

Believe me
My dear Mrs Cremer
Ever most truly
W. Windham.

It was not perhaps a very happy arrangement, but I cannot blame my great-great-grandmother for accepting it on her son's behalf. The advowson of Beeston did not belong to the Cremers, but was in the gift of the Duchy of Lancaster. Should the living fall vacant, there was no certainty that the Duchy would bestow it upon one of the family. Cremer had now reached the age of thirty, and had spent the summer of 1826 travelling in France and Switzerland. It was high time for him to settle down as soon as an adequate living should come his way. The Admiral's offer ensured him financial independence, a charming house in a pleasant village near his own home, and constant association with a family who had been his close friends since boyhood.

So he gladly accepted it, and next year was inducted into his livings and installed at Metton Parsonage. He did not remain there long alone. On 22 July 1829 he was married to Marianne Charlotte Wyndham, the eldest of the four sisters of the young owner of Cromer Hall. She was a woman of charm and character, and their marriage had every promise of happiness.

VI

I can say little about the remaining years of Admiral Windham's life. Few of his letters have survived, and he took little part in public or indeed local affairs. He carried on the Whig traditions of Felbrigg, but left active politics to his eldest son, and occupied himself entirely with the business of his estate. He was a genial and kindly man, and things went happily at Felbrigg during the nine years of his ownership. He died on 12 January 1833, at the age of sixty-four.

Chapter Twelve

WILLIAM HOWE WINDHAM

William Howe Windham's education and Grand Tour—love of farming and shooting—M.P. for East Norfolk—succeeds to the estate in 1833—quarrels with the Rev. Cremer Cremer—their reconciliation—Windham's application for a peerage—his activities at Felbrigg—his wife and son—his death in 1854—his brother General Charles Windham

I

THE eldest son of Admiral Lukin was born in London on 30 March 1802. He was named William Howe after his two distinguished godfathers, William Windham, the statesman, and Viscount Howe—not the famous Admiral under whom Lukin had served and who was now dead, but his younger brother the General. He was educated first at Norwich Grammar School under Dr Valpy, and later at Eton. In 1819 he was admitted a pensioner of Trinity College, Cambridge, and matriculated there in 1820. But he never cared much for books, and remained essentially a man of the open air all his life. Farming was his main interest, and shooting his favourite sport, from boyhood onwards.

These tastes are evident throughout his journal of the Grand Tour which he undertook, dutifully rather than enthusiastically, between September 1824 and April 1825. He was accompanied on his travels by George Wyndham of Cromer, who was engaged to be married to his sister Maria as soon as he came of age. They made the conventional round—Paris, Geneva, Milan, Venice, Florence, Rome, Naples, and so home once more. William Windham—he had ceased to be William Lukin earlier the same year—was an industrious sightseer, and filled his pocket-book with respectful comments on paintings and statues, churches and ruins, the ballet and the opera. He commented too, less respectfully, on the people: the inhabitants of Geneva were "a civil industrious set of fellows, not at all like the French"; "what would the old Romans think of the present generation, if they could see them?"

But at heart he was less interested in works of art and the Roman populace than in the crops, the oxen, the pheasant he flushed out of some wheat beside Lake Como, "which I flatter myself I could have killed."

Indeed his thoughts were constantly harking back to Norfolk. He was not impressed by his first sight of the Jura mountains—"they appeared about three times as high as Cromer Lighthouse cliffs"; and he felt no more sense of danger when traversing the mountain roads "than in going down Cromer Gangway." Most of his observations have the same down-to-earth quality. Nôtre Dame was "a very moderate Church for so large a Capital." Venice was "indeed a most curious and interesting town—you never see anything like it in other countries." St Mark's had "nothing inside particular except the gilding and precious stones." There must have been many travellers down the centuries who carried out their Grand Tour in just the same spirit, prosaic young gentlemen longing to return to their familiar acres under the cloudy skies of England.

Once back in Norfolk he resumed his accustomed life, farming the entire area of land within the park, helping his father in the management of the estate, and from the first of September until the first of February shooting day after day. From 1825 onwards the game-books are in his hand, and it is fascinating to compare them with the records of more recent times. The corn was still reaped by hand with sickles, and the knee-high stubbles afforded ideal cover for partridges, very different from the shaven fields of today. In consequence the annual bag of partridges was far larger than that of pheasants, for which in any case there was then less woodland cover. The number of hares shot is by modern standards quite extraordinary. Rabbits were substantially fewer. The annual total of all game averaged 3000 head, and seldom fell below 2000. The memorable year 1827 produced a bag of 4708 head, which remained unbeaten until 1834, when the estate record of 5383 was achieved. In 1842, 1846, 1852, and 1853 the bag exceeded 4000, but 5000 was never reached again.

The game-books are full of Windham's comments about rearing, poachers, harvests, gales, snowfalls, and the chance happenings of the day. "I never shot so well in my life—I killed seven double shots." "I believe the tenants killed as many hares coursing as I did shooting." "Billy Lines in shooting a rat in the fence stupidly shot off the tail of Simpson's favourite bitch." On one occasion he recorded in his own game-book an outstanding day with Lord Hastings in Swanton Wood, when a party shot 93 woodcock, and had killed 70 during the two previous days. I have already mentioned the Rev. John Cremer's bag of forty-eight snipe to his own gun. Another exploit worthy of remark was when "Charles Mills killed 2 woodpigeons at one shot *from his horse*, flying over his head, there being but two birds."

Meanwhile in the political world the battle for parliamentary reform raged furiously; and in 1832 it ended in victory. The Reform Act abolished one of Norfolk's pocket-boroughs, Castle Rising, and in place of it the county received two additional representatives. It was divided into two constituencies, Eastern and Western Norfolk, which were to return two members apiece. The Western division was safe for the Whigs, largely owing to the influence and prestige of Thomas William Coke, who now withdrew from Parliament after representing the county for more than half a century. The future of the Eastern division was less certain. It contained a number of influential Tory landowners, and the Reform Act was not universally welcomed even by the more cautious Whigs. Moreover the expense of a contested election was still considerable, even though much had been done under the Act to reduce it.

One Whig candidate, the Hon. George Keppel, was already in the field; but there was difficulty, and even some disagreement, in selecting his colleague. Finally William Windham was suggested. Locally his name bore honoured political associations; and although his friend and neighbour, that very ardent reformer the third Lord Suffield, doubted at first whether his views on certain points were quite as strong as might be wished, he was approached and agreed to stand. While anxious not to lose Suffield's support, he made it clear to him that "I am not disposed to shape my political conduct by the rules suggested by any person." He maintained this attitude of independence throughout the election, which took place in December 1832. The tide of feeling proved to be running strongly in favour of the Whigs all over the country; and Windham and Keppel beat the Tory candidates by a comfortable majority. The figures were:

William Howe Windham	3304
Hon. George Keppel	3261
Nathaniel William Peach	2960
Lord Henry Cholmondeley	2852

In those days of comparatively small electorates, when canvassing was forcefully conducted and voting took place in public, it was sometimes possible to forecast the outcome of an election with an accuracy that seems almost uncanny. The day before the contest, Windham wrote on a desk in one of the polling-stations his own computation of the result. His guesses were incredibly close: he was within thirty-four votes of his own total, and within ten of Peach's. The poll-clerk afterwards cut the piece of wood out of the desk and sent it to him as a memento. It still survives, an odd little relic of the first Reform Parliament.

In 1833 his father the Admiral died, and he entered into possession of the estate, which was henceforward the great preoccupation of his life. He was a vigorous and progressive landlord, tireless in looking after his property and always ready to seize any opportunity of enlarging it. Holkham was his model, in efficiency if not in acreage; and he was especially keen on bringing his farm-buildings up to date. From this time until his death in 1854 his building activities are marked by small stone tablets bearing his initials and the date of the work. These tablets appear all over his neighbourhood, and in scattered villages miles from Felbrigg where he owned a manor or perhaps a single farm. They are to be seen on farmhouses, cottages, barns, cartsheds, cowhouses, every sort of building. Even the rebuilding of a gable-end, or the addition of a few pigsties, would be commemorated in this way. They form an interesting record of an "improving landlord" who would be otherwise forgotten.

His Parliamentary life was brief—indeed it lasted barely two years. After the successive resignations in 1834 of two Prime Ministers, Lord Grey and Lord Melbourne, the King asked Sir Robert Peel to form a Government. A general election was held in January 1835; and although Peel did not secure a majority, and Melbourne returned to office shortly afterwards, there was a considerable reaction from the Whig triumph of 1832. Among the seats which changed their allegiance was East Norfolk. Windham and a new Whig candidate, Richard Hanbury Gurney, were defeated by two Tories, Edmond Wodehouse and Lord Walpole.

A few months later Windham married Lady Sophia Hervey. She was the youngest daughter of the first Marquess of Bristol; and the granddaughter of the "Earl-Bishop," Frederick Earl of Bristol and Bishop of Derry, the easy-going prelate who attained such celebrity as a builder, collector, and traveller, and whose name is still recalled by many a Hôtel Bristol in the cities of Europe. They had only one child, a son who was born on 9 August 1840. He was christened William

Frederick, but from his earliest years they always called him by the pet name of "Gla." It became evident before long that "Gla" was a very odd and unaccountable little boy.

II

In the meantime all had gone prosperously with the Cremers at Metton Parsonage. Children were born, Maria Ann in 1832, Thomas Wyndham in 1834: eventually their family consisted of three sons and three daughters. They were on the happiest terms with the Admiral until his death, with William Windham and Lady Sophia, whom Marianne pronounced "a most exceedingly agreeable person," and with all the Windham brothers and sisters.

Their only sorrow was the death in 1830 of Marianne Cremer's brother George Wyndham. He was only twenty-four when some mysterious wasting illness attacked him; and he died within a few weeks, leaving a young family, a son and two daughters. In the last days of his life, days of pain and delirium, he learnt that he had inherited a large property, Gayhurst in Buckinghamshire, through the death of an elderly cousin named Miss Barbara Wrighte. More will be said about Gayhurst presently, and the vexation that it brought into the family. The year after George Wyndham's death his widow—who was, it will be remembered, Maria Lukin (later Windham) of Felbrigg—married a second husband, Viscount Ennismore, son and heir of the first Earl of Listowel.

The tranquillity of Metton Parsonage was soon to be sadly broken. In 1836 and 1837 two separate storms blew up, which led to a complete breach of friendship between the Cremers and the Windhams for years to come. Family rows make unhappy reading, and I shall describe these as briefly and impartially as I can.

The Admiral's third son, Robert Courtenay Windham, was intended for the Law; but after giving that profession a very short trial he decided to become a clergyman instead. His eldest brother thereupon maintained that their father, the Admiral, appointed Cremer to the livings solely on the understanding that he would vacate them if any of his younger sons should enter the Church. It is perfectly clear, from the letter printed in the last chapter, that no such condition was attached to the Admiral's offer. Nevertheless Cremer felt he ought to relinquish the livings as soon as he could be sure of obtaining some equivalent preferment elsewhere. There were livings attached to the Gayhurst property, and Lady Ennismore assured Marianne that her husband would have the first offer of any of these when they fell vacant; or, if he preferred to remain at Metton, as she felt he was fully entitled to do, she would offer them to her brother Robert.

In 1835, however, the aged incumbent of Beeston Regis died; and Cremer told Windham that he would vacate the livings if he were appointed to Beeston, which was in the gift of the Duchy of Lancaster. Windham went up to London and saw Lord Holland, the Chancellor of the Duchy, who referred him to Thomas William Coke, still indefatigably looking after Norfolk affairs although now retired from Parliament. Owing to some misunderstanding Coke was not told that Cremer intended to resign his present livings, and formed the impression that he was a pluralist seeking to extend his preferment still further. He therefore nominated a Mr Langton to Beeston.

Cremer at once drove over to Holkham and explained the whole situation to Coke, who "received me very kindly" but could not cancel the presentation of the living to Mr Langton. In consequence he refused for the present to vacate the Felbrigg livings. As a man with a young and increasing family, he could not afford to do otherwise. But Windham and his younger brother Charles, a hot-headed young soldier, tried to exert pressure upon him. Tempers were lost on both sides. Angry interviews took place, followed up by even angrier letters. Windham asserted that as the result of his efforts to serve Cremer he had quarrelled with Mr Coke, "one of my father's oldest and best friends." Charles, in nine closely written pages, justified his conduct during an altercation at Metton in which Cremer may well have been extremely provoking, but he himself had descended to unworthy threats and abuse. Cremer described this letter as "in its general tone and language in the highest degree insulting."

It was a wretched quarrel between old friends. At the height of his indignation Charles still spoke of the Cremers as "a family from whom I have always received the greatest kindness." John Cremer tried to make peace, and Windham thanked him for "the friendly manner in which you have acted throughout the whole transaction." The eldest Windham sister, Mrs Henry Baring, and her kindly husband, who had lived at Cromer Hall since George Wyndham's death, wrote to lament "the circumstances which have so unfortunately arisen to separate the Felbrigg family and yours." But it is hard to recall words spoken in anger; and bitterness remained on both sides long after the situation about the livings had been resolved.

Mr Langton's incumbency at Beeston Regis lasted little more than a year. He resigned in the autumn of 1837, and this time the Duchy of Lancaster appointed Cremer to the living. He vacated his Felbrigg preferments in favour of Robert Windham, and settled at Beeston Hall for the remainder of his life. Even before he left Metton Parsonage, however, the second storm had broken.

In April 1837 little George Wyndham, the heir to Cromer Hall and to Gayhurst, died at the age of nine. There had been no reason to anticipate his death; but it had always been known to Marianne Cremer and her three sisters that Gayhurst was entailed upon them in default of the male line. It will be remembered that the elder George Wyndham had become owner of Gayhurst, through the death of his cousin Miss Wrighte, only a few days before his own death, and at a time when he was desperately ill. Nevertheless, it was now revealed that during these few days a document had been drawn up and supposedly signed by him, cutting off the entail, and thus depriving his sisters of the property in favour of his wife and daughters. It was doubtful whether he had the legal right to take any such step. It was even more doubtful whether, "whilst in a state of morbid insensibility and opium," he had the slightest idea of the nature of the document he was signing. It was more than suspected that his wife and her brother William Windham were jointly responsible for what had been done. Suspicion becomes certainty when one reads a significant letter from Windham to Lady Ennismore during a quarrel between them many years later. He analysed her conduct throughout her early years and during her marriage to George Wyndham, and continued:

> We now come to the Gayhurst business, of which I say nothing; it speaks for itself; except that upon my honour I have never ceased regretting that I was the cause that prevented that property going to his sisters, with whom at least but on this account I should have been good friends.

Such remorse, however, lay in the future. In 1837 the husbands of the four sisters did what they could to assert the claims of their wives to the Gayhurst property. They gathered much distressing evidence about George Wyndham's condition during his last days, took the opinion of Counsel, prepared what must certainly have seemed a formidable case. But none of them were rich men, whereas Lady Ennismore and her brother commanded wealth and influence. They could not face the uncertainties of an expensive lawsuit, and were obliged to submit to the injustice and chicanery that had been practised.

But the affair completed the severance between Felbrigg and Beeston. Marianne Cremer wrote to a sister in Kent: "I am so disgusted with Cromer and Felbrigg, and all belonging to both places, that I heartily wish I did not live in Norfolk"; and then, remembering that she was a true Wyndham, "What a shameful and wicked persecution we have suffered from the *Lukins*!"

Marianne Cremer died only five years later, at the end of 1842, suddenly and unexpectedly in her thirty-ninth year. Her husband was left with their six young children, "too young," in the words of her epitaph at Beeston, "fully to understand the irreparable loss they have sustained." He lived on sadly at Beeston, occupied with his parish, his farming, and his books—for he was a great reader, and amassed a considerable library. His mother looked after the household, and continued indomitably at the head of affairs until far into her eighties.

Gradually the old resentments died away; and shortly before the Christmas of 1847 he and William Windham met by chance and exchanged some friendly words. On Christmas morning he wrote the following note and sent a servant with it to Felbrigg.

Dear Sir

Perhaps you will permit me to express how much surprised and gratified I was at the manner in which I was met on Wednesday evening by you and Lady Sophia Windham. I can say with truth that my feelings towards you have been much changed for a length of time. I find now that, however fixed and certain my own impressions were on the unhappy subject of dispute between us, I must have been sadly wanting in Christian forbearance, when I was unwilling to admit that your view of the case might be founded on what you believed to be just and right. Not to dwell longer on a subject, that I never think of without pain, I will only add that if you are able sometimes to look over our wretched years of bitterness to those happy times, when we cordially wished well to each other, it will be very gratifying to me. At any rate I feel confident that you are much too open and candid a man, to address me in a friendly tone, if you still harboured feelings of enmity or ill will. And it is with much sincerity I hope you believe me to be

Dear Sir
Truly yours
Cremer Cremer.

Windham sent back the following note in return:

Dear Mr Cremer

I assure you I am much gratified with your letter. No one more regrets than myself the unhappy differences that arose between two friends; and I fully admit with you there were faults on both sides, and with this admission I am certain that our best course is to forget and to forgive, and this I hope has been and will be my motto.

Pray therefore for the future let us meet as if nothing unpleasant had ever passed between us; and with my kindest regards to your mother, towards whom I ever have felt and shall feel the warmest gratitude from past remembrances,

Believe me
My dear Mr Cremer
Very sincerely yours
W. H. Windham.

III

In 1837, at the accession of Queen Victoria, Parliament was dissolved. William Windham stood once again for East Norfolk; and once again he and his Whig colleague were defeated by the two Tory candidates. Marianne Cremer wrote to her sister—unkindly perhaps, but it was at the height of the bitter dispute over Gayhurst—that "poor Lady Sophia fainted when told her husband had lost the election. She said to a person we know, she had no idea he was so unpopular a man, and had such a bad name. She has learned truths which she never expected to hear during her canvass." However that may have been, Windham decided that he had spent enough money in trying to get back into Parliament, and asked Lord Melbourne for a peerage instead. The draft of his letter has been preserved.

My dear Lord

I have long been on the point of writing to your Lordship to beg you would be good enough to take into consideration my claims for a peerage at the approaching Coronation. I have been very reluctant to obtrude myself upon you, but have been so strongly urged by my friends that I feel I should not be acting justly towards myself did I any longer refrain from stating the nature of them. Upon family grounds, I need not remind you that my late uncle was twice offered a peerage. If he had accepted it my father would have of course succeeded to the title.[1] For myself, during the short period of five years that I have been in possession of my property, I have fought three successive contests for the representation of East Norfolk, which have cost me upwards of £15,000; and I regret to say, anxious as I am to support the principles of your Lordship's administration, I see but little prospect of anyone

[1] This was not true, as Lord Melbourne would have known perfectly well —unless, of course, the peerage had been created with a special remainder to Admiral Lukin.

of my politics succeeding in this division of the county. Under these circumstances I venture to make this application in the hope it will be favourably considered, and most willingly leave my case in your hands.

Lord Melbourne replied on 31 May 1838:

My dear Sir,

I beg leave to acknowledge your letter of yesterday. You know very well the respect which I feel for the memory of your uncle, and that I should be most happy to render any service to any of his connections. But when you recollect the limits within which my creation of Peers must necessarily be confined, you will not, I feel certain, be surprised at hearing from me that the various considerations, which I have to take into account, do not allow me to include your name amongst the few, whom it will be in my power to recommend to her Majesty.

Believe me,
My dear Sir,
Yours faithfully,
Melbourne.

This letter was accompanied by an informal note from Lord Melbourne's secretary, Mr Anson, to Lady Sophia.

If Mr Windham could conceive half the difficulties by which Lord Melbourne is surrounded, he would not be surprised at the conclusion which Lord M. is obliged to arrive at. There are above 100 applicants, and at the last two Coronations only 15 were created, including Irish and Scotch. When Mr Windham knows those who are made I do not think he will have any reason to feel aggrieved.

One of the new peers, incidentally, was the veteran Thomas William Coke, who became the first Earl of Leicester of the second creation.

With no further hopes of a seat in either House of Parliament, Windham turned to the further improvement and enlargement of his estate. He continued to drain, to plant, to erect new buildings on his farms. In 1841 he built new lodges in the Jacobean style, with direct references to the gables and chimneys of the Hall, at the three main entrances to the park. His architects were the Buckler brothers, and their name appears on a tablet over the fireplace in one of the Cromer lodges, which also states that 1841 was "the wettest season ever remembered—it rained from Midsummer till Christmas."

In 1845 he made the largest of all his acquisitions of land. To the south of Felbrigg, and intermixed with the property at many points, lay the Hanworth estate of some 1500 acres. For centuries the Doughty family had lived in its mellow red-brick Hall, and Windham's grandmother, the wife of the Dean, had been a daughter of the house. Hanworth now came into the market, and Windham bought the entire property for £65,000. It was a perfectly reasonable price; nevertheless its payment was a heavy additional charge on an estate already burdened by Windham's earlier purchases of land, his buildings, his election expenses, and the claims of his numerous brothers and sisters.

His vast expenditure on the estate, and the formidable mortgages which made it possible, prevented Windham from altering the house as he might otherwise have wished to do. There is reason to suppose that at one time he had thoughts of a complete Gothic refacing, complete with battlements, ogee windows, and arrow-slits, of the south and west fronts. He did, however, redecorate the interior of the Great Hall in a neo-Jacobean style, with over-elaborate spiky door-cases, a cornice of alternating masks and fleurs-de-lis, and a ceiling with huge bulbous pendants. At the same time the upper portions of the windows were filled with a remarkable assemblage of stained glass. I do not know who provided this glass, any more than I know who designed the neo-Jacobean features of the room. The well-known Norwich importer of ancient foreign glass, John Christopher Hampp, had been dead for some years; but some of it may have come from his stock. There are six panels of early seventeenth-century Swiss glass, exquisite in detail and colouring; several Flemish roundels in yellow stain; a quantity of Dutch and German armorial glass; two fifteenth-century French figures of angels; and a great variety of interesting oddments.

There are also several copies of panels in the great east window of St Peter Mancroft in Norwich. These were the work of John Dixon, an early nineteenth-century glass-painter and one of the Mancroft churchwardens. In 1837 Dixon executed a large figure of St Peter, which was inserted in the midst of the superb fifteenth-century glass in the east window. Several panels of the original work were removed to make way for this figure, and Dixon was presumably allowed to retain and dispose of them. At least three of these, and possibly five, found their way to Felbrigg together with Dixon's copies. It is a curious illustration of the indifference of that age to the value and excellence of genuine medieval glass.[1]

[1] Christopher Woodforde, *Medieval Glass of St Peter Mancroft* (1935), *passim*. Three of the five medieval panels at Felbrigg unquestionably came from St Peter Mancroft. The other two, although contemporary with them, cannot be related to any series of panels now surviving at Mancroft.

Windham added no pictures to the house, apart from his portrait, and those of his wife and child, by an unexciting painter named West. But he bought the noble and "heroic" bust of Napoleon by Canova, which in his day was regarded as the supreme artistic treasure of the house. He bought also the busts of the Duke of Wellington by Chantrey and of Sir Robert Peel by Bien-Aimé. I believe that the Nollekens busts of Fox and Pitt were of his purchasing, and had not, as one might have supposed, descended to him from William Windham the statesman, who had known them both so well. And I suspect that certain pieces of fine French furniture, and especially the Boulle cabinets and writing-tables, were his acquisitions likewise.

Only the library slumbered in his day, if we are to believe Charles Greville the diarist. Greville was a friend and correspondent of his eldest sister Mrs Baring, who still lived at Cromer Hall, and continued to do so after her husband's death in 1848. He sometimes stayed both there and at Felbrigg, and his name appears occasionally in the lists of guns in the Felbrigg game-books. In November 1842 he described a visit to Cromer in his journal.

> I am fond of that wild and bleak coast with its "hills that encircle the sea," the fine old tower of the church, and its lighthouse, whose revolving light it is impossible not to watch with interest. I went one day to Felbrigg, and looked into the library—a fine old-fashioned room containing Mr Windham's books, all full of notes and comments in his own hand, but library and books equally neglected now that they have fallen into the hands of a rough, unlettered squire.

IV

Rough and unlettered though Greville may have found him, "Old Squire Windham" was a potent figure in his day. I myself have talked with old men and women who could just remember him. My father's father knew him well, and many stories about him passed into family tradition. After the reconciliation in 1847 friendly relations between the Windhams and the Cremers were resumed; and my grandfather Thomas Wyndham Cremer was welcomed at Felbrigg both as a boy and a young man, since he was only six years older than "Gla," the strange little son of the house.

My grandfather remembered the old Squire as excitable and hot-tempered, and as having quarrelled with most of his relations. It was for this reason, apparently, that he pulled down the charming Parsonage or Cottage, which had been the happy home of earlier generations of his family. If it was demolished, he argued, none of his brothers and sisters could plague him by wanting to come and live in it. So down it came; and it is only just possible to descry in the grass the place where it once stood.

The little family—the Squire, Lady Sophia, and "Gla"—withdrew very much into themselves. "Gla" was extremely backward, could not learn to read or write for years, displayed an ungovernable temper, and was a very spoiled child indeed. He spent much of his time in the servants' hall, and was given a little suit of livery—blue coat, red waistcoat, red plush breeches—in which he waited at table. He helped to carry the food into the dining-room, and would return to the servants in the pantry afterwards. "Poor little fellow," his father used to say, "let him amuse himself; he has no playfellows." Dear old Mrs Martin, the cook and housekeeper, would be called up presently to make a fourth at whist. Many of the details of young Windham's childhood can be learnt from the evidence, kindly but not uncritical, which Mrs Martin gave later at the inquiry into his mental state. She loved the boy: she did not believe he was insane; but she clearly did not approve of the way in which his parents had brought him up.

Many of the boy's stranger habits reflected the habits of his father. Several witnesses at the inquiry, his servants and workmen, described how the old Squire would whistle and sing about the house, how he would shout and halloo when alone in the parlour, how he would fly into uncontrollable fits of rage. "I saw little difference between the way young Mr Windham went on," said Mrs Martin, "and the ordinary demeanour of his father in the house; both made a good deal of noise, and noise of the same kind—laughing, singing and whistling." Lady Sophia, according to another witness and a good deal of independent evidence besides, was also "an excitable person."

It was, in fact, a somewhat eccentric household; but outwardly all seemed well. The farming went on, the shooting went on, the estate flourished, the mortgages would be paid off one day, the Squire had all the reins in his hand and was in absolute control. Then suddenly at the end of 1854, after a few weeks of illness, this stalwart and active man died at the age of fifty-two.

"I can hardly realize the idea of Felbrigg without him," wrote his soldier brother Charles, amidst the frost and snow of the heights above Sebastopol. Charles Windham was as impetuous and hot-tempered as when he had hectored my great-grandfather at Metton Parsonage almost twenty years before; but disappointment in his profession had now added a sour edge to his hasty tongue. For twenty-nine years he had served Her Majesty for nothing; he was still only a Lieutenant-Colonel; he could not be said to be a lucky man. Such was the burden of his letters from the Crimea, and of the diary he kept there. In the Crimea, during that ghastly winter, there was plenty of scope for his acrid pen. The Generals were "a set of do-nothings," the Staff were "muddling muffs," many of the senior officers were "enough to frighten horses from their oats." Palmerston back at home was "an old petrified dandy." But Charles Windham, unlike most grumblers, was a very fine soldier. He was brave, resourceful, tireless in caring for the welfare of his men. Next year his opportunity came. He was chosen to lead the famous assault on the Redan on 8 September 1855. He behaved with extraordinary courage and coolness, in the face of what seemed almost the certainty of death. Although the Redan was not carried, his conduct throughout the action caught the public imagination, and converted this obscure and resentful man into a national hero.

He returned to England at the end of the war, a Major-General and "Redan Windham" to his countrymen, and the most illustrious member of his family. His two surviving elder brothers were not married. Robert was the rector of Felbrigg; Henry had a post in the coastguard service, was known as Captain Windham, and lived in Cromer. Charles, together with Lady Sophia, had been appointed guardian of the young William Windham; and in the event of the boy's death, he or his sons would succeed to the estate. In 1857, at the time of the Mutiny, he was sent to India; and his nephew was deprived of his influence and guidance, which might conceivably have averted the disasters that lay ahead.

Chapter Thirteen

WILLIAM FREDERICK WINDHAM

The childhood and schooldays of "Mad Windham"—his extravagances as a young man—his marriage to Agnes Willoughby—General Windham sets on foot the commission De Lunatico Inquirendo—the inquiry and its outcome—Windham's subsequent history—his sale of Felbrigg—his death in 1866

I

SOMETHING has already been said about the peculiarities displayed by William Frederick Windham as a child, and the haphazard and eccentric way in which he was brought up by his parents. His oddities in no way diminished as he grew older. As soon as he came of age, his relations instituted a judicial inquiry into his state of mind. This inquiry was conducted at enormous length, and with the utmost scandal and publicity. Day after day eminent lawyers dissected the life of this unhappy boy, and fought tooth and nail over each incident of his twenty-one years, no matter how trivial or how squalid. This chapter is largely based on the printed records of the inquiry. It has necessarily been much summarised, since the inquiry lasted for no fewer than thirty-four days; but I have done my best to construct, out of the wildly conflicting accounts of innumerable witnesses, an impartial record of the career of "Mad Windham."

II

At the time of his father's death William Frederick Windham was a boy of fourteen. Under the will his guardians were his mother and his uncle General Windham. When the General was ordered out to India, it was thought advisable to make William a Ward of Chancery, and to add his uncles Lord Alfred Hervey and Captain Henry Windham to the number of his guardians. Captain Windham, it may be remembered, held a post in the coastguard service and lived at Cromer; so it was found convenient that he should become receiver of the rents of the estate.

Young Windham was first sent at the age of eight to a small preparatory school kept by the Rev. Mr Bickmore at Hethel Hall near Norwich. Of all those who played some part at various times in his education, Mr and Mrs Bickmore, and a nursery governess called Miss Rauschen, were virtually the only people who felt able to give evidence on his behalf at the inquiry. He was obviously not their favourite pupil: they remembered him as rude, boisterous, and slovenly; but they believed him to be sane. His other tutors and schoolmasters, a large and exasperated band, could do nothing with him, and gave formidable evidence in support of those who sought to establish his lunacy.

He was next entrusted to a private tutor, the Rev. H. J. Cheales, who accompanied him when he went to Eton early in 1854, and returned to Felbrigg with him in the holidays. Mr Cheales gave striking evidence at the inquiry; and I have also, through the kindness of a friend, been enabled to read a series of extracts from his private diary which relate to Windham. It is a rather horrifying document, with its alternations of rebuke, chastisement and prayer. Yet what was Mr Cheales, or any other man, to do with a boy who would not work, who was habitually disobedient and untruthful, who laughed and yelled and screamed incessantly, whose language was filthy and profane, who ate voraciously, who blubbered like a child, and who never washed? Much of Mr Cheales's evidence was confirmed at the inquiry by Mr Hale, Windham's official tutor at Eton, who said that during his years there "he had never had a boy so low mentally, or so odd in his habits . . . he was looked upon by the boys as a buffoon, and he was generally called by them 'Mad Windham'."

Lady Sophia removed her son from Eton in 1857, but she failed to give him a satisfactory home background. Like many widows of ample means, she preferred the society of watering-places to an uneventful life in the country, and spent the greater part of her time at Torquay. Early in 1858 she became infatuated with a man half her age, the son of an Italian opera-singer named Giubilei, and presently married him, to the extreme displeasure of her relations. William was handed over to a succession of tutors appointed by the Court of Chancery. They travelled with him in Scotland, Ireland, and Switzerland. They accompanied him during long visits to Felbrigg and periods of residence in London and elsewhere. They were unable to teach him much, but kept him out of trouble as best they could. It was an aimless and desultory sort of existence; and they may have been, as was suggested by one of the counsel at the inquiry, a set of second-rate men. In any case their evidence was uniformly adverse to their former pupil. According to them, his manners and conduct were as uncouth as when he was a schoolboy, and his habits as unpleasant.

There can be no doubt at all that Windham's mental powers were well below the average. It was agreed, even by those who firmly upheld his sanity, that he was backward and weak-willed to an exceptional degree. For such a boy the circumstances of his upbringing could not have been less helpful. He was devoted to his mother, and he was very fond of the open-air life at Felbrigg. If they could have lived quietly there, among old servants and humdrum neighbours, his vagaries might have been held in check. But it was not to be. Lady Sophia remained at Torquay with her young Italian. His relations, Windhams and Herveys alike, seldom asked him to their houses or bothered with him in any way. He was indeed a most difficult guest. According to the tutors, his behaviour at evening parties and similar occasions was quite unpredictable. He might shout with unmeaning laughter, or imitate cats fighting, or burst into tears, or get pitifully drunk. "Take away this disagreeable boy," the indignant mothers of young girls would exclaim.

By preference he sought his amusements elsewhere. As he grew towards manhood, his tutors found it difficult to restrain him from doing very much as he wished; and the last of them, Mr Peatfield, who was appointed in June 1860, seems to have had little control over him at any time. He developed a passion for trains and everything connected with them. Occasionally he prevailed upon engine-drivers, strictly against the rules, to allow him to drive; and he became extremely proud of this accomplishment. But he was equally happy when acting as guard, ticket-collector, sorter of parcels, or porter. He obtained a guard's uniform, with belt, pouch, and whistle; and in this guise he became a familiar figure on the Eastern Counties Railway. The subordinate railway officials indulged his whims to an almost incredible extent. On one occasion, by blowing his whistle at the wrong moment, he nearly caused a serious accident on the Suffolk line.

When in London he used to haunt the Haymarket, at that time the centre of the city's night life. He frequented the brothels and was much in the company of prostitutes; but, on the whole, he seems to have found greater enjoyment in pretending to be a policeman. Although they did not provide him with a uniform, the police showed him the same kindly indulgence as the railway officials had done. They looked on tolerantly when he went up to groups of people in the street and ordered them, "in the voice and manner of a policeman," to move on. He used to threaten women that he would have them locked up—"he said there were too many women about the Haymarket, and he would not stand it any longer"—and the women would shout back, "Go away, you fool; you are not right in your head."

In May 1861 he and Mr Peatfield went to lodge with a Mr and Mrs Lewellin in Duke Street, St James's. He was now within three months of attaining his majority; and although the guardians had asked Mr Peatfield to remain with him until that event, they told him to let the young man be his own master.

Mr Peatfield had never been a very effective tutor; but this removal of the last vestige of authority led at once to disaster. Windham was marked down as an easy prey. At Ascot, early in the summer, he was introduced to a woman who went by the name of Agnes Willoughby. She was very different from the ordinary prostitutes whom he had encountered in the night-houses of the Haymarket—in fact he had probably never met anyone like her. She belonged to the same circle as the famous "Skittles," Catherine Walters, who appears so often in Victorian memoirs. They were accomplished women of the *demi-monde*, kept at great expense by rich men, riding or driving with them in the Park, hunting with them in Leicestershire. A good deal of glamour and publicity surrounded them. In music-hall songs and the more frivolous newspapers they were known as "the pretty horse-breakers"; and the name seems to have intrigued Windham and stuck in his mind. He was proud to become acquainted with a pretty horse-breaker, and still more proud when she showed signs of attachment to him.

Agnes Willoughby was said to be the daughter of a clergyman named Rogers. She lived in a handsome house in Piccadilly, which was maintained by a man named Roberts. He had been in the timber trade, and was therefore known to some of his acquaintances as "Mahogany Roberts"; and to others, perhaps more appropriately, as "Bawdyhouse Bob." Although she had long been upon affectionate terms with Roberts, Agnes was at this time kept by another man, from whom she received a generous allowance. But she was anxious to obtain an assured income; and Windham appeared likely to provide her with one. So she agreed to marry him.

In spite of his long minority, Windham would not come into a large income directly he was twenty-one. Owing largely to the purchase of Hanworth, there were mortgages on the estate amounting to £160,000.

Much of the property had been devised for the paying-off of these mortgages, which would not be complete until 1869. Lady Sophia's jointure of £1500 a year was a further charge on the estate. It appeared that until 1869, when the mortgages would be paid off and the devised estates would revert to him, Windham's income from all sources would not exceed £1400 a year, and might well be less.

This did not deter Agnes Willoughby and her advisers. A marriage-settlement was drawn up by a singularly uninhibited firm of solicitors, by which she secured £800 a year for life, to be increased to £1500 when her husband came into his settled estates in 1869. This settlement was signed on 29 August, the day before their marriage. In the meantime the engaged couple paid frequent visits to the shop of Mr Emanuel, a jeweller in Brook Street. In the course of a few months Windham bought jewellery for Agnes to the tune of close on £14,000. Her protector Roberts, the former timber merchant, cast an equally covetous eye on the woods at Felbrigg, which would pass into Windham's control as soon as he came of age. Fortunately timber is less easily negotiable than jewellery, and the scheme devised by Roberts was never carried through.

General Windham had returned from India in the spring, after having served there continuously for more than three years. He soon perceived his nephew's folly and weakness, and took the measure of the unsavoury gang who had gained control of him. He saw that strong and decisive action was the only way of saving Felbrigg from disaster. Windham's wild extravagance over Agnes Willoughby, and the extreme disrepute of all her associates, made it certain that the property would be doomed if he did not intervene. On the other hand, since he was the next heir to the estate, any such intervention would be to his personal advantage, and interested motives would certainly be imputed to him. A consultation took place at which he proposed an amicable rearrangement of the estate trusts, so that William would receive a larger income but be deprived of his power to bar the entail. This would have prevented the dispersal of the estates, but would have ensured the eventual succession of the General or his sons.

William flatly refused to give his consent to this plan. He had developed a great dislike for the General, whom in boyhood he had regarded as the family hero. The arrangements for the marriage went forward, and it took place on 30 August, three weeks after he had attained his majority. The honeymoon was spent in Paris, and shortly after their return Mr and Mrs Windham went down to Felbrigg, accompanied by Roberts. According to the guard on the Norwich train, Agnes and Roberts placed a large dressing-case in the middle of the carriage and covered it with cushions so as to form a bed. They pulled down the blinds, and Windham paid the guard to lock the door of the carriage. Then he spent the journey enjoyably between the guard's van and the engine-driver's cab. In this fashion the Squire of Felbrigg escorted his bride to his ancestral home.

III

There was now only one resource open to General Windham in the existing state of the law; and that was a public investigation of his nephew's state of mind. He petitioned the Lords Justices for the holding of a commission *De Lunatico Inquirendo*, an inquiry as to whether upon 1 August 1861 (a week before he came of age, and a month before his marriage) William Frederick Windham was fit and competent to manage himself and his own affairs. If the decision proved adverse to Windham, his marriage would be null and void; any issue of the marriage would not be recognised; and the legal transactions upon which he had embarked would have no validity. The General was joined in the petition by the entire body of Windham's relations on both sides of the family, Windhams and Herveys alike, with the sole exception of his mother.

The inquiry was held in the Court of Exchequer at Westminster before Samuel Warren, Q.C., one of the Masters in Lunacy, and a special jury. In his spare time Samuel Warren wrote novels, and his *Ten Thousand a Year* was widely popular. Varying opinions were expressed as to his conduct of the extremely difficult case which was now unfolded before him. Sir William Hardman wrote at the time that "he is snubbed and ridiculed most abominably by the counsel and witnesses engaged, and the papers very feebly convey in their reports the faintest idea of the stupendous folly and mismanagement of the whole concern. The scenes that take place in court are surprising and unheard of."

The counsel were certainly a formidable phalanx. Montague Chambers, Q.C., and two other lawyers represented the petitioners; Sir Hugh Cairns, Q.C., Mr Karslake, Q.C., and Mr Milward represented Windham; Mr Coleridge, Q.C., looked after the interests of Agnes Windham; and Mr Charles Russell held a watching brief for Lady Sophia. Whatever their behaviour may have been towards the learned Master, they did not themselves escape criticism from the newspapers and the general public. It was soon evident that the inquiry would take a very long time; that a fantastic number of witnesses would be called; that, whatever the verdict upon Windham's sanity might be, the legal costs were going to swallow up a very substantial portion of his estate. *Punch*, which commented freely upon the proceedings from week to week, had a cartoon showing the figure of Justice, the bandage tilted rakishly away from her eyes, lavishly dispensing oysters from a barrel marked *De Lunatico Inquirendo* to a horde of guzzling personages in wig and gown.

The opening speech of Mr Chambers, and the examinations and cross-examinations of the first witnesses, showed that no expense would be spared and no reticences observed. A succession of schoolmasters, tutors, doctors, and landladies testified to Windham's physical eccentricities. Their evidence was extremely detailed and often quite revolting. Enuresis, masturbation, uncontrollable dribbling (caused, in fact, by a malformation of the mouth), vomiting at table after excessive eating, discreditable diseases in his early manhood—everything was discussed at interminable length. Railwaymen and policemen described his activities as an amateur guard and an amateur constable. His purchases of jewellery, his proposed sales of timber, his various legal transactions were fully investigated. A formidable case was built up against him, especially by two of the concluding witnesses on behalf of the petitioners, medical men of the highest reputation—Dr Forbes Winslow, a well-known expert on mental disorders, and Dr Mayo, President of the Royal College of Physicians.

Nevertheless there was a good deal of sympathy for Windham, and public feeling outside the court ran strongly in his favour. It was observed—and the defending counsel repeatedly drew attention to the fact—that neither the General nor any other relation on the Windham side of the family was called to give evidence. The only petitioners who appeared in the witness-box were Lord Bristol and Lord Alfred Hervey, neither of whom would have derived any personal advantage from a verdict adverse to Windham. So it was easy for Sir Hugh Cairns and Mr Karslake to portray General Windham as a wicked uncle eager to seize upon his hapless nephew's estates, but unwilling to face their cross-examination as to his real motives. Mr Chambers protested that the General, having been absent in India for more than three years, could have no useful evidence to offer. But the jury, and the disgusted public outside, certainly desired to hear the evidence of Windham's next-of-kin, rather than examinations of housemaids and laundresses about the condition of his linen and his sheets.

The opening speech of Sir Hugh Cairns for the defence was long and impassioned, and at its conclusion "a burst of cheering rose from the audience, which the officers of the court were unable to repress." He produced in his turn two eminent specialists on mental diseases, Dr Harrington Tuke and Dr Seymour, who disagreed entirely with the views of Dr Forbes Winslow and Dr Mayo. Windham, in their opinion, was not a lunatic. He was, said Dr Seymour, "a very young man for his age, unable to judge properly, but I have seen no radical defect in his mind."

The impression made by these experts was confirmed, on a humbler level, by a large contingent of witnesses from Felbrigg and its neighbourhood, old servants and estate workers who had known Windham from infancy. For example, there was Nicholas Cawston, an aged carpenter, who remembered "the great Mr Windham" and was a relation of his faithful servant John Cawston. He had been discharged by Captain Windham in his capacity as receiver of the estate, and no doubt his evidence was influenced by the fact. But he regarded young Windham as perfectly sound in mind, and told Mr Karslake that "if he had your wig on his head, he would make a very good counsellor." An especially good witness was Mrs Martin, the wife of the bailiff at Felbrigg, whose evidence was full of sincerity and good feeling. She had been a confidential servant in the family for years, and was devoted to her young master. She did not attempt to deny his follies—the noise, the laughter, the singing and whistling. She had been shocked by his marriage, left the Hall as soon as it was announced, and went to live at the home farm. But she would never believe that he was anything but a headstrong and unruly boy.

Some of Windham's neighbours, men who had known him from boyhood, were also called as witnesses. With varying degrees of emphasis they voiced the local feeling that although he was noisy and obstreperous, there was no doubt as to his sanity. Among them was my grandfather Thomas Wyndham Cremer; and I may as well give the greater part of his evidence, since it was representative of opinion in Windham's own neighbourhood, and representative also of the general run of the examination of witness after witness:

I live at Beeston, in Norfolk. My father was a clergyman, and his property and residence are about five miles from Felbrigg. I knew old Mr Windham, and occasionally dined with him. The old gentleman used to tell comic tales in the Norfolk dialect, for the amusement of his friends, and he did it very well. I saw a good deal of young Windham when he was a boy. At the end of 1860 I dined with him at Felbrigg. Mr Peatfield was there at the time. Captain Windham and Captain Brereton were also of the party. Mr Windham sat at the head of the table, and behaved like a gentleman. The party played whist in the evening, and Mr Windham seemed able to hold his own. I visited Felbrigg after Mr Windham came of age, but before his marriage. After dinner we walked round the stables to look at the horses. Mr Windham seemed to be conversant with all subjects connected with horses, and his remarks upon them were sensible and rational. I shot with him in September 1859, and on other occasions. He was a rather bad shot, but managed his gun properly and carefully. I believe him to be a man of sound mind. (*Cross-examined*). Windham had a peculiarly formed mouth, but I cannot say that when a boy he had a particularly dirty face. He was always very noisy, and used to halloo and laugh in a loud tone. There was nothing otherwise to attract attention in his laugh. I have heard that he was in the habit of waiting at table, but never saw him doing so. . . . I have been told that he was in the habit of acting as a guard on railways: but I think it perfectly consistent with sanity in a gentleman of rank and property, after coming of age, to dress himself up as a guard and perform the duties of a guard on a railway. Pointing the attention of ladies to mules while staling is not gentlemanly conduct, but I cannot accept it as a proof of insanity. Windham was generally boisterous in his manner. When I was at Felbrigg in August last Windham did not tell me that he was about to marry Agnes Willoughby; if he had, I would have advised him not to marry such a person. (*Examined by the jury*). I attribute Mr Windham's boisterousness to high spirits, and not to unsoundness of mind.

Sir Hugh Cairns had stronger forces in reserve. A great deal of particularly repulsive evidence as to Windham's habits had been given by the people with whom he lodged in Duke Street, Mr and Mrs Lewellin. They were an odious and disreputable pair, and under cross-examination their statements had been badly shaken. The defence now produced several of their former servants—a cook, two housemaids, and a French valet—who completely gave the lie to everything they had said. To take one trifling example, Mrs Lewellin had sworn that Windham would eat anything up to seventeen poached eggs for breakfast, whereas the cook denied that he ever had more than two. The shadiness of the Lewellins and their establishment was progressively revealed; and it appeared also that General Windham, in his determination to establish a really convincing case against his nephew, had gone a great deal too far. A whole succession of witnesses maintained that he had tried, in one way or another, to suborn them.

Mrs Pritchard, a former housemaid of the Lewellins, testified that Mrs Lewellin had visited her in company with a military gentleman, and told her: "You must come to my house to see the General, for Mr Windham has been and married a bad woman and squandered all his fortune, and we want to do what we can in it for the General . . . the bad woman was going to bring Mr Windham a child, and the thing must be done quickly." In all Mrs Lewellin visited her four times, always urging her to bear witness to Windham's running naked about the house or otherwise misconducting himself; but she always refused.

She was followed by Mrs Lewellin's sister and brother, Eliza and Conway Dignam. Eliza had been at a meeting in the office of the solicitor for the petitioners when Mrs Lewellin's statement was taken down in the presence of General Windham. To the best of her belief, she said:

> It was entirely false. After she made it General Windham thanked her, said he was highly delighted with her, and extremely obliged to her. I left the office with my sister. When we got outside I said, "Oh, Augusta, what lies you have been telling " She replied, "Windham never did like me, I wonder what he will think of me now. I have given it him pretty strong, I think, and his lady-love too."

Eliza also told the court that the General said, in reference to herself, "This little woman would say what she knows, but I have never asked her. She is also very nervous, and I am afraid she would break down in cross-examination."

Their brother, Conway Dignam, was very much of a rolling stone, and frequently down and out. He had never lived in the establishment in Duke Street, or known Windham at all. Nevertheless Mrs Lewellin told him that "his uncle the General is going to bring him in mad"; and that he could give valuable evidence, and extricate himself from his financial difficulties, by swearing that he had waited on Windham and testifying to his madness. He replied: "I shall do no such thing. How can you ask me to come against a young man and put him in a madhouse, when I know nothing at all about him. . . . I would sooner remain in my present position than injure a young man I know nothing about."

Finally Mr Giubilei, the youthful husband of Lady Sophia, was called. His wife's health made it impossible for her to appear: she was described by Sir Hugh Cairns as lying "on a bed of sickness, and I fear on a bed of death," and she did in fact die less than two years later. But Mr Giubilei maintained that his step-son was sane, and repeated that Lady Sophia had at no time agreed to be one of the petitioners. When pressed by Mr Chambers upon this point, he replied, "No. General Windham offered Lady Sophia and myself two bribes to——" at which point his remarks were cut short by an altercation between Mr Chambers and Mr Karslake, and the delicate question was not pursued.

This type of evidence—and there was a good deal more of it—did great harm to the case for the petitioners. There can, I think, be no doubt that the General, that passionate and impetuous man, ever resolute to charge forward and surmount his objective, had been extremely indiscreet. He was determined to rescue his nephew, and his nephew's property, from the "cheats and sharpers of both sexes" who had gained control of him. But in the welter of corruption and recrimination in which all parties were involved, he too had touched pitch and was defiled. It was in vain that Mr Chambers described the Dignams as "wretched creatures," and attacked the characters and motives of other witnesses. The defence were successful in projecting an image of this distinguished soldier as an unscrupulous and cynical villain, whose sole purpose was to relegate his nephew to a madhouse and acquire Felbrigg for himself or his sons. It was the easier to do this as the General's popular laurels had somewhat faded since his exploit in the Crimea, and he was considered to have seriously mishandled an operation outside Cawnpore. Mr Karslake in particular now assailed him with extraordinary vehemence.

> In the privacy of the Court of Chancery he has ventured to defame and blacken the character of his youthful relative; but he has proved himself craven, recreant and coward enough to decline to sanction by his oath in the face of the public a story which he had foisted upon the Lords Justices, and which he has not hesitated to support by the evidence of hireling witnesses.

The entire petition was, in fact, "a cruel and wicked conspiracy got up by General Windham for the purpose of depriving his nephew of his property."

At last the proceedings drew to a close. Mr Russell addressed the Court briefly on behalf of Lady Sophia, emphasising once more that she had never concurred in the petition, repeating her conviction of her son's sanity despite "the faults which undoubtedly had stained his youth," and stressing the affection that had always existed between them. Mr Karslake, in a speech lasting the greater part of two days, mercilessly dissected the motives of the General and his fellow-petitioners, and drew a harrowing picture of Windham's fate if the jury should decide against him. Mr Coleridge delivered a flowery oration on behalf of Agnes Windham. He was so carried away by his own eloquence as to tell the Court (to the great amusement of *Punch*) that "I would far rather be the Magdalene who washed her Divine Master's feet with her tears and wiped them with the hairs of her head, than the self-complacent Pharisee who condemned the woman because she was a sinner."

The final speech of Mr Chambers for the petitioners lasted three days. He vehemently defended the General from the imputations made against him, reminded the jury of his splendid record as a soldier, reprobated "the epithets which a barrister has thought fit to bestow upon a hero." He went once more through the whole melancholy story of Windham's life, and urged the jury to conclude that he was utterly unable to manage himself or his own affairs. He must be saved from the consequences of his own weakness of mind.

> But if he is to be saved—saved from ruin of health and character, from disease and wretchedness of life, from disgrace, from scorn, from repulsion—from repulsion from the doors of his own wife, who will be living in luxury upon her £800 or £1500 a year—he must be saved through the instrumentality of these relatives who have come forward to do their duty, through evil report and gross abuse.

Mr Chambers concluded his speech on the thirty-third day of the inquiry, and the learned Master occupied the remainder of it with his summing-up. He spoke of the "vast body of contradictory evidence" which the jury had heard; and endeavoured to direct their attention to the one cardinal point—"whether you found the state of mind of Mr Windham to be such as to bring him within the scope of the protection of the law." He had decided that at the conclusion of the hearing Windham should be examined before the jury in a closed court, and that the jury might put questions to him. It was an opportunity that the jury, their heads awhirl with the speeches of counsel and the conflicting testimony of 140 witnesses, must undoubtedly have welcomed.

So next morning the Court assembled for the last time. "The Master announced that he was very poorly, the result of his great exertions in the case." (Several of the jurymen had made similar announcements in the course of the inquiry, and one had been obliged to withdraw seriously ill.) Windham's counsel protested against his being examined in a closed and not in an open court, but was over-ruled. The rest of the proceedings were summarised in the printed report as follows.

It was then arranged that the examination of Mr Windham should take place in the court, from which all strangers were ordered to withdraw. This was at about twenty minutes past eleven, and Mr Windham was introduced. He was questioned on all the matters which were brought out in evidence—the places he had been to, his early life, his tutors, his acquaintance with Agnes Willoughby, his marriage, his and her subsequent conduct, the jewels, &c. He is reported to have answered all the questions put to him unhesitatingly, straightforwardly, coherently, and consequentially.

The Jury retired at three o'clock, and returned in half an hour with a verdict, "That Mr Windham is of sound mind, and capable of taking care of himself and his affairs."

The announcement was received with loud cheers.

IV

The great inquiry was over, and the press was no longer filled day after day with columns of squalid and salacious detail. The excitement of partisanship died away, and everyone realised how absurd and undignified the whole affair had been, and how unnecessarily prolonged. *Punch* summed up the general feeling very neatly:

Windham is sane: but England must be cracked
To bear such process as hath fixed the fact.

Windham had been pronounced, as Hardman put it, not a madman or an idiot, "but simply a damned young spendthrift and fool." The plaudits that had greeted him were soon heard no more; and the newspapers, while approving the verdict, vied with each other in denouncing his folly and wickedness. The *Daily Telegraph* provided a masterly summing-up.

Grotesque as the finding seems, in contrast with the timber sales, the diamond bargains, the orgies, the sins, the stolidities of this pitiful young prodigal, it is still a supremely just one. Competency to manage is right to mismanage; and it was not because a noble array of petitioners watered at the mouth for pearls going visibly to swine, that the ownership was to be unjustly transferred, and the fool pronounced a madman . . . The verdict of the Windham jury is not a hesitating one; it pronounces him sane and competent; and in doing so in face of the immense mass of evidence collected to prove him fool, liar, brute, and prodigal, it simply asserts that these are disgraceful names, but not the names of madness.

The expense of the inquiry had been fantastic. It had lasted thirty-four days; 140 witnesses had been examined; they had been brought from all over the British Isles and the Continent, and kept in London for weeks at a time. A galaxy of the most eminent lawyers had been engaged on the case throughout that period. In short, someone would have to meet a bill that was in the neighbourhood of £20,000. It was obvious that the payment of such a sum would ruin Windham, following upon the havoc that he had already made of his finances. He therefore appealed to the Lords Justices that the petitioners should be required to pay the expenses of the case which they had brought, and in which they had been defeated. But the Lords Justices rejected the appeal on grounds which were briefly summarised as follows:

First, that the original petition was made *bonâ fide*, and not from personal motives or considerations on the part of the petitioners; and secondly, that, assuming Mr Windham to have been always of sound mind, it must be considered that his own acts and conduct were the occasion and cause of the proceedings, which were necessarily expensive to him and others.

As *The Times* remarked, "to make a man pay for what is tantamount to a declaration of his own innocence looks hard; but the Judges had to make the best of a bad job."

So the £20,000 of costs was added to the mountain of Windham's debts. Besides obtaining her settlement for life, Agnes had succeeded in obtaining large sums of cash from him. In his closing speech at the inquiry Mr Chambers had shown that his bank account had been reduced, by payments to her and to Roberts, to a balance of £17—and this before any provision had been made to meet the £14,000 bill of the jeweller Mr Emanuel. Under the influence of the shady solicitor who had drawn up the marriage settlement, he had immediately afterwards executed a deed disentailing the Felbrigg estate, except for that portion which was secured for the paying-off of his father's mortgages. As the excitement of the inquiry faded, many people came to feel that there was much to be said for the petitioners' point of view.

The crazy marriage soon foundered. I do not propose to discuss the details of their intimate relations as disclosed at the inquiry; but it seems certain that Agnes felt no affection for Windham at any time. Physically he repelled her: and even for the sake of the settlement, the cash, the jewels, she could not overcome her distaste. A few months after their wedding she suddenly left Felbrigg, and was next heard of in Ireland with a former lover, an opera singer named Giuglini—not to be confused with Lady Sophia's young husband Giubilei. Later she returned, and for the sake of appearances was reconciled to Windham during the course of the inquiry. They were together at Felbrigg in February 1862, although even at that time Windham found it necessary to disclaim responsibility for her debts by means of a newspaper advertisement.

Later in the same month they were still living together at a house in Westbourne Terrace, Paddington, when Windham was brought before the Hammersmith magistrate for threatening to cut his wife's throat. According to her evidence, as reported in *The Times*, she had gone out in the evening with his consent, accompanied by two men friends, guests who were staying in the house. After they returned Windham became violent, produced a large clasp-knife, and said that "he was determined to shed the blood of all three." He had threatened her life before: "on two occasions he threw knives over the table at her." Windham said in his own defence that the two gentlemen had poured water down his ears when he was lying drunk upon the sofa. The magistrate bound him over to keep the peace in the sum of £500, with two sureties of £250. "The defendant was not provided with bail, and he was removed by the gaoler."

Soon afterwards, understandably, they parted. Windham returned to Felbrigg. Agnes divided her time between London and Paris, usually in the company of Giuglini. A deed of separation was executed between them in June. In the meantime Windham, continually pressed by his creditors, had borrowed very large sums from Robert John Harvey, a leading Norwich banker, giving a bill of sale upon his disentailed estates as security. The house and shooting were let; and by the end of 1862 most of the property that was at his own disposal had passed into the ownership of the banking firm of Harvey and Hudson. Early in the following year Felbrigg Hall and a considerable portion of the estate was acquired from them by John Ketton, a Norwich merchant. Mr Ketton's purchase comprised approximately the four parishes of Felbrigg, Aylmerton, Metton, and Sustead.

The formal conveyance and release to him, by certain trustees and by Windham himself, bear the dates of 8 and 9 April 1863.

V

Both before and after his departure from Felbrigg, Windham continued to fling away all the money he could obtain. He still played the fool on the railways in his guard's uniform. He set up a large coach, which he drove from one East Anglian town to another, "taking up gratuitously all the stray passengers he could collect on the way," and thereby causing much vexation to the proprietors of coaches plying for hire along those routes. In the course of 1862 he instituted divorce proceedings against Agnes, citing Giuglini as the co-respondent. The hearings dragged on for several months, but next year the case was withdrawn. Agnes was forgiven; Giuglini faded into the background; husband and wife were reconciled, and lived together for a year or more. A son was born to Agnes on 19 April 1864, and was christened Frederick Howe Lindsey Bacon Windham.

During this period of reconciliation Agnes contrived to obtain the whole of what was left of Windham's property. He made over to her, in return for a ludicrously small sum, the reversion of Hanworth and the other settled estates, as well as his insurance policies, his personal effects, and indeed everything that he possessed. He then filed his petition in bankruptcy. In the summer of 1864 he and Agnes parted, and for the last time. She had obtained everything, and had a son to whom she would pass it on.

Windham was now virtually penniless. His uncle the General tried to save something from the wreck, and to come to an arrangement with Agnes. There was talk once more of divorce proceedings, and of contesting the legitimacy of her child; but she held all the cards, and she knew it. Windham passed his time, not disagreeably, among the inns and pot-houses and livery-stables of Norwich; and there he made the acquaintance of a coach-proprietor named Tom Bingham, who proved a true and loyal friend. He gave Windham steady and congenial employment, put up with all his drunkenness and violence, and kept him from utter dereliction during the last year and a half of his life. The employment was modest enough—driving the "Express" coach between Norwich and Cromer at a guinea a week; but Windham was a brilliant if erratic whip, never had an accident of any consequence, and may well have found more genuine enjoyment in his coaching career than at any other time.

WILLIAM FREDERICK WINDHAM
("Mad Windham")

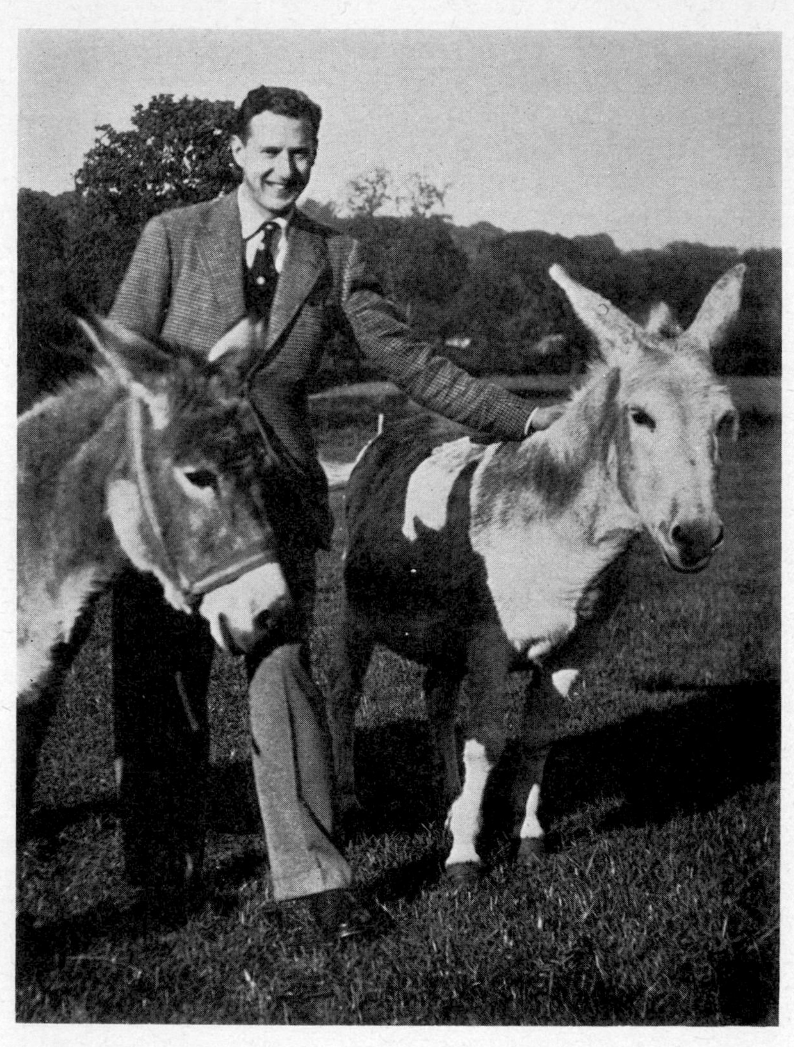

RICHARD KETTON-CREMER

On one occasion the future editor of *Punch*, Sir Francis Burnand, was a passenger. He described in his reminiscences how Windham during part of the journey "played the gentleman," and talked of Eton and a man whom they had both known there. Then:

> He suddenly threw care and refinement to the winds, exchanged some coarse chaff with the passers-by, laughed with the guard, used the most outlandish expressions, whipped up his team, and took us up to the inn in fine style, when, after having thrown the reins to an ostler and descended from the driving-seat, he with a true coachman-like touch of his hat and in broad country-tongued dialect, said, "Good-day, sir," and accepted his two crowns as a tip from us; and when we subsequently encountered him among his boon-companions at the inn he did not bestow upon us any further recognition, nor appear to be anything else but a rough, jolly sort of loud-voiced, easy-drinking, country driver of the Norfolk coach.

I have some of the cards which advertised the "Express" coach. It left the Belle Vue Hotel at Cromer each morning (Sundays excepted) at 8 a.m.; was at the Hanworth Post Office at 8.30, at the Black Boys Hotel at Aylsham at 9.0; and reached Norwich in time for the 10.45 train to London. The return journey started from the Norfolk Hotel in Norwich every afternoon at 4.30. The cards were signed by

H. Bingham & Co., Proprietors.
W. F. Windham, Esq., Coachman.

Eventually Windham had a disagreement with Bingham, and would drive the coach no longer. He continued to live in a little bedroom in the Norfolk Hotel, overlooking the yard, from the window of which "he used to thrust his strange-looking countenance and singularly-formed mouth, and grin and whistle to the ostlers below." Bingham remained cordial and kind, and he had another friend in a coachman named Tom Saul, who presently succeeded him as driver of the Cromer coach. But drink and nervous excitement had wrecked his constitution. He was suddenly taken ill on 1 February 1866, and died on the following day. Tom Bingham and Tom Saul were with him: the General was sent for, but did not arrive in time. He was buried in the family vault at Felbrigg. Agnes did not appear, but was represented by her sister and two gentlemen. The real mourners were the two Toms, Bingham and Saul.

General Windham did his best to recover the settled estates from Agnes and her son, but without success. The boy was pronounced to be legitimate and his father's heir, and in 1869 his mother brought him to live at Hanworth Hall. She married a second husband, Mr George Walker; and she professed—and indeed proclaimed on more than one public occasion—the deepest penitence for the sins of her past life. Her conversion was due to the ministrations of a London clergyman, the Rev. Mr Veitch, who arranged for her confirmation by the Bishop of London, and acted as her spiritual adviser thereafter.

Her son—"Fred Windham"—went to Eton and Cambridge, and entered into possession of the settled estates when he came of age. My father, six years his junior, knew him well, and described him as tall and good-looking, impulsive, excitable, a fine horseman and shot. He died in the autumn of 1896, at the age of thirty-two, a few months after his mother. He was married but left no children. Years ago, in a sun-drenched *quinta* in Madeira, I received much hospitality and kindness from his widow; and her relations, my neighbours and friends, although Hanworth is no longer their property, still own a substantial portion of the former Windham estates.

Chapter Fourteen

JOHN KETTON and ROBERT WILLIAM KETTON

Early history of John Ketton—he purchases the Felbrigg estate in 1863—life at Felbrigg as described in Mrs Ketton's diaries—marriage of Anna Ketton to Thomas Wyndham Cremer—death of John Ketton in 1872—Robert Ketton's life at Felbrigg—his sisters—his Liberal inclinations—he becomes a recluse and neglects the house and estate

I

THE Victorian self-made man was a favourite subject in the fiction of the day. John Ketton was, I think, on the whole a creditable example of the type in real life. I know less of his career than I could wish; and most of my knowledge of his character is derived from the diaries kept for seven years or so by his wife. But he was, by any standards, an exceptional man.

The name of Kitton had been a common one in Norwich for some centuries. Its bearers had never achieved the smallest distinction, in civic life or in any other way. They were tradespeople of very modest station—cordwainers, glovers, tallow-chandlers, grocers. But in the eighteen-thirties and eighteen-forties one of them, John Kitton, built up a prosperous business in oil-cake and other feeding-stuffs for cattle. His enterprise and foresight brought him some valuable contracts at the time of the Crimean War, and eventually the business became one of the most important in Norwich. He acquired an attractive small estate on the outskirts of the city, Sprowston Grange, where he farmed and raised stock on a considerable scale. While at Sprowston, in 1853 or thereabouts, he changed his name to Ketton, a variant which appears to have been used occasionally during earlier centuries.[1] As the terms of his will obliged my family to add his name to our own when

[1] Rye, *Norfolk Families*, pp. 442–3. He records the occurrence of the spelling Ketton in 1306.

we inherited Felbrigg in 1924, I do not regret that he adopted this slightly more euphonious form.

John Ketton's portrait and photographs show a face clean-shaven, pale, full of intelligence and character. There was great character also in the woman he married, Rachel Anne, the daughter of Robert Blake of Norwich. The Blakes were a Quaker family, and some of their tombstones remain in the burial-ground of the Gildencroft.[1] John Ketton and his wife lived first, I think, in Ber Street, and later moved to a house in the Close, which they retained throughout their years at Sprowston and Felbrigg. They had two sons and five daughters. The elder son, John, went into the business at an early age. His brother Robert, the youngest of the family, was still a small boy when his father bought Felbrigg in 1863.

John Ketton's purchase of Felbrigg caused considerable surprise and comment at the time. At no period of English history has it been unusual for a tradesman to acquire a small estate and establish his family in the countryside. But it is seldom that a historic house with its entire contents—pictures, furniture, books, documents, everything—is transferred from one family to another. That, however, is precisely what occurred at Felbrigg, owing to the suddenness and completeness of the ruin that "Mad Windham" had brought upon himself. Like most men who have achieved success through their own efforts, John Ketton had his enemies; and he and his family at first had to withstand a good deal of abuse and ill-nature. Snobs and fools made ample use of their opportunity; and even kindlier men must have regretted the passing of the Windham heirlooms into alien hands. In fact it proved the means of preserving the greater part of them intact to the present day.

John Ketton did not sever his connection with the Norwich business after his move to Felbrigg. No doubt he hoped to hand over the management in due course to his elder son. But it soon became apparent that the young man was both incompetent and idle; and his father was obliged to pay constant visits to Norwich, and keep a close watch on all that went on. Nevertheless, he took the home farm at Felbrigg into his own hands, planted up a good deal of land which had

[1] I have the birth-certificates of all the children of "Robert Blake, junior, Manufacturer, and Martha Elizabeth his wife" as endorsed at Monthly Meeting by Joseph John Gurney and other prominent Quakers. Most of them bear the comment "Parents not in membership," and they seem in later years to have drifted entirely out of the Quaker fold.

hitherto been little more than heath, and in general kept the estate in very good heart. He built some excellent cottages, and was also responsible for the Sexton's Gate Lodge, an uncommonly attractive little house for the architecturally barren eighteen-sixties. His zeal for improvement went even further. He bought a large tract of land in the distant parish of Kelling, and spent much time and trouble in attempting to bring that light and sandy soil under proper cultivation.

The Ketton family moved to Felbrigg on 26 March 1863. The diaries kept by Mrs Ketton begin on 2 August, and continue for the next seven years. For the most part they give only a brief record of the occurrences of each day, sometimes no more than a couple of lines. They are not in the least reflective or introspective. Little is said about matters of deep concern, such as the growing antagonism between John Ketton and his elder son. Mainly they describe the placid round of Victorian country life, when people seldom moved farther from home than their horses could carry or draw them, met their few neighbours almost every week of their lives, and enjoyed a modest range of social pleasures to the full.

The neighbourhood for the most part received the new family at Felbrigg in a friendly and indeed a cordial spirit. John Ketton was involved in one or two disagreements about estate boundaries, and politically he was a Tory in an area predominantly Liberal; but in general he got on well enough with the squires who were his neighbours. Mrs Ketton could display when necessary the gentle firmness of her Quaker forebears, whether dealing with an arrogant local matron or with the "detrimentals" who sought the hands of her daughters. A power of sardonic description appears in her diaries now and then; but she and her sister Priscilla Blake, who had long lived as one of the family, preferred peace and harmony, and did their best to obtain it. I think, however, that the ready acceptance of these newcomers was mainly due to the attractions of the five daughters. Anna, the eldest, was the beauty of them all. I well remember her delicate features and her grace of carriage in old age, and her early photographs are exquisite. Margaret, the second daughter, with less beauty, had much gaiety and vitality. Ellen, the third, was a rather negative personality. Of the two youngest girls, Marion partook of Margaret's vivacity, and Gertrude promised to rival Anna's beauty.

Within the comparatively restricted neighbourhood the diaries are full of riding-parties, croquet-parties, dinner-parties, dances, and the everlasting ritual of calling and being called upon. The summer brought cricket-matches, bathing in the sea at Cromer, picnics on the Lighthouse Cliffs above; and also the local horticultural shows, one of which was "only enlivened by Mr Cozens-Hardy having a row with Mr Girdlestone and the judges about partiality." With the autumn came what Mrs Ketton called "the hateful shooting season"—I do not know why she disliked it so. In the hard winters there were long days of skating and dancing on the ice, with great bonfires blazing at the lakeside. On at least two occasions Aunt Priscilla escorted the elder girls for a few weeks of shopping and theatre-going in Paris—a Paris radiant with the deceptive lustre of the Second Empire.

At this time the social life of Norfolk was inseparable from religious activity. The feeling of the neighbourhood was strongly evangelical; and the closely intermarried families of the Buxtons, Barclays, Gurneys, and Hoares—collectively known as "the Clan"—were much addicted to prayer-meetings, addresses by missionaries, and similar forms of edification. These occasions were dominated by Hannah, Lady Buxton, widow of the philanthropist and emancipator Sir Fowell Buxton, who lived at Northrepps Hall. Lady Buxton was a formidable dowager, one of the Gurneys of Earlham, a sister of Elizabeth Fry and of the Louisa Gurney, afterwards Mrs Samuel Hoare, whose childhood impressions of Felbrigg were quoted in an earlier chapter of this book. She moved about the district with a retinue of pious nieces and promising curates, and overawed the clergy for miles around. On one occasion she failed to appear at a luncheon party at Felbrigg, and explained afterwards that she had "an interesting Sacrament" instead. Another aspect of this serious view of life was the fondness of the neighbourhood for private lectures. The Kettons drove miles through the winding lanes to listen to Mr Mott's discourse on Home Scenes, "in the course of which he quoted twelve different poets," and to young Henry Upcher on the Holy Land, and to Charles Buxton, M.P., on Parrots.

John Thomas Mott of Barningham Hall was a pleasant and congenial neighbour; but he was also an enthusiastic Liberal, and at the general election of 1865 he decided to find out how matters stood at Felbrigg. On 17 July of that year Mrs Ketton wrote:

John went to see Bond Cabbell. While he was gone Mr Mott came and told me he wanted to see John about politics, and said he was a Whig himself and had been so all his life. I told him Mr Ketton was a Tory and had been so all *his* life. He asked if there was any objection to his canvassing the tenantry. I said Mr Ketton had promised his vote and interest to Howes and Read; and he said it was of no use his stopping.

In this election the Tory candidates, Howes and Read, were returned for East Norfolk with a large majority. Politics change with the changing generations; and the great-grandson of this Whiggish Mr Mott has long sat in Parliament on the Tory benches.

The surviving members of the Windham family appear occasionally in the diary. General Windham called once or twice when staying in the neighbourhood. Mr and Mrs Ketton sent game and fruit to Captain Windham, now sinking into invalidism at Cromer; and when they failed to do so, he "called to say that Felbrigg fruit was necessary for his health." The figure of "Mad Windham," driving his coach between Norwich and Cromer, was a familiar sight to them. In the autumn of 1863 he is mentioned as "shouting very loud," and a few months later as driving over a Mr Johnson and breaking his arm. Nevertheless they had no hesitation in entrusting their small son Bobby to Windham's care when it was time to send him off to school.

And so the diaries go on, with all the daily happenings of a century ago. They convey a curious impression of luxury mingled with discomfort—the blazing fires, the leisurely carriage-drives, the hothouse grapes in December; the throngs of servants, with their frequent changes and easy replacements (twenty-nine applications for a sewing-maid's place, twenty-six for a footman's); the headaches and fainting-fits, the agonising visits to the dentist, the chimneys on fire, the burst pipes, above all the long winters and the bitter cold. "Norris [the butler] accidentally locked up Margaret in the water closet where she passed the whole night, suffering very much from cold, at six o'clock one of the housemaids let her out." Such calamities did not often occur; but Anna Ketton, my grandmother, remembered the cold of the house to the end of her days. Bedrooms on the first floor, in that Spartan age, were not allotted to the five daughters. They clambered, in their great crinolines, up the narrow stairs to a little range of rooms in the attic, giving on to the leaded balcony behind the parapet. Only one of the these bedrooms had a fireplace; and on the coldest nights the sisters would all crowd into it, and called it "the balcony hotel."

II

On 9 August 1864 Mr and Mrs Ketton and their daughter Anna dined for the first time with the Cremers at Beeston Regis Hall. The other guests were Sir Henry and Lady Robinson of Knapton. "Altogether it was the pleasantest dinner party since we have been here." It was also an auspicious dinner-party, since Anna was to marry

Thomas Wyndham Cremer and live for many years at Beeston, and her sister Margaret was to marry the Robinsons' son.

We last saw Tom Cremer three years back, testifying in court to his belief in the sanity of "Mad Windham." He was now a man of thirty, living at Beeston with his father and his sister Arabella. His elder sister and younger brother had married; the youngest sister and brother were dead, the latter a midshipman who perished at the age of eighteen when his ship caught fire off Calcutta. Tom looked after the home farm at Beeston, shot and fished and collected rare birds, and now fell in love with Anna Ketton.

He did not feel able to approach her father, that formidable man of commerce, until he could offer her a home of his own and a sufficient jointure. But his father died early in 1867, and at Christmas of that year he proposed to her. He was rejected, in what circumstances I do not know. Mrs Ketton recorded in her diary that one of his letters "made us unhappy for the rest of the day." But he and Anna continued to meet at dances and dinner-parties, and he continued to shoot at Felbrigg and fish for pike in the lake. On 14 January 1869, a twelvemonth after his first rejection, he called the morning after a dance at Felbrigg and stayed an hour. "Anna did not come down." All came right a few months later. He complained in a letter that he could never see her alone, without her phalanx of sisters, and spent his time "wandering about day after day longing to meet you and never doing so." But in July they became formally engaged, in the rather unexpected *milieu* of a horticultural show held in the grounds of Holt Hall. Everyone knew what was afoot, "the company generally congratulating and looking on," as Mrs Ketton expressed it, adding that the Felbrigg garden obtained prizes for cherries and pelargoniums.

I still have the letter he sent her the same evening. It is a very moving letter, as are the others which this rather inarticulate man wrote to his future wife during the next few weeks. Matters were soon settled with her father to the satisfaction of both parties; and Mrs Ketton, who had supported the cause of Tom Cremer from the start, wrote in her diary that she "felt very triumphant." The marriage took place in Felbrigg Church on 13 October. Three weeks later the whole family "went to Beeston to see the newly married come home. A grand triumphal arch was erected over the gate with *Welcome Home, Health and Happiness*, and about a hundred men dragged the carriage the last mile." On 3 August 1870 their first child, my father, was born, and subsequently three daughters.

III

John Ketton's last years were clouded by ill-health and the constant disagreements with his elder son. He developed a great irritability of temper, and fretted intensely over matters which once he would have taken in his stride. "John's temper very easterly" is a frequent entry in his wife's diaries, and "John dreadfully cross all day." She had to endure exhausting scenes and sleepless nights. I do not know what led to the final breach between the younger John and his father. But something happened which caused him to be completely disinherited, "cut off" in the best Victorian tradition. His father died not long afterwards, on 15 August 1872, in his sixty-fifth year. The new owner of Felbrigg was the younger son Robert, a boy at Eton, sixteen years old at the time of his father's death.

I remember Robert Ketton as a rather frustrated and decidedly eccentric old man. At Eton and afterwards at Oxford—he went up to Merton in 1875—he showed considerable promise. He was highly intelligent, with strong radical leanings, in contrast to the conservatism of his late father. Small, spare, and active, he was passionately fond of shooting and a very good shot. He supervised every detail of his farms and woods, and began to take an active part in local affairs soon after he came down from Oxford. Feeling ran high at that time, in the northern division of Norfolk, between Conservatives and Liberals. He supported the Liberals with a young man's enthusiasm, and especially so in the general election of 1885. On this occasion, with an extended franchise and a revision of boundaries, the Liberal candidate Herbert Cozens-Hardy first won the seat which he was to hold unassailably for many years. Robert Ketton preserved a great bundle of posters, notices of meetings, and the like, which show the extremely active part which he himself played during this election, speaking night after night all over the division.

As a Liberal who carried his views into practice, he appears in an agreeable light in the autobiography of that remarkable man George Edwards, the pioneer of the Agricultural Workers' Union. Edwards had been victimised on account of his political activities, and was unable to find employment. Robert Ketton gave him work on the home farm at Felbrigg, but was at first unable to find him a cottage, so that for eighteen months he had to walk six miles each day to work and six miles home again. Eventually a cottage became vacant at Aylmerton, and Edwards was installed there. It was a time of severe agricultural depression, with much unemployment and wages at a fearfully low level, but:

happily for me I had at last got under a Liberal employer, who not only was favourable to the men, but showed his sympathy by paying them a shilling per week above the rate paid by other employers, and I was able to breathe freely without any fear of victimization. My employer also assisted me by lending me books and papers on political problems. He also put every kind of work on the farm in my way to enable me to earn extra money.

Robert Ketton also encouraged the activities of the Union, and allowed Edwards, as district secretary, to leave work an hour early whenever he required to do so.

Apart from a few years on the Norfolk County Council, Robert Ketton's public activities took him no farther afield than the local Bench of Magistrates and the local Board of Guardians. But his progressive views were at this time a good deal in advance of the genteel Whiggism professed by most of his Liberal neighbours; and for various other reasons he came to be regarded—with increasing justification as the years went by—as something of a crank. "Young Ketton is an awful Radical, and he does not show any sign of marrying." The sentence, typical of much family disapproval, comes from a letter of an old neighbour, the Rev. Edgar Montagu, who had married Arabella Cremer of Beeston. The Radicalism was not destined to survive the budgets of Lloyd George; nor did Robert Ketton ever take a wife. His mother died at Felbrigg in 1885, and henceforward he lived there with his two youngest sisters. They were women of much personal charm and still greater force of character. I do not think it is unfair to suggest that they dominated their brother, and would scarcely have given any warm encouragement to the idea of his marriage.

For they loved Felbrigg, and impressed their personalities strongly upon the house and gardens. There are many photographs of them in their pony-carriage or among their flower-beds—Marion short, vivacious and forthright: Gertrude tall, graceful, gentle. They are always together, never with their brother. Several people have talked to me about them, and invariably with warm affection. Lady Battersea (Constance de Rothschild) remembered them well, and indeed described them in her book of reminiscences—putting the manorial records in order, regaling the Empress of Austria with figs in the kitchen garden. It was Marion who really grappled with the intricacies of court hand, and was responsible for classifying and arranging the whole vast accumulation of deeds and manor-court rolls. Both sisters were fond of music and books, and the library was their favourite room. They liked to welcome to Felbrigg the writers and men of learning who stayed at Frederick Locker-Lampson's house at Cromer, and with the Batterseas at Overstrand. There were even such unexpected visitors as Oscar Wilde and his wife, who took rooms at Grove Farm in the village—the cards they left at the Hall have chanced to survive. I remember Augustine Birrell, Locker-Lampson's son-in-law, describing his visits to the library at Felbrigg in the days of my great-aunts. He liked to recall the occasion when they silently placed in his hands a substantial packet of ballads and verses whose wrapping a more outspoken age had endorsed with the single word "Bawdy," and left him alone for the rest of the afternoon.

The two sisters died unexpectedly young, both in their forties, Gertrude in 1895 and Marion three years later. The light had gone out of Felbrigg, and for the next quarter of a century it was a house of solitude and gloom. Robert Ketton became almost entirely a recluse. Apart from his shooting-parties, he never entertained and was seldom seen. He continued to sit on the local Bench, and served as High Sheriff of Norfolk in 1914, but otherwise ceased entirely to take part in local affairs. And the estate began to go downhill. Repairs were neglected, to farmhouses and farm-buildings and cottages alike. Land was undrained, watercourses became choked, nothing was done to the drives or roads. I do not think that during the whole of his forty years of ownership he built a single new cottage; and this at a time when cottages could be built for less than £200 apiece. After the year 1900 he does not appear to have planted a single tree, thus creating a lamentable gap in the woodland rotation, which was made even worse by the heavy fellings required during the First World War.

It was the same in the house and its surroundings. Damp began to soak everywhere through the roofs. The shrubbery grew into an entanglement and the lawn into a hayfield. The kitchen garden was let to a market-gardener. The Orangery and the Dovehouse fell into decay. The church became a byword for its fantastic condition of neglect. There were no financial reasons for Robert Ketton's indifference to the estate in which he had once taken such pride; and his physical health remained good. It was as though he had just lost heart.

IV

My father had happy boyhood memories of Felbrigg as his mother's home, and knew the estate intimately. As it became more certain that Robert Ketton would not marry, his thoughts inevitably turned to his future inheritance. At the same time he could not but notice, every time he shot at Felbrigg or went pike-fishing in the lake, the progress of neglect and decay; and I think he felt increasingly that he would himself never be able to live there.

Remonstrance was out of the question. He was on the pleasantest of superficial terms with Robert Ketton, who in age was more like an elder brother than an uncle—there were only fourteen years between them. They used to go to Scotland together every year for stalking, shooting, or fishing. At election times they would solemnly "pair"—my father was a Conservative, his uncle still a Liberal—so that neither need have the trouble of going to vote. But although there was great friendliness between them, there was also an iron curtain of reticence.

Robert Ketton would occasionally come to Beeston, and was always there on Christmas Day. The small grey figure, in the invariable pepper-and-salt suit and knitted red tie, would walk down from Felbrigg and then walk back again. He never owned a motor car, and never made use of his dog-cart if his objective was within possible walking distance, whatever the weather. I would sometimes accompany my father shooting at Felbrigg, and later would be allowed to bring my own gun. "Uncle Bobby" was invariably friendly and kind, but I do not think he and my father ever exchanged a word about the mounting problems of the future.

His conduct became unreasonable and unpredictable. Just after the end of the First World War, in November and December 1918, he was obliged to raise some money to pay off a small family trust. It was a time when the price of land was high, and the sale of a couple of small detached farms would have brought in all that was required. But to my father's dismay he elected to sell all the china in the house, some of the best furniture and plate, and the cream of the books. The sale in London was insufficiently advertised; the prices were poor; it is impossible to look through the catalogues without a feeling of resentment. The china in particular was superb—old photographs show the rooms loaded with the Oriental porcelain, the Sèvres, the really outstanding Meissen figures and ornaments, dishes and services, all vanished now. My father attended this sale; and I have his priced catalogue, with a note of the few modest lots of Sèvres which he was able to buy as a present for my mother.

The best of the books were sold early in 1919. The priced catalogue of this sale is for me a particularly exasperating document, not merely on account of the low prices obtained, and even though some of the gaps made in the Felbrigg shelves were in due course filled with editions of the same works from my great-grandfather's collection at Beeston. In several instances sets were sold with one or more volumes missing, and were thus rendered almost valueless, when the missing volume or volumes were in the library all the time, and so remain. One at least of Admiral Lukin's log-books was included in the sale, and has now vanished. Among the works sold, and not so far replaced, were a fine set of the original editions of Hakluyt; Turberville's volumes on hunting and falconry; *Purchas his Pilgrimes*; Loggan's *Oxonia* and *Cantabrigia*; voyages, county histories, a large volume of seventeenth-century plays; a number of important Americana; the first edition of White's *Selborne*. The three huge albums containing George Steevens's unique Hogarth collection accounted for nearly half the total sum realised by the sale. It is a consoling thought that these volumes, after further vicissitudes, have come to rest in Mr W. S. Lewis's great library of the English eighteenth century at Farmington in Connecticut.

My father had known many of these things from boyhood—the Hogarth volumes, the great Chippendale suite and four-poster, the *tour de force* in porcelain known as the Temple of Fame which stood on a table in the Cabinet bow-window. He hated to see them go. Nevertheless by far the greater part of the contents of Felbrigg remained—not a picture had been sold, and only a little of the furniture. He was far more distressed by the steady deterioration of the house itself, of the farms and cottages, of the land and woods. But there was nothing to be done; and for several more years he waited at Beeston, with patience and good temper, while affairs at Felbrigg drifted into worse confusion.

Chapter Fifteen

MODERN TIMES

Later years and death of Thomas Wyndham Cremer—the author's recollections of his parents and his brother—life at Beeston—the move to Felbrigg in 1924—Richard Ketton-Cremer is killed in Crete in 1941

I

MY grandfather, Thomas Wyndham Cremer, died suddenly at Beeston on 3 November 1894, at the age of sixty. He had spent his entire life quietly at his home, farming, shooting, and adding to his impressive collection of Norfolk birds. He was a blunt but kindly man, a capable magistrate and a good landlord, much beloved in his small neighbourhood, and especially by the fishermen of Sheringham and Beeston. The fishing community consisted of a few families much inter-related, and therefore distinguished by an extraordinary variety of nicknames. Tippoo Cooper, Anyhow Cooper, Key Cooper, Snuffer West, Scotter West, Cutty West, Doy West, Rumbelow West, Jockey Grimes, Saffron Grimes—these and many more constantly recur in certain private records kept by my grandfather.

For records in general, however, he had no use at all. He destroyed —an act for which I find it hard to forgive him—most of the correspondence and other family papers of his forebears, apart from those relating directly to the estate. They were used, according to my father, to light the greenhouse fire during the whole of one winter. Nor did he often open a book, apart from Yarrell's *Birds* and the three green volumes of Stevenson's *Birds of Norfolk*, which were in use as constantly as his gun. Those were the days when ornithology meant the shooting of rare birds, and in due course their elaborate mounting in glass-fronted cases by Mr Gunn of Norwich. My grandfather would often put up at an inn at Blakeney or Salthouse, and spend happy days shooting over marshes and sandhills which are now among the most carefully guarded sanctuaries in the land. But some of the rarest specimens fell to his gun on his own land at Beeston, on the wooded heaths or the grassy cliffs.

He was buried, as his ancestors had been, in the windswept churchyard at Beeston. As a memorial to him, a host of friends subscribed to fill the east window of the church with excellent stained glass. But I think he would have been as well content to be remembered by a modest paragraph in the *Shooting Times*. A correspondent in that periodical, after describing his collection of rare birds and the charms of his house and garden, concluded:

> With the gun he had few equals. I recollect one day at a shooting party in the Cromer Hall woods, when it was blowing half a gale, and the pheasants, if not stopped, were "rocketing" over the town of Cromer to the sea, he was observed quietly taking them at a great altitude left and right, two birds being sometimes dead in the air at once; there was no "tailoring" or wounding, every bird falling dead.

II

My father went to Harrow and Trinity College, Cambridge, and afterwards lived with his mother and his three sisters at Beeston. He led much the same sort of life as his father had done—farming and local administration, shooting and fishing, the occasional unexacting duties of a subaltern in the Norfolk Yeomanry. It was while shooting in Scotland with his uncle Robert Ketton that he first met my mother, on a moor in Caithness. Her name was Emily Bayly, and she was acting as hostess for two of her brothers in a remote shooting-lodge.

The Baylys originally belonged to Poole in Dorset, where they were shipwrights and shipowners from the sixteenth century onwards. In the eighteenth century one of them, John Bayly, was taken into partnership by his uncle, Captain Brabant, a shipowner and timber merchant at Plymouth. He succeeded his uncle in 1752; and under him and his descendants the timber business flourished greatly, as it continues to do to this day. My mother's father, Robert Bayly, lived in a house called Torr, on the high ground behind Plymouth and then still in the unspoiled countryside. She was the youngest but one of a large family, three sons and five daughters. She and my father were married in the summer of 1905. I was born at Torr in the following year, and my brother Richard in 1909.

In an age when so much autobiographical writing is clouded with sadness and self-pity, one is almost ashamed to confess to a happy childhood. I do not mean to describe in any detail my early years; but if I tried to do so there would be little to tell beyond a deeply thankful record of family happiness. This book is dedicated to my parents and my brother. Every day I look back to them with gratitude and love. "Their very memory is fair and bright," and not least when I revisit the places where I first remember them.

Owing to the First World War and other circumstances, Dick and I spent much of our childhood at Torr with my mother's dear and kindly sisters, or at another family house called Elfordtown, looking down the Meavy valley on the southern confines of Dartmoor. Tall, square, ugly, and extremely comfortable—rebuilt in the 'eighties to replace a charming small Georgian house—Torr then stood alone in its fields high above Plymouth, with a glorious view over the Sound and Mount Edgcumbe and the Cornish hills. At night I used to watch from an upper window the Eddystone winking far out at sea. Now the suburbs of Plymouth have spread over the fields, across the parks of neighbouring Widey and Manadon, up to Crownhill, and far beyond. The sleepy little country church of Pennycross, where my parents were married and I was christened, is submerged in a vast housing estate. Torr itself is a Home for the Blind. If I go there now I can still recognise a few old beeches, the mounting-block by the stables, some vestiges of the garden which was so impressive to us as children, so much more elaborate, with its hot-houses and its lily-pond, than anything we knew at home. Everything else is altered beyond recognition.

Home was at first a long white house on the hills behind Sheringham, which my parents built directly after their marriage. It was called Sheringham House; and now, greatly enlarged, it has become a convalescent home. Its terrace looked across to the sea and to Beeston, where my grandmother and her daughters continued to live. But in 1920 they moved to Sheringham, and we to Beeston; and it is round Beeston that my most vivid memories still linger.

The house had been much altered by my grandparents. Sundry Victorian additions had obscured its simple eighteenth-century lines; and I do not now regret the bomb which damaged it during the last war, and gave me an excuse to restore the exterior to something of its original character. It was not a beautiful house, and is not now. But it was a singularly happy house; and a happy house I like to think it remains, with those once quiet rooms filled today with the cheerful uproar of a boys' preparatory school. It lay secluded in its large garden, sheltered from the sea-winds by its grove of trees. Fields, since sold and built over, were still under pasture or plough. The little church stood alone, sentinel over unfrequented cliffs, as it had done for hundreds of years.

By this time I had gone to Harrow, where Dick followed me in due course. My years there were much interrupted by illness. Three times I was brought back by ambulance from Harrow with a form of rheumatic fever; and once, later on, from Oxford, after which it ceased to plague me. If I never became a very fervent Harrovian, it was owing to the bedevilment of my school life by this wretched malady. If I cannot sing *Forty Years On* with much conviction, it is because I am rather less "rheumatic of shoulder" than I was forty years ago.

Although I was thus cut off from much activity, the delights of country life were not debarred. How well I remember those summers at Beeston in the early nineteen-twenties, months suffused with a golden haze of contentment—the garden with its oaks and ilexes, the tulip-tree and the old gnarled mulberry; the cliffs and the beach; walking in the sunset across the stubble-fields to shoot rabbits in the wood called Whitebarns; flighting duck as they came in at twilight to the rushy ponds; the calling of the owls at night.

And then the winter holidays, and those long evenings with the books which my great-grandfather had brought together. I have said that the Rev. Cremer Cremer was a tireless reader; but his tastes lay mainly in the eighteenth century and earlier. If he ever read Dickens and Thackeray, or even Scott and Jane Austen, he borrowed them from some library or book-club. He owned the collected works of Wordsworth and Byron, but not a Shelley or a Keats or a Tennyson; I suspect that Cowper was his favourite poet. The next two generations had added to his library little if at all. So my own tastes followed his: and night after night I would sit over the fire of beech-logs or apple-wood, reading Ben Jonson, *Hudibras*, Clarendon, the plays of Fielding, *A Sentimental Journey*—almost anything but the books which most bookish boys of my generation would have read. My ignorance of the great Victorians remained extreme, and to this day I have never caught up with them.

Occasionally we used to go over to Felbrigg. Shooting was now virtually my great-uncle Robert Ketton's sole interest, the organisation of his shooting-parties the only thing he took any trouble over. These parties seemed very grand to Dick and myself, accustomed as we were to rough shooting over the few hundred acres at Beeston; and I do not suppose that we noticed, as my father was noticing all the time, the defects of the farm-buildings and the bad state of much of the land.

But when we went to the house itself I do recall the sad impression made by the overgrown garden, the weedy paths, the lawn roughly cut for hay, the dying trees rising from tangled shrubberies, the beds of nettles in the park, the "hateful docks, rough thistles, kecksies, burs." Only the camellias in the Orangery survived beneath its makeshift roof of corrugated iron, thanks to a former coachman, who still did a little in the garden and made them his special care.

I remember, too, that my great-uncle would sometimes invite me to spend an afternoon in the library. He would welcome me kindly in his little room, and presently leave me alone among the Gothic bookshelves upstairs. The shelves bore the scars of the sale that had taken place a few years before, and the gaps in the rows of calf and vellum were filled with the strangest miscellany of substitutes—cheap novels, old Bradshaws and Baedekers, copies of *Kelly's Directory* and *Whitaker's Almanac*, volumes of the *Badminton Library* and *Punch*. The sun would pour in through the unshaded windows, cracking and fading the bindings that it reached. Flies buzzed against the panes, the only sound in the silence of the room. And there I would examine shelf after shelf, from the ponderous folios at floor-level to the jumble of little books packed close beneath the cornice. The early atlases, the Aldine classics, the voyages and travels, the collections of eighteenth-century poetry, the volumes of pamphlets and plays—I understood little enough about books at that time, but I shall never forget the excitement of those first afternoons in the library which I was to know so well.

III

I have already spoken of my father's doubts as to whether he could afford to live at Felbrigg at all, still less to restore house and estate to the condition from which they had fallen. My mother loved Beeston, and had no wish to move. But in 1923 my great-uncle suddenly decided to leave Felbrigg, and spend the rest of his days elsewhere. He offered to make over the property to my father immediately; and in the end my father accepted. Robert Ketton left Felbrigg at the beginning of 1924, and never once returned there during the eleven years that remained to him.

We moved from Beeston to Felbrigg in May of the same year. It was a long and exhausting business for my parents, involving months of preparation. I took little part in it myself, as I was recovering from one of my attacks of rheumatic fever, and was sent to Devonshire to be out of the way. But an immense amount had to be done to bring the house even remotely up to date. Robert Ketton's long ownership had not resulted in any alteration, either architectural or decorative. There had been neglect and decay, but not the slightest change. The house had just slumbered for a full half-century. In view of the fate of many houses during just that period—the additional wings, the Gothic refurbishings, the conservatories and porte-cochères, the hideous fittings for gas and electric light, the plate-glass in the windows—one can only be thankful. But there were no bathrooms, since Robert Ketton had remained faithful to the hip-bath all his days. There was the most extraordinary sanitation. All the water was still raised from a well by a huge wheel worked by a mule. There was, needless to say, no telephone. There was no heating, and no form of power or artificial light.

The roof was in a fearful state, with rain soaking through perished lead and displaced slates. By some miracle, dry-rot was not seriously present at any point; but great areas of the roof-timbers had been so softened by the wet as to become easy prey for the death-watch beetle, that pest against which I continue to do battle even now. Samwell's cornice on the west wing was rotting away; large holes were to be seen in it, and several of the modillions had fallen. My father lost no time in restoring the entire cornice to its former state. The ceiling of the library, with its elaborate geometrical pattern, was so damaged that it had to be taken down altogether. Here a complete reconstruction would have been too costly, so a plain ceiling was substituted, only the cornice being restored where necessary, and the original decoration being left in the bays, where the damage was less.

My parents were devoted gardeners. Beeston had always been full of the colour and scent of flowers, of roses in particular. At Felbrigg not a flower had been grown for years. The kitchen-garden had long been let to a market-gardener, and the greenhouses had collapsed in a welter of splintered wood and broken glass. My father could just afford to reconstruct two of them out of the ruins of the rest. The Dovehouse was likewise almost a ruin, with gaping holes in the roof, the principal timbers rotted through, and the cupola leaning drunkenly awry. My father was not able to include this building in his programme of reconstruction, and it continued to moulder until I found myself in a position to reconstruct it in 1937.

The general decay had extended also to the church in the park. My great-uncle had latterly taken not the smallest interest in the structure, or indeed in any parochial activity. The rector had kept the sister-church at Metton in good order, but was unable to cope, without the encouragement of the squire, with the repairs necessary at Felbrigg. "The dilapidated appearance of parts of this old and interesting church occasioned some little surprise," reported the local Archaeological Society after a visit in 1921. In fact it was in a condition of the most shocking neglect—holes in the roof, green slime dripping down the walls, windows broken, doors rotting, jackdaws and bats befouling everything. The great monument to Thomas Windham had grown so insecure that the rector would never venture near it, even at moments of the service when the rubric required him to do so. The churchyard was choked with thistles and nettles. All this, thanks to the energy and devotion of my parents, was put right within a couple of years.

How well I remember those first months at Felbrigg. I recall the sound of rain dripping through the leaky ceilings into basins placed in the bedrooms; our first Sunday in the church, when my mother recoiled from the Hall pew, upholstered in red baize crawling with moths and maggots, and insisted on seats elsewhere; my father's irritation at the necessity, under the peremptory terms of a clause in John Ketton's will, of adding the name of Ketton to our own, and the difficulty we all had in getting accustomed to it. I remember the streams of people who came to call, now that a house so long and so firmly barred was opening its doors once more. Most of all, from that far-off spring, I remember the brilliance of the beech-leaves and the calling of the plovers, as I explored for the first time those unknown woods and fields.

IV

During the next years my father applied himself calmly and steadily to the work of restoring the estate to order. It was a time of agricultural depression. Rents were low, and farms were difficult to let. The approach of each Michaelmas Day brought anxiety lest a tenant should give notice, in which case his farm might have to be taken in hand. (The position is very different now, when even the rumour of a vacant farm brings a flood of applications.) Although he had farmed most of his life at Beeston, he had no time and no desire to do so at Felbrigg; nor, in the event, was it ever forced upon him. Forestry by then had become his passion, as it is mine. Several of the outlying farms were sold, at prices which seemed reasonable then, but which would be derisory nowadays. One picture was sold—a large Van Goyen—and certain pieces of furniture. These sales were a dire necessity, in view of the menace of death-duties which hangs over every estate.

My father was a quiet and somewhat reticent man, gifted with great tenacity of purpose, and with a foresight for which I cannot be too grateful. I went up to Balliol in the autumn of 1924, and the novelty and delight of Oxford life took possession of me. I spent most of the vacations at home, and noted each time the improvements in the garden, the woods, the fields; but it was only later that I came to realise the full extent of what my father had done.

I think those years at Felbrigg were happy ones for him, despite the worry and the hard work at a time when most men begin to take things more easily. He had always loved the place, and had longed for the day when he could begin to repair the neglected farms and replant the ravaged woods. He delighted in the garden, the shooting, the fishing in the lake. Fond though he had been of Beeston, the steady growth of nearby Sheringham, with its visitors and its motor-traffic, had much encroached upon its privacy. At Felbrigg he found the space and seclusion that he longed for.

My sweet and gentle mother had been so content at Beeston that she did not at all welcome the move to a much larger house in an indescribable state of disrepair. But she too coped valiantly with a host of problems, and brought order out of chaos in an almost miraculous way. And she created at Felbrigg, as in every house in which she lived, an atmosphere of quiet happiness. Everyone loved her, everyone wanted to see more of her. She was able to conceal her great dislike of social occasions, and the old hospitalities of Felbrigg were renewed. But flowers were her real delight, and animals and birds of all kinds—dogs, cats, peacocks, ducks; and the long tranquil days of family life.

The strain of much business in late middle age gradually told upon my father's health. It became evident, soon after I left Oxford, that I would have to live at home, assist him, learn all I could from him, and take over by degrees the management of the estate. In any case I would have preferred this to most other ways of life, since it gave me time for the writing which had already become my ambition. Thanks to my father's kindly and patient instruction, I learnt enough to act as my own agent and manage the estate unassisted for many years to come—not, it is true, very efficiently, but without any serious disaster. With the increase of duties and preoccupations in recent years, I have placed its day-to-day running in other hands; but I have not forgotten how to hold a rent-audit or to measure a tree.

My father became seriously ill in the summer of 1932, and died on 22 April of the following year. His uncle Robert Ketton died two years later. There was a period of acute anxiety about the payment of death-duties. But these were eventually settled; and I found myself able to continue at Felbrigg, and to lead the life which I have led ever since, among my books and my trees.

V

Of all the young men, generation after generation, who have moved through the pages of this book, my brother Dick was the only one to die in battle, or by any form of violent death. Such things are a part of the bloodstained nightmare of our own century. It is twenty years ago, this very month, since he was killed; yet even to read his letters is like the reopening of a wound.

We spent our childhood together, at Torr, at Beeston, at the same preparatory school. Despite the three years' difference in our ages, we were devoted, inseparable, completely in accord. The differences in our tastes and temperaments did not seem to matter. At that early age, and throughout his life, he displayed the same sweetness of temper, the same sincerity and goodness of heart.

Intellectually he developed late. He had none of my bookish precocity, my knack of passing examinations. He could play games, was good at cricket and tennis, clever with cars and wireless. But at Harrow, where we were together only a few months, he was not happy. There was a change of house-masters soon after I left, a clumsy and insensitive new régime just at the time when Dick most needed kindness and sympathy. He never rose high in the school, or found much enjoyment there. He was far happier, and learnt a great deal more, at Wye College in Kent, where he spent some years after leaving Harrow and obtained his diploma in agriculture.

He inherited Beeston on my father's death in 1933. The house was let, the farms were occupied, and in any case he was only twenty-three at that time, too young to settle down. My mother had moved to her own small house at Metton, and he lived sometimes with her and sometimes with me. But he also spent months and sometimes years in travel. He went all over the world—to Mexico, to Australia, to China and Japan; spent months of blissful idleness in Tahiti; drove all over the United States, and all over Europe. A few albums of splendid photographs are all that remain from those gay and carefree years. Naturally my mother and I complained of his long absences; and prudent friends talked about a job in the City or at least a farm in the country. This *Wanderlust* was the only subject on which he and I ever had a serious disagreement, and I remember it now with remorse. He knew what he was about—it was as though he had some premonition that his time was short, and must be enjoyed to the full. I am thankful that he saw so clearly what he wanted to do, and listened to none of our advice, and went his own way.

Those were the years of the gathering storm, the state of the world growing more ominous with every month that passed. Yet few of us could believe that the horror of 1914–18 was to be repeated; that total war would not somehow be averted in the end. It is against that black cloud that I remember Dick when he was at home with us—riding, going to dances, learning to fly an aeroplane, and obtaining his pilot's licence.

Then Munich came, and the long suspense of 1939, with hope fading fast. Felbrigg had never seemed more beautiful than during those late summer days, with sunset after calm sunset throwing the shadows of the oaks and beeches across the grass. I recall a sad walk down to Beeston, where Dick was at last thinking that he might live in years to come, if only the nightmare would fade. And then war was upon us, the first sirens, the first searchlights, Chamberlain's voice droning over the wireless, the destruction of all our happiness in the present and all our ambitions for the future.

During the first weeks of the war—that period of uncertainty and anticlimax, the "phoney war"—Dick joined the Royal Air Force Volunteer Reserve. As the holder of a pilot's licence he had hoped for flying duties. It turned out, however, that his eyesight was not up to the standard required. He had used spectacles for reading for some while, and had not otherwise noticed anything wrong; but it was enough to exclude him from operational duty. At the beginning of 1940 he was posted to the Middle East, as Equipment Officer to No. 113 Squadron of the Royal Air Force. He said goodbye to us in January, and to Jester his large horse and Mimi his little cat, both of whom were to live with me for many years. We never saw him again.

VI

It is difficult to carry one's mind back to the mood of 1940. So much has happened during the intervening twenty years—such heroism and tragedy, a victory supposedly won, a cold war dragging on today and far into the perspectives of the future. Our memories are blurred by the lapse of time; our judgment is confused by the writings and speeches, complacent or apologetic, of a host of soldiers and politicians.

Turning over the little packet of Dick's letters from the Middle East, I can find no trace of resentment towards those well-intentioned and honourable men who are blamed nowadays for their failure to avert the war. He wrote to me with extreme frankness, and always with the same complete independence of mind. He reluctantly accepted the necessity of the war, but had great doubts about its probable outcome. At first, in Cairo and Heliopolis, there was nothing but boredom and frustration, sometimes great depression. Things seemed absolutely static—routine, perpetual rumours, the flashy night-life of Cairo, the "phoney war" still prevailing in England and reflected in the ragged *Tatlers* in the mess.

Then came the German surge into Norway, Denmark, the Low Countries; the collapse of France; the entry of Italy into the war. His squadron was moved up into the Western Desert, and there, in camp at Maaten Bagush, he was happier. He was grateful for the climate, the sea, the beauty of the desert at evening, compared with which things the haphazard Italian bombing was a small disadvantage. Now and then he took part—unofficially, I suppose—as an observer in raids over Bardia and Tobruk. He had a particular friend in the squadron, John Ward, whose company was a great delight until he was taken prisoner. John Ward survived the war; his son, born a few months after his father's capture, is Dick's godson and bears his name.

And so the months dragged on, with the fortunes of war swaying to and fro, and a pervasive sense of doubt and indecision. "Exalted persons fly out here now and then, and give apologetic and uninspiring little talks, mince round in the sand for a few minutes and fly off again, to the relief of all." Some day I shall print, for private circulation among his friends, a few of Dick's letters, and particularly his description of the Western Desert campaign which resulted in the taking of Derna and Tobruk—the unorthodox conduct of the Australian troops, the elderly Italian Generals who were captured in their baths, the enthusiastic evangelical padre.

As I read these letters on their flimsy blue air-mail paper, I am thankful for their recurrent note of personal optimism. He was often lonely and depressed. He hated war, and cruelty, and destruction. He had no belief at all in the assurances of politicians and publicists that the world would be a better place when the tyranny was overpast. But he thought incessantly and with gratitude of the ten happy years that had preceded "this whole silly business," and repeatedly wrote of his conviction that he would survive. This may have been partly his desire to reassure my mother and myself; thoughtfulness and consideration were in the fibre of his being. But I think he truly held the belief that he would come through, and I am glad indeed that it should have been so.

There are few letters from the winter of 1940, and some of those to my mother were accidentally destroyed. But I know that during that winter he got some leave and spent it in Jerusalem, staying in luxury at the King David Hotel. He made an expedition to Amman and the ruins of Jerash—it was all, he wrote, like the old sight-seeing days that he had loved so much.

In the autumn of 1940 the Italians had invaded Greece, and had been valiantly repulsed. Early in 1941 a German invasion of the Balkans, directed against Yugoslavia and Greece, was obviously only a matter of time. Allied reinforcements were despatched to Greece in March, and No. 113 Squadron was among them. Dick did not go with the squadron to Greece at this time; he had been unwell—I am uncertain of the details—and was only able to rejoin them early in April. By this time the sheer weight of the German attack had prevailed, and the resistance of the Greeks was collapsing. The convoy in which Dick was travelling to rejoin his squadron in Greece was diverted instead to Crete. He was there attached to another squadron, and remained with them to the end. Shortly afterwards his own 113 Squadron, evacuated with the rest of the Allied forces from Greece, put in for a day or two at Crete on their way back to Egypt. They wanted him to rejoin them, and it seems more than reasonable that he should have been allowed to do so. But someone in a position of authority decided otherwise, and his friends sailed away to Egypt without him. It was a cruelty of fate to which I shall never reconcile myself.

Only one letter has survived from those few weeks in Crete, written on 24 April. He was not allowed to disclose his whereabouts, but a reference to "cretinous creatures" indicated where he was. Indeed by the time the letter arrived the evacuation of Greece was complete, and we were being loudly assured on the wireless that "Crete will be held." Dick knew otherwise, a month before. Raids were incessant; the Germans were in full control of mainland Greece; but no arrangements at all had been made for the evacuation of the island. "If the whole lot are Dunkirked again there can really be no excuse, as it must have been obvious weeks ago that there was hardly a chance of success."

Even so it was a joy to see mountains again, some still capped with snow, and green fields and olive-groves after the endless desert. The verdure and the sea reminded him of that other island, Tahiti, where he had once been so happy. He had got a black kitten, which he called Mimi after his little cat at home. And so the letter ends, with words of comfort and reassurance which I can still hardly bear to read.

From then onwards we were to hear no more—nothing but the vaguest rumours, for months and years. Towards the end of May the German bombers and paratroops attacked Crete with obliterating force and fury. A magnificent resistance was unavailing, and the island was evacuated with heavy losses. Dick was not among those who got away. Even so, there was some chance that he might be among those who escaped to the hills and were sheltered by friendly Cretans until they could escape. I remember my mother, so brave and patient, clinging to this fading hope.

Eventually news came trickling through from prisoner-of-war camps in Italy and Germany. Dick had been stationed, it appeared, at the airfield of Maleme, the objective of the most powerful German attack and the first airfield to be captured. It was pounded on 20 May by relays of bombers, and heavily encircled by parachutists and by troops brought in gliders. After long and bitter fighting, the hopelessly scattered survivors of the British and Dominion forces were ordered to make their way, if possible, to the southern coast of the island.

Dick escaped from the shambles of Maleme in company with a naval officer who had known him at Harrow. They passed the night in an olive-grove not far from the airfield; but the country was alive with parachutists, and in the course of the night they became separated. Although organised resistance had ceased, sporadic fighting was still going on. Some time next morning—so far as I can make out, it was 23 May—two young airmen came upon Dick, who was known to them, about two miles south-east of the airfield. He was bleeding from a stomach wound, could not take the water they offered him, and ordered them to leave him and continue on their way. They were both captured later, and I saw one of them when the war was over. He told me that he thought Dick was drifting rapidly into unconsciousness, and could not have lived long afterwards. I am not certain whether he was speaking in kindness or in truth. No one will ever know how many hours Dick had lain, and had still to lie, in agony and loneliness on that Cretan hillside.

Chapter Sixteen

EPILOGUE

I END this book, as it was begun, in the month of May. It is exactly twenty years since my brother died in Crete, when we waited for news of him, and heard none, in just such another spring. Day after day the verdure increases—the brilliance of the beeches, the endlessly diversified green of the oaks, the chestnuts richly flowering, the reluctant ashes, the hawthorns "white again, in spring, with voluptuary sweetness." As always, the plovers cry in the meadows. As always, the cold winds sweep in from the sea.

I end the story here. Felbrigg survived the war, shaken now and then by bombs, a few windows broken, a few additional cracks in the ceilings, nothing worse. Since it was then still without electricity, it could not be adapted for any military or civilian purpose whatever. In contrast to its neighbours, occupied from cellar to attic and ringed round with camps and hutments, it remained undisturbed.

And so it stands, with all its associations and memories, confronting the unpredictable future. It may be the scene of happiness, kindness, hospitality in centuries to come. It may be burned to the ground this very night. The story of its first three and a half centuries has now been told; and who can know what lies ahead?

POSTSCRIPT

The National Trust was bequeathed Felbrigg Hall and Estate by the late R. W. Ketton-Cremer in 1969. Through his foresight and generosity the Hall and Park are now preserved for all time.

BIBLIOGRAPHY

General

This book is based throughout on the papers which have been preserved at Felbrigg by successive generations of its owners, from the seventeenth century until the present time. The political correspondence of William Windham the statesman, however, is now in the British Museum, together with many of his personal papers; and these have been used in the chapters which relate to him.

Chapter Two

For the early history of the Wyndham family I stand greatly indebted to *A Family History, 1410–1688: The Wyndhams of Norfolk and Somerset*, by the Hon. H. A. Wyndham (now Lord Leconfield), 1939.

For certain details about the Felbriggs and the earlier Wyndhams I have also drawn upon *The Paston Letters*, ed. James Gairdner, 3 vols., 1895; Blomefield's *History of Norfolk*, 11 vols., 1805; and (with caution) Walter Rye's *Norfolk Families*, 1913. The suggested derivation of Felbrigg is quoted from *The Concise Oxford Dictionary of English Place-Names*, by Eilert Ekwall, 3rd ed., 1959.

Chapter Three

In this chapter I have again made much use of Lord Leconfield's *Wyndhams of Norfolk and Somerset*, which contains a full account of Florence Wyndham's resurrection, and valuable details of the early career of Thomas Windham of Felbrigg.

The papers defining the attitude of Thomas Windham during the Civil War, and his letters to Sir John Potts and Sir John Hobart, are among the Tanner MSS. in the Bodleian Library—Vols. 62, 64, 66, and 69.

Chapter Four

The elections in Norfolk, described in this chapter, have been treated from a more strictly political angle by Mr J. Rees Jones in the *Durham University Journal*, 1953, pp. 13–21.

For the architect William Samwell see H. M. Colvin's *Biographical Dictionary of English Architects*, which contains the little that is known about him. Roger North's architectural essay quoted on page 75 is in B.M. Add. MS. 32540.

Other sources:

The Letters of Sir Thomas Browne, ed. Geoffrey Keynes, 1930.
The Diary of John Evelyn, ed. E. S. de Beer, 6 vols., 1955.
John Aubrey, *Miscellanies*, 1696.
———, *Brief Lives*, ed. Andrew Clark, 2 vols., 1897.
The Life of the first Duke of Newcastle by his Duchess.
Savile Correspondence, ed. W. D. Cooper, 1878.
H.M.C. Le Strange MSS. 1888.

Chapter Five

The experiences of the Windhams during the South Sea Bubble were described in fuller detail in my *Norfolk Portraits* (1944). The lifelong association of Ashe Windham and Patrick St Clair was the theme of my *Country Neighbourhood* (1951). Several passages from both books have been reproduced almost without change in this chapter.

Other sources:

J. H. Plumb, *Sir Robert Walpole: a Statesman in the Making*, 1956.
——, *Sir Robert Walpole: the King's Minister*, 1960.
John Lord Hervey, *Memoirs*, ed. Romney Sedgwick, 3 vols., 1931.
John Nichols, *Illustrations of Literature*, Vol. III, 1818.
Letters of Humphrey Prideaux to John Ellis, ed. E. Maunde Thompson, 1875.
The Wentworth Papers, 1883.
H.M.C. Townshend MSS. 1887.

Chapter Six

There is much about William Windham's Grand Tour and the Common Room at Geneva in *The Literary Life and Select Works of Benjamin Stillingfleet*, 3 vols., 1811; and also in my *Early Life and Diaries of William Windham*, 1930.

For Windham's collection of paintings see "The 'Cabinet' at Felbrigg," by F. W. Hawcroft in *The Connoisseur*, May 1958.

The descent of the Lukins is given in *The Lukin Family*, by Sir Algernon Tudor-Craig, 1932.

Chapter Seven

Windham's militia activities were described in greater detail in the chapter "Norfolk and the Threat of Invasion" in my *Norfolk Portraits*, 1944, from which a few pages have been incorporated in the text.

Garrick's mention of his visit to Felbrigg, and Windham's letter to him, occur in the Garrick volumes of the Forster MSS. in the Victoria and Albert Museum (Garrick vols. 27 and 48 respectively). Johnson's reference to the elder William Windham is in B.M. Add. MS. 37934, f. 63.

Chapter Eight

Much of the material in this chapter was used in my *Early Life and Diaries of William Windham*, 1930. From 1784 onwards the passages from Windham's diaries are quoted from *The Diary of the Right Hon. William Windham*, edited by Mrs Henry Baring, 1866. Some use has also been made, in this and the two following chapters, of *The Windham Papers*, 2 vols., 1913, although I have given on pages 159–60 the reasons why this compilation should be treated with caution.

Lady Beauchamp Proctor's journal of her tour in Norfolk, which contains her description of Felbrigg, is more fully treated in my *Norfolk Assembly*, 1957.

Other sources:

The Torrington Diaries, ed. C. Bruyn Andrews, 1934.

Hester Lynch Piozzi, *Anecdotes of the late Dr Samuel Johnson*, 1786.

James Woodforde, *Diary of a Country Parson*, ed. John Beresford, 1924.

Nathaniel Kent, *Hints to Gentlemen of Landed Property*, 1775.

———, *General View of the Agriculture of Norfolk*, 1796.

The Norfolk Tour, 1808.

William Marshall, *Rural Economy of Norfolk*, 2 vols., 1787.

James Boswell, *Life of Johnson*, ed. G. B. Hill and L. F. Powell, 6 vols., 1934–50.

J. C. Loudon, *Landscape Gardening and Landscape Architecture of Humphry Repton . . . with a Biographical Notice*, 1840.

Chapter Nine

Mrs Baring's edition of the *Diary* is again much used. The correspondence between Burke and Windham was edited for the Roxburghe Club by J. P. Gilson, 1910. Use is also made in this chapter of Windham's *Speeches*, edited in 3 vols. by his secretary Thomas Amyot in 1813.

For fuller description of Johnson's books now at Felbrigg, see my article in *The Book Collector*, Winter 1956.

The letters to Wyatt are B.M. Add. MS. 37914 f. 67 and 37915 f. 272.

Other sources:

James Boswell, *Life of Johnson*, ed. G. B. Hill and L. F. Powell, 6 vols., 1934–50.
Letters of Samuel Johnson, ed. R. W. Chapman, 3 vols., 1952.
Diary and Letters of Madame d'Arblay, 6 vols., 1842–6.
Antony Dale, *James Wyatt*, 1956.
Christopher Hobhouse, *Fox*, 1934.
William Field, *Memoirs of Samuel Parr*, 2 vols., 1828.
Life and Letters of Sir Gilbert Elliot, first Earl of Minto. 3 vols., 1874.

Chapter Ten

The *Diary*, edited by Mrs Baring, and the *Speeches*, edited by Thomas Amyot, are again the principal sources for this chapter.

A few paragraphs have been reproduced from the chapter "Norfolk and the Threat of Invasion" in my *Norfolk Portraits*, 1944.

The unpublished journal of Louisa Gurney, which contains her description of Felbrigg, is quoted by the kind permission of the owner, Mr Desmond Buxton.

Other sources:

The Farington Diary, ed. James Greig, 8 vols., 1923–8. (More particularly Vol. III, which shows the extent to which private people of all parties were surprised and distressed by Windham's speech about the memorial to Pitt.)
Edward Lascelles, *Life of Charles James Fox*, 1936.
Sylvester Douglas, Lord Glenbervie, *Diaries*, ed. Francis Bickley, 2 vols., 1928.
Robert Forby, *Vocabulary of East Anglia*, 2 vols., 1830.
A New Election Budget, Norwich, 1802.
Norfolk Election Budget, 1806.
Mrs Thistlethwayte, *Memoirs of Dr Henry Bathurst*, 1853.

Chapter Eleven

In this chapter I have drawn upon some correspondence preserved by the Cremers at Beeston Regis Hall, and now kept with the bulk of the Windham papers at Felbrigg.

The letters quoted from George William Lukin to his mother, and from William Lukin to William Windham, are in B.M. Add. MSS. 37,911 and 37,913 respectively.

Other sources:

Journal of Elizabeth Lady Holland, ed. the Earl of Ilchester, 2 vols., 1908.

John Marshall, *Royal Naval Biography*, 1823.
S. D. Kitson, *The Life of John Sell Cotman*, 1937.

Chapter Twelve

The reference to the "rough unlettered squire" in *The Greville Memoirs* is under the date of 17 November 1842.

The stained glass at Felbrigg was fully described by the Rev. Christopher Woodforde (now Dean of Wells) in *Norfolk Archaeology*, Vol. XXVI, pp. 73–84.

The Crimean Diary and Letters of Lieut.-General Sir Charles Ashe Windham, edited by Major Hugh Pearse, was published in 1897.

Chapter Thirteen

Two reports of the inquiry into the state of mind of William Frederick Windham were issued in 1862. The version under the imprint of W. Oliver, Catherine Street, Strand, claimed to be the "illustrated and unabridged edition," and has been mainly followed in this chapter. The other version, printed by E. Harrison, Exeter Change, Strand, aimed at being more sensational—"disclosures in high life," etc.—and espoused more openly the cause of Windham against the petitioners.

I have also consulted the reports (and more particularly the comments) in contemporary newspapers—*The Times*, the *Daily Telegraph*, the *Norwich Mercury*, the *Norfolk Chronicle*—and, of course, *Punch*.

The complications of the married life of William and Agnes Windham, with which I have dealt rather summarily, are more fully described in an entertaining essay, "Mr and Mrs Windham," by Donald MacAndrew in *The Saturday Book*, 1951. Windham's last days and death are luridly depicted in *The Norfolk Handbook*, 1866, in a sketch "from the graphic pen of the editor of the *Norwich Argus*."

Sir William Hardman's comments on the inquiry occur in *A Mid-Victorian Pepys*, ed. S. M. Ellis, 1923; and Sir F. C. Burnand's encounter with Windham in his *Records and Reminiscences*, 1904.

Chapter Fourteen

Besides Mrs Ketton's diary and a few other family papers, I have quoted from:

Sir George Edwards, *From Crow-Scaring to Westminster. An Autobiography*, new ed., 1957.
Constance Battersea, *Reminiscences*, 1923.
Frederick Locker, *My Confidences*, 1896.

INDEX